DATE DUE

~~JE 6 07~~			
~~AP 25 08~~			
~~MY 22 08~~			
~~AP 29 09~~			
~~MY 20 09~~			
~~FE 11 10~~			

DEMCO 38-296

EXPLORATIONS
Contemporary Perspectives on Religion

Lynn Davidman, Gillian Lindt, Charles H. Long, John P. Reeder Jr.,
Ninian Smart, John F. Wilson, and Robert Wuthnow, *Advisory Board*

Transformations of the Confucian Way

John H. Berthrong
Boston University
School of Theology

Westview Press
A Member of the Perseus Books Group

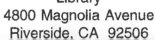

Explorations: Contemporary Perspectives on Religion

Copyright © 1998 by Westview Press, A Member of the Perseus Books Group

Published in 1998 in the United States of America by Westview Press, 5500 Central Avenue, Boulder, Colorado 80301-2877, and in the United Kingdom by Westview Press, 12 Hid's Copse Road, Cumnor Hill, Oxford OX2 9JJ

A CIP catalog record for this book is available from the Library of Congress.
ISBN 0-8133-2805-5 (hc) — ISBN 0-8133-2804-7 (pbk)

The paper used in this publication meets the requirements of the American National Standard for Permanence of Paper for Printed Library Materials Z39.48-1984.

10   9   8   7   6   5   4   3   2

Contents

5 The Flourishing of the Yüan and Ming   115

The Turn Toward the Mind, 116
The Ming Transition, 118
Wang Yang-ming, 123

6 Korean and Japanese Confucianism and the
   Ch'ing School of Evidential Research   144

The Rise of Korean Confucianism, 144
Japanese Confucianism: The Tokugawa Achievement, 151
New Directions for the Ch'ing Summation of the Tradition, 161
The School of Evidential Research, 167

7 Confucianism in the Modern World   174

The Chaos of First Impressions and Reactions, 178
The Transition to Modern China and East Asia, 179
The New Confucians, 185

Acknowledgments

First, I want to thank the long line of Asian and Western scholars who have provided the scholarship upon which this study is constructed. As a young graduate student I had the privilege of hearing T'ang Chün-i lecture at Taiwan National University at the end of his career. I also had the opportunity to spend an enlightening afternoon in Hong Kong talking about Chu Hsi with Mou Tsung-san, one of the most learned scholars I have ever encountered. His grasp of Chinese, Buddhist, and Western philosophy was truly phenomenal. His kindness to a young graduate student was a model of Confucian graciousness; I hope that I have picked up some of the corners of learning that Mou lifted for me that afternoon.

As I continued my studies of the Confucian tradition, I was fortunate to meet many other scholars who have enriched my understanding of the variety of the tradition. Wing-tsit Chan and Wm. Theodore de Bary stand out as representing the doyens of modern Confucian studies. I have also been able to discuss these matters with Tu Wei-ming, Cheng Chung-ying, Liu Shu-hsien, Julia Ching, Will Oxtoby, and, of blessed memory, Edward Ch'ien. The list needs to be expanded to include another international generation of Confucian scholars scattered around the globe: Mary Evelyn Tucker, Dean Rodney Taylor, John Chaffee, Thomas Lee, Lisa Raphals, Conrad Schriokauer, Lionel Jensen, Thomas Wilson, Hoyt Tillman, Thomas Metzger, Kim Heup Young, Peter Lee, Mathew Levey, Kim Sung Hae, Roger Ames, David Hall, Chen Lai, Anne Birdwhistell, and Zheng Jiadong.

Second, I want to thank my friends at Boston University, beginning with Dean Robert Cummings Neville for his unfailing friendship and support— support encouraged by Chancellor John Silber, President Jon Westling, and Provost Dennis Berkey. Peter Berger has always provided a wonderfully irenic and ironic check on my flights of fancy. Joseph Fewsmith, David Eckel, Merle Goldman (who never ceases to marvel that I can actually like the Neo-Confucians), Chung Chai-sik, Robert Weller, and Harry Gelber share in worrying about how to teach Asian studies effectively in a large urban research university. At various stages of the production and editing of the manuscript, Dorothy Rogers and Tracy Deveau provided superb assistance.

Third, at Westview Press I want to thank Spencer Carr for his initial interest in adding a work on Confucianism to a distinguished series. Laura Parsons, Elizabeth Lawrence, and Michele Wynn provided encouragement and support during the production process. I also want to thank the various readers who rendered such insightful comments on the manuscript. I thank all for their encouragement and ask for their collective forgiveness where I have misconstrued their work.

John H. Berthrong

A Note on Conventions

The problem of romanizing Chinese characters is notorious. Unlike the Korean and Japanese systems, where there is just one excellent romanization system, Chinese has suffered the imposition of a number of different systems. There are two major forms commonly in use, the older Wade-Giles and the newer Pinyin. There are good arguments for demanding uniformity within one text; but there are equally compelling arguments for honoring the original forms used by translators over the years. One of the strongest arguments for using Pinyin is that it is now the official romanization supported by the Chinese government and hence is likely to become more and more the norm for scholars in the future. However, Wade-Giles, at least for the English-speaking world, has been the scholarly standard for decades, and most serious publications have employed it for generations. I have decided to retain the romanization form used by the original authors and translators. I do this for two reasons. First, it remains faithful to the valuable scholarly convention that we should quote accurately from our sources. Second, I believe that it is still necessary for any student of Chinese intellectual history to master the two most common forms of romanization. To this end, I have provided a conversion chart for Wade-Giles and Pinyin at the end of the text.

Although Wade-Giles and Pinyin are the most commonly used romanization systems, students will encounter other styles from time to time. For a discussion of the rules governing the use of Pinyin and a cogent listing of a number of the systems of romanization, see John DeFrancis, ed., *ABC Chinese-English Dictionary* (Honolulu: University of Hawaii Press, 1996), pp. 835–855.

Concerning my citations within the text, I have employed what the University of Chicago's *A Manual of Style for Writers* calls the parenthetical references in the author-date system. The bibliography is organized in four sections. The first section provides a list of general reference works about East Asia; it contains general and specialized histories of East Asian countries, philosophies, and religions. The second section lists works on the history of Confucianism in China; the third, on Korea; the fourth, on Japan. All works cited in the body of the text will be found in one of the four sections.

Dynastic Chart

Era of the Legendary Sage Kings and Empires

Fu Hsi

Shen Nung

Huang-ti

Yao Shun Yü

The Three Eras of High Antiquity

Hsia ?–ca. 1751 B.C.E.

Shang ca. 1751–1045 B.C.E.

Chou 1045–249 B.C.E.

Western Chou 1111–771 B.C.E.   Eastern Chou 770–256 B.C.E.

Spring and Autumn 722–481 B.C.E.   Warring States 480–221 B.C.E.

The Imperial States

Ch'in 221–206 B.C.E.

Han 206 B.C.E.–220

Western Han 206 B.C.E.–9   (Hsin 9 – 23)   Eastern Han 25–220

Three Kingdoms 220–280

Wei 220–265   Wu 222–280   Shu-Han 221–263

Western Chin 226–316

The Period of Division (316–589)

Eastern Chin 317–420

Northern and Southern Dynasties 386–589

Southern 420–589

Sung 420–479   Ch'i 479–502

Liang 502–557   Ch'eng 557–589

Northern 386–581

Northern Wei 386–534   Eastern Wei 534–550

Northern Ch'i 550–77   Western Wei 535–557

Northern Chou 557–581

Sui   581–618

T'ang   618–907

Five Dynasties   907–60
Later Liang   907–23   Later T'ang   923–36
Later Chin   936–47   Later Han   947–50
Later Chou   951–60

Liao (North China)   916–1125

Sung   960–1279
Northern Sung   960–1127   Southern Sung   1127–1279

Chin   1115–1234

Yüan   1260–1368

Ming   1368–1644

Ch'ing   1644–1911

Introduction:
Transformations and Variations
on Confucian History

THE TWENTIETH CENTURY has been cruel to the Confucian tradition throughout East Asia. At the beginning of the century it was painfully obvious that traditional China was in terminal dynastic decline as well as being under persistent attack by the powerful Western colonial powers. Korea was already partially incorporated into the reinvigorated Japanese imperial system. Vietnam was a French colony. The Confucian tradition was likewise considered moribund because its fortunes were assumed to be inextricably intertwined with the fate of the late Chinese and Korean imperial states. Joseph Levenson, at the end of his great trilogy about the fate of the Confucian tradition, wrote, "When Confucianism finally passed into history, it was because history passed out of Confucianism. Intrinsic classical learning, the exercise of divining from canonical historical records how men in general should make history for all time, lapsed" (1968:3, 100).

Although Levenson mourned the shattering of the Confucian world under the hammer blows of Maoist ideology and Western modernism, it was clear both to him and to the revolutionaries that there was much to be condemned in the Confucian past before East Asia could rise again.

However, the predicted demise of Confucianism and the Chinese empire proved premature. Confucianism now shows signs of rejoining the history of East Asia and is expanding rapidly into the larger global community of nations. But just as the projected demise of Confucianism proved chimerical, so the renewal is likewise subject to various interpretations. At one end there are scholars who firmly believe that we are witnessing a renewal of the tradition, albeit in a remarkably different manner than ever before. What we are seeing, according to this positive reinterpretation, is the emergence of an ecumenical Confucianism, at once chastened by the failures of the past and open to the influences of the modern and primarily Western world. At the other end of the spectrum there are those who note that whatever else may happen with Confucianism, the traditional pattern of what Mark Elvin (1996) has perceptively called "scriptural Confucianism" will never be revived in East Asia or anywhere else. According to this less sanguine prognostication, although we will certainly observe vestigial Confucian habits of the heart, there will never be anything like a scriptural tradition that will command the study, attention, affirmation, and then total commitment to a life lived in conformity with the Confucian Way. What is the truth of the situation? It is probably somewhere in the middle and probably impossible to ascertain at this time.

The Confucian tradition has changed so many times before, due to the pressure of history's dance to the music of time, that we must expect it to do so again. New Confucianism will retain a fascination with its classic texts and history; but it will change. And this change, because it embodies new patterns of response and transformation, will be something unexpected, unanticipated, and, it is hoped, exciting. Just as Confucius, after starting his travels, would have been surprised about becoming the great teacher of ten thousand generations and just as Chu Hsi would have been surprised by Wang Yang-ming's critique, so too will we be astonished by the ceaseless transformations and creativity of the Confucian Way in the future. Therefore, the task before us is to chronicle the developments and transformations of the Confucian Way. As we shall see, the Confucian Way has known some periods of resplendent glory and others of intense self-doubt and despair. But if China is poised to dominate the twenty-first century of the Pacific Era, it is supremely ironic that Confucian habits of the heart will help guide this remarkable transformation from an early colonial defeat to the growing wealth and power of the contemporary technological world.

I will display the pageant of the tradition's actual and intrinsic beauty (and blemishes) as a complicated and compelling creation of generations of East Asian people. There really were and still are good reasons for generations of Chinese, Korean, Japanese, and Vietnamese people to find a source of inspiration for ordering their lives in the philosophy of the first teacher, as Confucius is often called in East Asia. I believe that these great scholars, farmers, soldiers, rulers, poets, painters, doctors, historians, writers, civil servants, provincial officials, local teachers (both men and women), merchants, and common people had every right to embrace and promote the Confucian Tao. The Confucian tradition is one of the great intellectual achievements of humankind. As with all such variegated cultural systems, it has had its internal and external critics; it also has a history of failures and perversity. Nonetheless, the Confucian Tao represents one of the supreme human systems of study, contemplation, speculation, and action.

Of course, Confucians, as appears in Confucius' own reflections on the ambiguities and perils of public service, pondered the connection and all-too-probable misalliances of public service with the ruling powers and the seductive pleasures of assuming the mantle of an official state ideology. The Confucian problematic was in managing to remain committed to public service while avoiding the just critique of misguided, tyrannical, and corrupt state power. The problem was that neither were all rulers paradigmatic sage kings such as Yao or Shun, nor were their ministers paragons of virtue or wisdom like the duke of Chou. Like people in other parts of the world, Confucians had to put up with the general ebb and flow of humanity as far as their rulers went. Whatever the moral, intellectual, or cultural state of the ruler, the Confucian intellectual was bound by a sense of loyalty to the political process, by the need to make things better.

However, in the midst of the spiritual, intellectual, aesthetic, social, and political decay of the twentieth century, there has been a rebirth of scholarly attention to the richness and diversity of the Confucian Way both in East Asia and in the West. None of this would be surprising in this most historically prone intellectual tradition. Confucianism has known periods of great power and influence, of intellectual and cultural creativity. It is fair to say that from the Sung dynasty (960) to the end of the Ch'ing dynasty (1911), Confucians of various sorts controlled the workings of the family, of education, and of state service. From the time of the Ming dynasty (1368) on, Confucianism became even more important in the cultures of Korea and Japan.

Primary Focus

The primary focus of this study concerns the intellectual development of the Confucian Way in East Asia. There are two reasons for this. First, it is impossible to anticipate all the social, economic, political, artistic, literary, technological, gender, scientific, and material history that will be written about the Confucian Way in the years to come in a single work. The task of this study is to describe the general outlines of the intellectual development of the tradition from its beginnings to its modern revival. The selected bibliography is designed to point the reader toward the extensive and growing world of contemporary scholarship about the Confucian tradition. At best, we can capture moments of the history through the thought and words of significant Confucian scholars across the centuries. Furthermore, the history of Confucianism is also an international phenomenon, requiring separate studies of the Confucian impact on Korea, Japan, and Vietnam as well as China. Confucian philosophy has moved into the Western world along with the East Asian diaspora, making Confucianism now a part of Western intellectual history.

Second, I believe that there is something intrinsically fascinating in reviewing how Confucian intellectuals and scholars throughout East Asia have used the tradition in order to understand, interpret, and then order their social and physical worlds. In Levenson's memorable image, they sought to make history as well as to live it. For centuries, the peoples of

East Asia have found the Confucian tale to be a compelling story, although not one without problems. There have been many internal and external critics of the Confucian Way who have been more than willing to point out where the Confucians have gone wrong. The task of this study is to allow the Confucians to describe, explain, interpret, and then commend their tradition in terms of its intellectual content.

One of the truly unexplored frontiers for Confucian studies is the examination of the spread of the tradition in Vietnam. However, there is nothing comparable to the scholarship available about China, Korea, and Japan when it comes to describing the role of Confucianism in Vietnamese history. I have been told by a Vietnamese colleague who became interested in the impact of Confucianism in Vietnam that when he went to explore the previous literature he found no general, comprehensive studies in either Vietnamese or French on the topic. I have thus had to make a difficult choice here. Rather than relying on the very few sources presently available for the study of Confucianism in Vietnam, I have decided not to include any of this material. Perhaps if there is a second edition of this book, or if other scholars in later decades return to a general account of the Confucian Way, there will be enough parallel Vietnamese material to allow for its inclusion along with the Chinese, Korean, and Japanese material.

Regional Issues and Variations

This study chronicles the spread of the Confucian tradition from its Chinese home to the rest of East Asia—and into the wider world of the global city of the modern world. Although it is true that the Chinese carried their love of the Confucian tradition everywhere they traveled and that visitors to China often became fascinated by its teachings, the serious appreciation and indigenous appropriation of Confucianism occurred at different rates in Korea and Japan. For instance, whereas Japanese scholars knew that the Confucian tradition had an early impact on the formation of the first Japanese imperial institutions, it is fair to say that the flowering of Confucian philosophy in Japan did not take place until the Tokugawa period in the sixteenth century.

Korean Confucianization took place much earlier than that in Japan and had an even greater impact on the whole of Korean society. The Koreans, from late in the fourteenth century to the nineteenth century, actually tried to adopt consistent Neo-Confucian patterns of thought and practice for all aspects of their personal and social lives. They were so successful in this endeavor that later, especially after the Manchu conquest of Ming China in 1644, they asserted that they were the most faithful of Confucian countries because of their upholding Chu Hsi's imported Sung Neo-Confucian orthodoxy.

Confucianism thus became an essential part of Korean and Japanese intellectual life. Moreover, there were periods when the most interesting philosophical and intellectual activities in the Confucian world were in Korea and Japan rather than China. In short, Korean and Japanese intellectuals actively identified with the Confucian tradition and shaped their lives around its teachings, ritual, and institutions. And more than that, Confucianism was transformed and adapted in unique and creative ways within Korean and Japanese cultures. In trying to determine just when this happens, I have been guided by the self-understanding of these regional traditions and by the judgments of modern scholarship. Accordingly, I will not directly address the history of the Korean and then the Japanese variants of Confucianism until discussion of the fourteenth and fifteenth centuries. It was only then that Confucianism became a multicountry symphony throughout East Asia.

Defining the Confucian Way

What *is* Confucianism? The answer is not quite as clear as it might seem at the outset (see the section "Further Readings and Contentious Issues" at the end of the book for further discussion of this issue). The burden of modern study of the Confucian Way has been to uncover the complexity of the vision, life, conduct, meditation, conflict, compromise, and creativity that is hidden by the generalization of the word "Confucianism." But even if we can define what we mean by Confucianism, there is still the question of what Confucianism signifies as an intellectual tradition worthy of serious study in the modern world. But why should anyone be interested in exploring this?

I mean to defend the thesis that Confucianism is intrinsically valuable as an intellectual, moral, and reflective system beyond the historical and sociological fact that its impact on East Asian civilization is as great as that of Christianity has been in the West. I do not know how anyone could write a history of Western European thought without recourse to the interpretation of Christianity in all its multifarious guises. Nor can one study East Asian history without trying to place Confucianism in its diverse regional contexts.

Beginning with their first encounter with Confucianism, Western scholars wondered what they had found. Was Confucianism a religion, a form of social ethics, a species of Asian wisdom literature, an account of history, or a particular kind of Asian primordial philosophy? It is instructive that both the early Catholic and Protestant missionary-scholars called the canonical Confucian texts "classics" rather than scriptures. This shows their profound ambiguity as they tried to categorize the Confucian Way in terms of familiar Western intellectual concepts such as religion or philosophy. A classic could be either religious or philosophical in nature. Early Western scholars rightly recognized that the Confucian Way was founded on a comprehensive philosophical and religious worldview.

It is crucial to remember that the Confucian tradition does not see itself as actually beginning with Confucius. Such a notion would have shocked the First Teacher, who saw himself as a transmitter of a tradition that was already old by his day and stretched back to the primordial teachings of the great sages of high antiquity. Whereas we now recognize how creative Confucius was in his presentation of the way of the ancient sages, this does not obviate the fact that for him and his followers, the real claim was not the novel creation of some new doctrine or ritual system but the respristination of the essence of the inherited way of the former dynasties and sage kings. Confucius and the early Confucians took their history with deadly earnestness. They truly believed that the records of "this culture of ours" pointed out the correct way to be a human being among other human beings. If one properly understood the classics of the ancient sages, as supposedly edited and preserved by Confucius, then one had a chance to merit the name of a civilized person.

Were these early *ru*/ritual scholars, the classical Chinese name used to describe early Confucians—the ancestors of classical and early modern Confucians? Although there is no consensus on this issue, it is a safe generalization to note that *ru* as a designation does define many of those who considered themselves Confucians. Such ruminations on early Chinese intellectual nomenclature demonstrate the complexity of matching modern Western concepts of religion and tradition to a term like *ru*. But at least no one seriously doubts that Confucius' own life and teaching mark a dramatic change in the history of the developing tradition. He is the first teacher and is universally recognized as having given the tradition its distinctive characteristics and orientation for the rest of its history.

We need to remember that the use of labels such as Confucian, Taoist, and Legalist—all the terms that are in common use today to describe the various schools of pre-Han thought—are actually derived from the historical and bibliographical writings of the great historians of the Han dynasty just before the beginning of the Common Era. For instance, the Han historians Ssu-ma T'an, his son Ssu-ma Ch'ien, and finally Pan Ku, as they sought to order the exuberance of the late Chou and early Han intellectual world, created a list of six major schools that we still use today to classify early Chinese thought. These terms have stuck because, as with all such good typologies, they are a rough-and-ready way to make sense of what has gone on before, even if this is not the way Confucius or Chuang Tzu might have seen their thought.

Confucians become Confucians by the reading, interpreting, and living out of these canonical texts. The range of how they understand these texts runs from the purely pragmatic to the obviously spiritual; in fact, for many Confucians none of this reading makes any sense at all without the religious encounter with the ultimate or transcendent referent indicated in the texts by terms such as the "Tao" or the "Supreme Ultimate." This range of reactions to reading the Confucian texts has caused a perennial debate about whether Confucianism is a religion. The answer is probably that some Confucians interpret their tradition in a highly spiritual way and discover in it a transcendent referent point that defines and transforms their lives for the better.

More specifically, the modern Chinese scholar Tu Wei-ming (1989) has maintained that it is much better to talk about the religious dimensions of the Confucian tradition than to define Confucianism as a religion in the mold of Judaism, Christianity, or Islam. At least part of the reason for this difficulty in defining Confucianism as a religion is that Confucianism is an open or inclusive humanism in the sense that it begins with events and documents from human history and not from some revealed scripture. The direction of these reflections may be spiritual, but the focus is always on humanity and the virtue of humaneness. All the same, there have been many Confucians who were completely uninterested in the spiritual side of the tradition and yet would always have been recognized by other Confucians as members of the tradition. To be Confucian, let me stress again, means being dedicated to the canon and its interpretation rather than to any one philosophical or religious reading of the text.

The Six Epochs of the Confucian Tradition

During its spread throughout East Asia, there have been six paradigmatic historical transformations of the Confucian tradition.

1. The rise of the classical tradition in Shang and Chou China (ca. 1700–221 B.C.E.)
2. The commentary of the Han dynasty (206 B.C.E–220)
3. The defense of the Confucian Way: The challenge of Neo-Taoism and Buddhism, from the Wei-Chin to the T'ang dynasties (220–907)
4. The renaissance of the Sung and the flowering of the Ming dynasties (960–1644) and Confucianism's spread to Korea and Japan
5. The evidential research of the Ch'ing dynasty and Korean and Japanese appropriations of the tradition (1644–1911)
6. New Confucianism in the modern world: Variations on an East Asian theme (1911 to the present)

Such a historical analysis based on paradigmatic change challenges the view that the Confucian tradition was a perpetual formalism of ritual and social domination. A chapter is devoted to each one of these distinctive periods in this study. The classical period begins with Confucius, is reshaped by Mencius (371–289 B.C.E.), and is concluded by Hsün Tzu (fl. 298–238 B.C.E.). In framing his vision of the Tao, Confucius relied on a number of early traditions, including historical documents, governmental decrees, poetry, and ritual texts that were later given the title "classics." The number of classics grew from the initial recognition of five to thirteen in their final canonization during the Sung dynasty. Most of these texts were assumed to have been in existence prior to Confucius' lifetime. In fact, contrary to modern scholarly opinion, the tradition maintains that Confucius was the first great commentator and editor of the Confucian classics. As concerns the intellectual development of the tradition, Confucius, Mencius, and Hsün Tzu are commemorated as the foundational masters, and in fact they do indeed provide the basic structure for Confucian thought down to the modern period.

The second transformation of the Confucian Way began with the founding of the great Han dynasty (206 B.C.E.–220 C.E.). The second stage was marked by the formulation of a state-supported imperial Confucian ideology to replace the discredited Legalism of the Ch'in dynasty. This is also the grand era of commentary as the technique for understanding the words and meanings of the sages. In one form or another, this Han mixture of Legalist realpolitik, Confucian ethics, and Five Phases cosmology—and much else, as we shall see—came to dominate the Chinese political, social, and intellectual world right up to the end of the imperial state and the founding of the Chinese republic in 1911. However, many Confucians were extremely disconcerted about the inevitable misuse of Confucian symbols by state authority. Balancing this fear of serving an unworthy prince was the perennial Confucian desire to bring good government and social order to the world. The Confucians saw that this service of theirs must be tied closely to the government for it to be effective. Three of the most representative of the Han Confucians were Tung Chung-shu (c. 179–104 B.C.E.), Yang Hsiung (53 B.C.E.–18 C.E.), and Hsün Yüeh (148–209).

The third era begins with the Wei-Chin period and the revival of a form of Taoist thought called Neo-Taoism. Many of the greatest intellectuals of this era, such as the precocious Wang Pi, mixed their Confucian reflections with Taoist cosmology and metaphysics. Even more momentous was the arrival of Buddhism in China. The Chinese intellectual world was never the same after the impact of the Buddha's dharma. Although Confucianism never lost its place in the Chinese state or family, it is entirely accurate to say that the most acute religious, artistic, and philosophical minds in China · from the third to the ninth centuries devoted themselves to the appropriation and Chinese transformation of the Buddhist dharma. Great temples were created; the huge Buddhist *sangha,* or monastic community, was formed; entirely new and elaborate schools of Buddhist thought such as

T'ien-t'ai, Hua-yen, Pure Land, and Ch'an were created and sustained. The rise and flourishing of this great Chinese Buddhist world formed the background for new epochs of transformation of the Confucian Way.

Toward the end of the T'ang dynasty, a number of Confucian scholars saw their task as defending the Confucian Way against the challenge of Buddhism. The three most famous of these scholars were Han Yü (768–824), Li Ao (fl. 798), and Liu Tsung-yüan (733–819). Along with continuing the Han Confucian interest in government service, commentary, family ritual, and historical writing, these scholars framed the major lines of the Confucian response to the Buddhist philosophical and religious challenge.

The fourth stage of the development of the Confucian Tao is the justly celebrated revival of Confucian thought known in the West as the Neo-Confucianism of the Northern and Southern Sung (960–1279). The Sung scholars of the Neo-Confucian revival invented a new name for their teachings, calling it the Learning of the Way, or *tao-hsüeh*. The revival itself began in the Northern Sung period and reached its great conclusion with the synthesis of Chu Hsi (1130–1200). Regarding the scope and influence of his work, Chu has been likened to St. Aquinas in the West, and there is little doubt that except for Confucius, no one has been more important in defining the course of the Confucian tradition. Chu Hsi's form of Confucianism, which he based on the writings of the Northern Sung masters Chou Tun-i, Shao Yung, Chang Tsai, Ch'eng Hao, and Ch'eng I, was spread by his followers to Korea and Japan. Neo-Confucianism actually replaced Buddhism as the principal form of Chinese thought from the Sung to the modern period.

According to Confucian scholars, the great Neo-Confucian reformers of the Sung, Yüan, and Ming dynasties are only second to the great classical Chou founders in terms of their impact on Chinese culture. From the Confucian point of view, no higher praise can be given. If the classical Confucians—Confucius, Mencius, and Hsün Tzu—defended the learning of the sages during the Spring and Autumn and Warring States periods of the late Chou dynasty, the Sung and Ming Neo-Confucian masters did the same in countering the challenge of Taoism and Buddhism in their own age. Even though there were great changes and transformations of the Way after Chu Hsi, no one can deny the pivotal role that he played in the renewal and definition of the tradition. Although others could contest Chu's synthesis in the name of the tradition, no one could overlook his contribution to it.

The most important challenge to Chu Hsi's summation of the Way came during the Ming dynasty in the form of Wang Yang-ming's (1472–1529) epic struggle to come to terms with Chu Hsi's rationalistic study of principle. Wang is remembered as the founder of the School of Ming, or *hsin-hsüeh*, in contradistinction to Chu Hsi's School of Principle, or *li-hsüeh*. Wang, along with being a brilliant critic of Chu's thought, was also an outstanding general and civil servant, poet, and teacher. Wang held that principle was in the mind-heart of the sincere student of the Way. He further taught a doctrine of the unity of thought and action based on this understanding of true principle being in the mind-heart.

The fifth epoch of Confucian learning is itself a reaction and transformation of the great Neo-Confucian achievement of the fourth phase of the Sung and Ming dynasties. I believe that the Ch'ing School of Evidential Learning, also called the School of Han Learning, is unique in its concerns and its self-conscious rejection of a great deal of Sung-Ming scholarship. Its great leaders were thinkers such as Wang Fu-chih (1619–1692), Huang Tsung-hsi (1610–1695), and Tai Chen (1723–1777). By turns, these Ch'ing scholars castigated the needlessly abstract thought of the Sung and the equally debilitating subjectivism of Wang's thought in the Ming as wrong turns for the Confucian Way. They believed that Confucianism must be of some concrete use for the people. Hence, they often stressed strict, accurate, indeed, empirical historical research. Likewise, they argued that much Sung and Ming thought was infected with an unhealthy Buddhist and Taoist love of meditation without proper attention to what ought to be Confucian self-cultivation, namely, the practice of service to self and others in practical ways. All of their empirical studies of the history of taxation and flood control were defended as being more in tune with the true nature of Confucian thought than Buddhist or Taoist sensibilities.

The sixth epoch of the Confucian Way is dramatically different from the first five. With the arrival of the expansive and aggressive Western powers, the Confucian tradition, like every other aspect of Chinese culture, was disrupted. This agitation continues today as Chinese intellectuals, along with their Korean, Japanese, and Vietnamese colleagues, struggle to come to grips with the interruption of the West. Although there is an early analogy to the arrival of the Buddhist dharma, there are profound differences because the Buddhists never arrived with such overwhelming military, political, and economic power.

East Asian Confucian intellectuals have responded to this great challenge from the West by searching for a modern identity for the Confucian Way. This modern movement is called "New Confucianism" in order to distinguish it from the earlier Neo-Confucian synthesis. The contemporary Confucian scholar Tu Wei-ming describes the New Confucianism as the third wave of the Confucian tradition (Eber 1986). Tu uses the metaphor of a great ocean wave to express the movement of the tradition within the East Asian cultural world and into the broader world of the modern global city.

Enduring Themes in the Confucian Way

One constant feature of the Confucian tradition is the lack of any formal or enforced systematic list of official teachings or dogmas as is the case for the great West Asian religions of Judaism, Christianity, and Islam, and even various well-defined Buddhist schools. Although in China from 1313 to 1905, there were official lists of texts and commentaries to be mastered for the purpose of passing the vital civil service examinations, there was no set of official guidelines or revealed dogmas concerning how these texts were to be understood, save for the fact that Chu Hsi's interpretations of the classics were used as the basis for the examinations.

However, it is equally true that there are a number of enduring themes or traits common to all Confucian discourse from the time of Confucius to the current New Confucianism. It is better to think of these traits as clusters of overlapping concepts, prototypes, or metaphors as the tradition is lived by than as a substantial, absolute, eternal, or unchanging core. Over its long history, classical Chinese, the common language of East Asian philosophy, used a common set of written characters that often hid the fact that there was transformation of the philosophical meaning of these terms over time. Hence, what a Chou aristocrat like Confucius thought about ritual differed markedly from what Chu Hsi wrote about in the Southern Sung. Any list of shared prototypical traits needs to be treated with care; it is a heuristic device designed to help bring order to the vastness of the Confucian tradition and must never be confused with the living reality of the tradition itself. At best, it is a list of complex ideal types.

In summary, the eight persistent traits are:

1. *T'ien-ming,* as the Mandate of Heaven, the very source of creation itself; this is the ceaseless productivity of the Tao;
2. *Jen,* as creativity mediated by the primordial concern for self and others; this is the Tao as manifested in proper human conduct and relationships;
3. *Li,* as timely ritual actions or civility of conduct between and among people;
4. *Hsin,* as the mind-heart functioning and as the locus of the experiential unity of concern-consciousness, the proper response to the Way as mandate, morality, and civility between and among people;
5. *Hsing,* as human nature in its role as the active creation of new life-values for civilized human society and guidance for forming human character;
6. *Tao wen-hsüeh* (or *chu-ching ch'iung-li*), as serious study and reflection or residing in reverence in order to exhaust principle; this is the self-reflexive function of critical reason as an aspect of the cultivation of humane wisdom;
7. *Ch'i,* as matter-energy, the dynamic force/matrix from which all objects and events are manifested and to which they return;
8. *Chih shan,* or *ho,* as the highest good or harmony, the peace and perfection of human nature that comes from the measured realization of the ethical personal and social life.

Is there some root metaphor or enduring prototype that can capture the sensibility of the tradition embodied in these eight traits? Even a list of eight common themes omits important concepts such as *tao*/the Way and can easily oversimplify the true details of the historical situation and the uniqueness of each great thinker. Nonetheless, I believe that the New Confucians Hsü Fu-kuan and Mou Tsung-san are highly suggestive when they observe that it is impossible to consider the vast sweep of the Confucian tradition without paying attention to what they call concern-consciousness as a root metaphor for the Confucian Way. They tell us that Confucians cannot be part of the tradition without being concerned with getting the Tao for themselves and being concerned about the welfare of others. This is why Confucianism is so often defined as a form of social ethics or applied political philosophy.

All of this is true. If Hsü and Mou are correct, then this distinctive Confucian sense of concern-consciousness for self and others expands to include what in Western thought encompasses religion, art, political science, medicine, technology, science, and philosophy. Concern-consciousness becomes the grand theme, the single thread through which the tale is told and deemed to constitute proper thought, passion, and action. To be rightly concerned about self and others is the crux of the Confucian path of self-cultivation. But what makes for such a rich story is that our concern with human flourishing must be conditioned by our historical circumstances. This is one reason that Confucians placed emphasis on intuition, correlative thinking, metaphors, and examples as the way to reason through the human condition. The Confucians resist a priori deductions of completely formal sets of transcendent rules. It is custom, ritual eminence, and example that provide guidance as we try to broaden the Way with excellence and humane conduct.

It is now time to examine how Confucius, Mencius, and Hsün Tzu illumined the Confucian Way.

❀ 1 ❀

The Classical Tradition
from Confucius to Hsün Tzu

CONFUCIUS WOULD HAVE BEEN SURPRISED, perhaps even shocked, to discover that he had invented Confucianism. Just as Judaism holds that there was a great deal of Jewish history before the revelation to Moses at Mt. Sinai, Confucians advertise that Confucianism existed long before Confucius. In fact, Confucians maintain that they are simply reminding humanity of the profound truths to be found in the teaching of the great founding sages of Chinese high antiquity. Confucius did not invent *jen*/humaneness; he taught a primordial wisdom culled from the teachings of the ancient sages.

The three classical Confucian masters of the later part of the Chou dynasty (551 B.C.E.–206 B.C.E.)—Confucius, Mencius, and Hsün Tzu—contemplated the great legendary yet paradigmatic sage rulers beginning with Fu Hsi; Shen Nung, the Divine Farmer; Huang-ti, the Yellow Emperor; Shao Hao; and Chuan Hsü. These great cultural heroes and semidivine figures were followed by the equally exemplary and more human Yao, Shun, and Yü, the master of the floods and the purported founder of the first great "historical" dynasty, the Hsia. No shortlist of these founders and heroes would be complete without also referring to Kings Wen and Wu of the Chou dynasty (founded somewhere around 1045 B.C.E) and Wu's brother, the duke of Chou. The duke of Chou is famous for acting as the wise and faithful regent for the young son of his brother Wu. The duke of Chou becomes the chief exemplar of a worthy minister within an imperial order and the patron saint of later Confucians, who believed one way any ruler proved to be a good prince was by listening to the sage advice of wise ministers.

From modern archaeology we now know that the traditional Confucian view of Chinese predynastic history is not what scholars consider history in any verifiable form. There are many important cultural artifacts predating the traditional founding of the Shang dynasty that demonstrate the great Bronze Age culture in North China. Nonetheless, the traditions that

Confucius so revered about the predynastic sage kings and the Hsia, Shang, and Chou dynasties already had a long history by the time he sought to revive them in the sixth century B.C.E. Although much of Chinese history is vague before the eighth century B.C.E., we know that the Shang dynasty is certainly historical and that perhaps the Hsia dynasty itself represents an earlier version of Bronze Age literate culture that eventually became the Shang civilization. Although he did not know as much about previous cultures as he would have liked, Confucius still revered their teachings as expressing the way civilized human beings should act toward each other. According to Confucius, we must all learn from the ritual, poetry, music, and morality of these early sage kings and their ministers.

Confucius stands at the pivot of the Axial Age in China. The great ancient cultures of the world—such as those in Shang and Chou China, ancient Egypt, the nations around the eastern end of the Mediterranean, the Mesopotamian lands, and Vedic India—were being transformed by thinkers and seers as diverse as Confucius, the Buddha, the prophets of Israel, and the pre-Socratic philosophers of Greece. The cultural capital of the Hsia and Shang civilizations was passed to Confucius; but in their passing they were transformed. These thinkers are collectively the founders of the Axial Age because the great intellectual movements and religious traditions that they founded or shaped are with us today. In a sense we still live in the world of Socrates, the prophets of Israel, the Buddha, and Confucius.

The Confucian tradition, as a ramified cumulative culture of concern-consciousness, shows a profound continuity with what can only be called pan-Chinese civilization. By "culture" I mean the constellation of the five distinctive realms of social interest including art, morality, religion, science and technology, and philosophy. For instance, the question of the role of religion has always been a perplexing one in the Confucian context. However, as Jordan Paper (1995) and other students of Chinese culture have argued, the Chinese certainly have an indigenous and primordial religiosity that has worked itself out in a myriad of ways over time. The best religious question to ask in East Asia is "To whom do you owe sacrifice?" and not "What religion do you belong to?" As Paper has noted, many uneducated and educated Chinese will argue that they "do not belong" to any particular organized religious tradition such as Christianity, Judaism, or Islam but will invariably have definite opinions concerning the sacrifice they owe their ancestors.

Other scholars have debated the role that Confucianism played in either preventing the growth of science and technology in modern China or promoting its emergence in the classical and medieval periods. Joseph Needham, the great historian of Chinese science, warned us that it is important to define what we mean by science. Needham argued that the Chinese were leaders in the worlds of ancient and medieval science; East

Asia only fell behind Europe during the period of the rise of modern, ecumenical science. However, no one would deny the great impact Confucians had on Chinese art—though again there are those who both praise and blame Confucian theories and artistic practices. And finally, Western intellectuals have been fascinated or repelled by Chinese philosophy since the European Enlightenment.

Confucius' favorite term for the fullness of humanity, the primal Confucian virtue of *jen*/humaneness, speaks volumes about a condition of human life that makes sense only within a community of shared interests. Furthermore, this communal aspect of humanity always, from the Confucian perspective, arises out of the family, because for Confucius the crucible that forges the human being is the family. Family ritual and conduct has always and everywhere played a tremendous role in the Confucian world. We hasten to add that the empirical family provided Confucians with abundant social and psychological problems as well. Beginning with Confucius, Confucians became aware of the fact that not all families are perfect.

One of the problems with trying to be too precise about what Benjamin Schwartz (1985) calls the "early cultural orientations" of the Chinese world of the Shang and Chou cultures is that we have so little evidence when we compare our early conjectures with the later records of Chinese civilization. Schwartz went on to note that "when one examines the oracle bone inscriptions one is immediately struck by the persuasiveness of what we call ancestor worship" (Schwartz 1985:20). The formalized worship of the ancestors specifies a persistent feature of Chinese and Confucian thought: the role of ritual, or *li,* in human civilization. Many intellectual historians and students of religion have noted that no great human cumulative tradition places more emphasis on the role of ritual, organized civility, or appropriate action in human culture than Confucianism.

Nonetheless, Confucius' intellectual world lacks the recognized philosophical schools as they were finally arranged in the second century B.C.E.. It is true, save for the arrival of Buddhism in the second century C.E., that almost all the familiar themes and philosophical concepts and metaphors that came to dominate East Asian thought originated between the time of Confucius (551 B.C.E.) and the beginning of the Han dynasty (206 B.C.E.). Alfred North Whitehead once remarked that the history of Western thought is a series of footnotes to Plato; much the same can be said about the history of Chinese philosophy after Confucius, Mencius, and Hsün Tzu.

Confucius (551–479 B.C.E.): The Way of Virtue and Tradition

Without a shadow of a doubt, Confucius is the dominant intellectual figure of East Asia. No one can understand the history of China, Korea, and

Japan without the influence of the "teacher of the ten thousand generations"—one of the most revealing of the titles ever attached to Confucius
by his followers. Yet we know remarkably little about his life. In many
ways this is not surprising; we know little about the lives of many of the
Axial Age thinkers such as the Buddha, the prophets of Israel, the pre-
Socratics of Greece, or the great *rishis* of India. Furthermore, it is a mistake
to look in the *Analects* for a systematic account of Confucius' thought or
life because this book is a record of conversations with students and not a
critical intellectual biography of Confucius.

Confucius' path of *jen*/humaneness, as the supreme marker of the Tao of
Heaven, is the virtue of virtues and the defining characteristic of true civilization. Although he never defines just what he means by the way or by humaneness in a purely propositional form, it is clear that he insists that there
really is a way of humaneness in the world that we ignore to our peril. This
way is the way of proper conduct, hence it is linked to a second great notion, that of *te*/virtue, as power. Confucius invented neither humaneness
nor virtue, and the entire history of early Chinese thought is an extended
argument about the nature and the way to achieve these virtues. Even the
modern critic of the Confucian tradition, Chad Hansen (1992), has observed that all Chinese thought aims to teach people a regulative rule about
how to guide their action, either as individuals or as members of a group.

Even in the midst of difficulty, the proper way can be learned, but learning or study is never easy according to the Master. Yen Hui, Confucius'
most famous and best-loved student, reported that

> Yen Yüan, heaving a sigh, said, "The more I look up at it the higher it appears.
> The more I bore into it the harder it becomes. I see it before me. Suddenly it is
> behind me.
>   The master is good at leading one on step by step. He broadens me with cul-
> ture and brings me back to essentials by means of the rites. I cannot give up
> even if I wanted to, but, having done all I can, it seems to rise up sheer above
> me and I have no way of going after it, however much I may want to."
> (Confucius 1992:79)

Although Confucius was a stern judge of his own life and character, what
shines through all of his writing is the joy that he felt in trying to teach his
students about the Way of the sages. When asked about how he would describe himself, the Master said, "Why did you not say something to this effect: he is the sort of man who forgets to eat when he works himself into a
frenzy over some problem, who is so full of joy that he forgets his worries
and who does not notice the onset of old age?" (Confucius 1992:61).

Another facet of Confucius' personality that speaks across the centuries
is his humility. Not only did he never claim to be a sage or even a worthy
gentleman, but he believed that he had never even encountered such a person. However, he was convinced that we can become like his favorite im-

ages of human perfection, embodied in such as the duke of Chou, if we love to study enough to put true virtue into practice. Although perfection is difficult, it is not something that is impossible or something that we need not seek. It is, as his student Yen Hui noted and as Spinoza would have said, something that is as wonderful as it is rare.

As is the case with so many other traditions, the *Analects* is filled with what we might call fruitful ambiguities. For instance, Confucius' comments on *hsing*/human nature have provided the Confucian tradition with an endless opportunity to divine what the Master really meant by our common humanity. "The Master said: 'Men are close to one another by nature. They drift apart through behaviour that is constantly repeated'" and then "The Master said: "It is only the most intelligent and the most stupid who cannot be budged'" (Confucius 1992:171). Mencius and Hsün Tzu, basing their arguments on their interpretation of what Confucius must have meant, began a perennial debate about the true nature of human nature. Did Confucius hold that our basic human nature is good and that we only later learn evil? Did the Master hold that there are people who cannot be reformed even by contact with a sage? Or are there people who are already born sages?

However arduous the path of true virtue is, Confucius outlined a path for his own intellectual and spiritual biography. The Master said, "At fifteen I set my heart on learning; at thirty I took my stand; at forty I was never in two minds; at fifty I understood the Decree of Heaven; at sixty my ear was attuned; at seventy I followed my heart's desire without overstepping the line" (Confucius 1992:11).

In an innovative study of Confucius, David Hall and Roger Ames (1987) employed Confucius' chronology of his intellectual development in order to present the major themes of Confucian philosophy. They begin their account by stressing "the conditions of learning" that dominate the Confucian quest for virtue. According to Hall and Ames, the process of intellectual reflection in Confucius revolves around the interplay of *hsüeh*/learning and *ssu*/reflecting and then realizing what has been learned by means of *hsin*/living up to one's word. As the *Analects* say, "The Master said, 'If one learns from others but does not think, one will be bewildered. If, on the other hand, one thinks but does not learn from others, one will be imperiled'" (Confucius 1992:15). Hence, the act of learning and thinking is a performative action "that is an activity whose immediate consequence is the achievement of a practical result" (Hall and Ames 1987:44).

A. C. Graham developed a hypothesis about a pan-Chinese theory of knowledge that could be applied to any of the early schools. Graham called this a "quasi-syllogism" with a common structure.

In choosing how to act we are accustomed to recognise an imperative, "Face facts", which imposes itself whenever emotional bias makes us reluctant to acknowledge things as they are. . . .

In awareness from all viewpoints, spatial, temporal and personal, of everything relevant to the issue (= viewpoints from which I do find myself spontaneously moved in one direction or the other) I find myself moved towards X;
overlooking something relevant I find myself moved towards Y.

Be aware from all relevant viewpoints . . . Therefore let yourself be moved
towards X (a goal which may be here or there, now or then, yours or mine).
(Graham 1992b:17, 23)

Graham argued that this kind of discernment, based on spontaneity and
awareness of the facts, has the advantage of avoiding the persistent problem of separating facts from values in ethical thinking. Of course, what
marks the particular Confucian twist on Graham's general thesis is that
Confucius did not just start with a series of value-neutral "facts"; rather,
the Master began with learning about the rituals, music, and institutions of
the early Chou, especially the work of Kings Wen and Wu and the duke of
Chou.

At thirty, Confucius took his stand in the world of Chou rituals, or *li*.
Ritual is civility, a basic recognition that life without ritual as appropriate
action is barbaric in the sense that without ritual the only real law would
be that of brute force over all other concerns. Moreover, ritual for
Confucius was something much more than a prophylactic against the rule
of the strongest barbarian. Confucius loved ritual because it was beautiful.
In this sense, ritual conjoins itself with the ebb and flow of life, all the minor and major social graces that make life worth living from day to day.
The mundane quality of ritual must not be lightly dismissed. We all live by
our little rituals—the way we go about our lives, the way we shape the
meanings, metaphors, and times of our very being human together. In his
influential study of Confucius, Herbert Fingarette (1972) said that for
Confucius the secular was really the sacred. What Fingarette means is
neatly captured in one of his chapter titles: "Human Community as Holy
Rite." In fact, the later Confucian tradition was always fond of saying that
it was a teaching about reality as opposed to Taoist teachings about non-
action or Buddhist teachings about nothingness.

Fingarette deemed that for Confucius the essence of the spiritual quality
of life was not to be found in some world beyond human social life. The ultimate values of human life were always found in human community. And
human community was only civilized to the extent that it was founded on
good rituals. As Hall and Ames have argued, ritual "enables one to determine, assume, and display his personal stance" (1987:85). As they noted,
Confucius believed that you could not really be a person until you were
able to appropriate ritual as the way of action. "Unless you study the rites
you will be ill-equipped to take your stand" (Confucius 1992:167). Hall
and Ames went on to note that there is a linguistic link between the notion

of ritual and the body such that one can make the case that without ritual one does not really have a body, that is, a place to stand among other human beings.

However, how does one know what ritual to follow? D. C. Lau (1989) has observed that for Confucius, a person's appropriation of ritual is always governed by considerations of righteousness or justice. Further, Hall and Ames cited the fact that "throughout the early philosophical and philological literature, *yi* is consistently defined in terms of its homophone, *yi*, 'right, proper, appropriate, suitable'" (1987:96). Of course, one could argue immediately that we find ritual through the study of the rituals of the worthy sages of antiquity. This would be correct as far as it goes, and Confucius was definitely interested in such study. But such study does not go far enough; even ritual must be judged in the context of righteousness. How then do we understand the conjunction that allows ritual and justice to become the basis for human virtue?

A ritual is just or righteous because it is *jen*/humane. The person of humaneness is a truly authoritative person in terms of ritual and wisdom. As Hall and Ames have pointed out, "The authoritative person is perpetually self-surpassing, to be evaluated in open-ended, qualitative, terms rather than in terms of 'completion' or 'fulfillment'" (1987:115). Of course, *jen* has long been recognized as the primary Confucian virtue. Confucius transformed an aristocratic virtue of noblesse oblige into the virtue around which all the other Confucian virtues revolve. According to Confucius, only a person of *jen* can truly be counted a civilized person. Or as Hall and Ames put it, "We have defined 'authoritative person' (*jen*) as a process of integrative person making in which one incorporates the interests of others as his own and conducts himself in a manner that addresses the general good" (1987:122).

Confucius repeatedly noted that there was nothing supernatural about *jen* even if it was a very difficult thing to achieve. "Now, on the other hand, a benevolent man (*jen*) helps others to take their stand in that he himself wishes to take his stand, and gets others there in that he himself wishes to get there. The ability to take as analogy what is near at hand can be called the method of benevolence (*jen*)" (Confucius 1992:55). Perhaps achievement is the wrong way to express what humaneness really is. We must remember, as Yen Hui pointed out, that even if one worked hard at the cultivation of virtue, real humaneness would rise up again and remain as elusive as ever. As D. C. Lau pointed out in his translation, "This awareness that what is appropriate changes with the times was one of the outstanding features of Confucius' thought, so much so that Mencius describes him as 'the sage with the sense of what is fitting to the times'" (Confucius 1992:xlviii).

The next question to address is this: How does one become a good person? Ideally, such a person will manifest *jen*/humaneness in proper ritual action, guided always and in every circumstance by justice or righteousness. Once this is done, and Confucius was profoundly aware how difficult such an achievement was, then the person is worthy of being called a *chün tzu,* an exemplary or authoritative person. The term *chün tzu* is also often translated as "gentleman" for the simple reason that women in classical China, as in the rest of Eurasia, were excluded from much social, artistic, political, and intellectual life. Nonetheless, there is nothing about the union of humaneness, civility, and justice that is alien as a basic philosophical ideal to women, as we shall see later.

Hall and Ames noted that "first, the model is not only a means of sustaining continuity with the sages of the past, he is a means of stimulating novelty, as well. . . . models may, indirectly, take the form of institutions (*li*) as well as persons" (1987:179). Furthermore, they argue that there is a distinctive aesthetic quality to the profound person because that person is the author of himself or herself. Ultimately, the *chün tzu* is accorded this title because of the way he or she achieves a balance of virtue and circumstance in a timely and appropriate way, of not being of two minds, of avoiding being a divided and conflicted person. "His existence is in pursuit of the fullest disclosure of the concrete detail as a contribution to the harmonious order of the whole" (Hall and Ames 1987:192). This is a person of sincerity, or *ch'eng,* as the self-realization of humaneness in all its personal and social dimensions.

However noble any one achievement may be, life moves on and at the age of fifty, Confucius realized the *ming* of *t'ien*. The phrase *t'ien-ming* introduces another pair of crucial concepts: *ming*/fate, circumstances, destiny, or mandate; and *t'ien*/heaven. Both concepts guide us into the world of Confucius' vision of ultimate reality. Confucius was hesitant to speak too much about the complicated matters of heaven and fate. "The topics the Master did not speak of were prodigies, force, disorder and the gods" (Confucius 1992:61). Given that heaven was the author of all of these things, it may surprise us that Confucius was not willing to speak of them. As Hall and Ames have suggested, "Where *t'ien-ming* means the causal conditions constituting the whole of existence as perceived from a particular perspective, *ming* can mean the same, or can also mean the causal conditions constituting a particular phenomenon, without reference to the whole" (1987:213).

As an ultimate vision of reality as the Tao, Hall and Ames attested that "Confucius' cosmology is a generalized sociology, a vision of the manner in which human beings emerge from within a social context grounded in a tradition, while remaining open to novel articulations insofar as these might be called for by the *ming* of present circumstances" (1987:248). Of course, another name for this reality is the Tao itself as the matrix of all order, especially the order as recorded in the records of the early sages. Or as Confucius put it,

Kung-sun Ch'ao of Wei asked of Tzu-kung, "From whom did Chung-ni (Confucius) learn?

Tzu-kung said, "The way of King Wen and King Wu has not yet fallen to the ground but is still to be found in men. There is no man who does not have something of the way of Wen and Wu in him. Superior men have got hold of what is of greater significance while inferior men have got hold of what is of lesser significance. From whom, then does the Master not learn? Equally, how could there be such a thing as a constant teacher for him? (Confucius 1992:197)

The Tao is a road, and it can be followed, but the journey is never easy and never comes to an end as long as the person is alive. The focus for Confucius is always on the person who follows and even creates the way in terms of humane action and ritual beauty. "The Master said, 'It is Man who is capable of broadening the Way. It is not the Way that is capable of broadening Man'" (Confucius 1992:157). No one statement better captures both the glory and agony of the process of finding the Tao than the passage quoted earlier on Yen Hui's famous lament and praise of his teacher.

Even if the sheer rising of the Tao before the eyes of the student dedicated to humaneness is daunting, there is even more to Confucius' pedagogy because as he said, "at sixty my ear was attuned." What is to be done when even the ear is attuned to the Mandate of Heaven? Again, Confucius has a wonderfully cryptic answer to this question, the famous doctrine of *cheng ming*/the rectification or ordering of names. This is the act of the social ordering and communication of the Way. Because the Way is public, it must be communicated, but communicated in a special way, by the rectification of names. The term *ming* means both to have a meaning and to give a name. The emphasis in Confucius' thought is to stress the performative and prescriptive nature of learning about the Way. In this regard, as Hall and Ames tried to show, it is very much a *li*, or specific ritual action, in this case the correct ritual action of ordering things themselves.

Confucius reported that there is a single thread that unifies all of his thought. Although the highest virtue is, of course, *jen*/humaneness, "The way of the Master consists in *chung* (doing one's best) and *shu* (in using oneself as a measure to gauge the likes and dislikes of others). That is all" (Confucius 1992:33). In another section, Confucius defines *shu* as follows: "The Master said, 'It is perhaps the word *shu*. Do not impose on others what you yourself do not desire'" (Confucius 1992:155). Other ways to translate *shu* include "deference," "altruism," "reciprocity," and "consideration." Hall and Ames have summarized *shu*: "The methodology of *shu* requires the projection or recognition of excellence as a means of eliciting or of expressing deference. *Shu* as a methodology requires that in any given situation one either displays excellence in oneself (and this anticipates deference from others) or defers to excellence in another. Again, *shu* is always personal in that it entails *chung*: 'doing one's best as one's authentic self'" (1987:287). To actually defer to the Tao in all things is something that Confucius had never seen, nor had he expected to see it, though he was convinced that it was possible for a sage to do just this very thing.

Nonetheless, the pursuit of the Confucian Tao is not a thankless, loveless, or sorrowful task, even though it is immensely difficult. As Confucius said, "And at seventy I could give my mind-heart free rein without overstepping the mark." What Confucius had done was to create (or as he would prefer to say, preserve and promote) a new high culture out of the ideals of his beloved Chou dynasty. This culture is high both in the sense that it embodies reflection on what it means to be a civilized person and high also, as Yen Hui learned, because it is a lofty goal that is not easy to attain. Yet Confucius finds joy in seeing the Tao. "In the eating of coarse rice and the drinking of water, the using of one's elbow for a pillow, joy is to be found. Wealth and rank attained through immoral means have as much to do with me as passing clouds" (Confucius 1992:61).

Furthermore, the image of Confucius as some kind of remorseless pedant is false when we comprehend the joy he found in studying the ancient worthies and in the practice of music and poetry. In one of the most revealing passages in the whole of the *Analects*, Confucius asked his assembled disciples what they would truly like to accomplish. Most of the disciples gave properly stoic and public-minded responses, just the kind of answers about duty and justice that we would expect from such worthy students. However, Confucius himself sides with the more bucolic delights of his student Tien, who responded to the question this way:

> In late spring, after the spring clothes have been newly made, I should like, together with five or six adults and six or seven boys, to go bathing in the River Yi and enjoy the breeze on the Rain Altar, and then go home chanting poetry.
> The Master sighed and said, "I am in favor of Tien." (Confucius 1992:105)

Two ideas that Confucius devoted less attention to in the *Analects* but that became the objects of intense debate for his later disciples are the notions of *hsin*/mind-heart and *hsing*/human nature. For both Mencius and Hsün Tzu, these two motifs of Confucian discourse join other elements of Confucius' own thought to form the perduring background of all Confucian discourse. Along with these various themes, who could not recognize the element of concern-consciousness that pervades all of Confucius' thought? Here is a man, who in his own words, knows he will not always be successful, but keeps on trying because he can do no other. It is his profound concern to get the Way for himself and for others.

Challenges to the Confucian Way and Mencius' Defense

There was a long gap between the death of Confucius and the birth of Mencius (371–289 B.C.E.), the second sage of the Confucian tradition. If Confucius believed that he lived in a world where the great cultural values of the early sage kings were in deep decay, Mencius lived a world where these values were being destroyed by the ever-increasing warfare of the period the Chinese came to call, for good reason, the Warring States period (480–221 B.C.E.) The larger states were destroying and annexing the smaller ones, and all the rulers were claiming the title of king as they tried to replace the leaders of the Chou dynasty. In fact, Mencius believed that there was no way to restore the Chou leadership and that what must happen was for some state to reunite the Chinese world under the aegis of an enlightened ruler.

Philosophically, there was now a great debate about the definition of *hsing*/human nature. On solid Confucian grounds, Mencius needed to know what it means to be a human being in order to be able to transform petty individuals into worthy members of the human race. After a person has discovered what it means to be human, then Mencius, like most Chinese thinkers, stresses a regimen for self-improvement that allows the person to be of service to the larger community. We must remember that for Mencius, self-cultivation is not merely a private enterprise but a public necessity.

Chuang Tzu, a great Taoist and near contemporary of Mencius, is credited with discovering the individual as a concept for philosophy and is known as a wonderfully humorous critic of Confucian piety. As Graham has shown in his various studies and translations, we can discover in Chuang Tzu a thinker who has uncovered the self as something of great philosophical interest. Furthermore, Chuang Tzu finds the self and its ramifications so absorbing that he often ignores the social dimension of the self as a member of a family, a clan, and the larger state. What is so shocking about Chuang Tzu from the perspective of more socially minded Chinese thinkers is that he simply does not worry about how his thought will play in the public sphere. Chuang Tzu is interested in the powers of the individual as a spontaneous self-referencing entity. In discovering the self, Chuang Tzu also discovers that there is profound power in spontaneous action, that things are so of themselves, or *tzu-jan*, as he would say. From Chuang Tzu's relativistic perspective, all the Confucian rules and regulations are useless. And more than useless, they are simply a silly way to look at the world. In and of themselves, rituals may be individually harmless, but if we take them seriously in a collective way, as a way of describing what it means to be human, then we run the risk of deforming ourselves. Chuang Tzu is interested in giving advice about how to live beyond the bounds of convention, but his advice, to use the words of Lao Tzu, recommends no political action at all.

Nonetheless, Mencius wants us to pay special attention to the social cultivation of the mind-heart. In fact, it is really with Mencius that the Confucian tradition begins to probe the various ways in which the mind-heart can be cultivated in order to achieve sage virtue. In debating with other philosophers, Mencius is particularly concerned with developing a theory of the mind-heart and explaining how the virtues can be cultivated within it.

One wonders why Mencius, who was so keen on defending the Confucian tradition, is not more alert to the intellectual world around him. Benjamin Schwartz (1985) has made the astute observation that Mencius was not a disinterested historian of Chou philosophy; rather, he was a passionate defender of the Confucian tradition and hence operated much more like a religious preacher than a disinterested scholar providing a neutral account of the doctrines of his adversaries. Like modern politicians, Mencius did not want to give undue attention to those he believed were wrong about human nature. And when he did argue, Mencius often distorted the teachings of his favorite heretics.

For instance, Yang Chu is defined as the prototypical arch-individualist and hedonist. According to Mencius, Yang Chu would not even try to save the world by the sacrifice of a single hair from his body. What is much more likely is that Yang Chu held that he would not sacrifice a hair in order to *gain* the world. There is a genuine world of difference in this slight Mencian modification of Yang's original teaching. As with so much Chinese thought, what Yang was trying to do was to give good advice about how to live in a politically dangerous world. According to Yang, in order to live successfully in the world of late Chou China, one ought not to seek high office at the peril not only of good health and mental repose but also the distinct possibility of losing one's life in the service of some rapacious feudal lord.

Mencius was also a harsh critic of Mo Tzu, the founder of the Mohist school. This is a particularly instructive debate because, in so many ways, Mo Tzu is so close to the Confucian position. In fact, there are traditions that suggest that Mo Tzu began as a Confucian but became disgusted by the morbid ritualism of the Confucians, or *ju,* of his day. Mo Tzu objected to the way the doctrines of Confucius were presented in his day; from his point of view, they harmed rather than served the people and caused true virtue to be held in contempt. Mencius was forced to respond to Mo Tzu's accurate criticisms of Confucius' later disciples.

Mencius was appalled by Mo Tzu's utilitarian stance on the efficacy of morality. Most specifically, Mencius did not approve of linking morality to benefit or profit, even if this were a general profit for the people. Mencius believed, rightly or wrongly, that if you continue to ask about what benefit morality justifies, you will lose sight of the sovereign nature of what morality ought to teach, which is humanity and righteousness. One suspects that

Mencius would not have been totally aghast at Mo Tzu's doctrine of universal love if this prime Mohist idea had been governed ultimately by the Confucian virtue of *jen*. But Mencius believed that this is precisely what did not happen. According to Mencius, the Mohists gave up on real virtue and were merely interested in what is beneficial rather than holding out for what is just, even if this is not always beneficial or profitable.

Mencius fervently believed that he was defending the correct Confucian view that the natural inclination of human nature is to do good, but only if a person is correctly cultivated and placed in a proper environment. Mencius asserted that heaven itself gave every human being human nature. But merely having this nature in its purely natural state was not enough for Mencius. *Hsing* must be developed, nurtured, and cultivated in order for it to be fully realized. Another important Confucian aspect of the theory is the utter seriousness with which Mencius views social relations. Although he averred that heaven gives us our common nature, if this seed falls on barren ground—and given the terrible conditions of the Warring States period in China, there was a lot of infertile ground—then even cultivation of the person may not be enough to transform the natural into the civilized.

Mencius begins his account of the structure of human *hsing* by positing the fact, which he takes to be empirical and normative at the same time, that we all have some kind of innate moral sensibility within us. The main task of moral self-cultivation is to nurture this innate moral sensibility and to let it be what it really can and ought to be. Mencius' way of stating the issue is to say that each human being has what he calls the four *tuan*/sprouts, germs (Lau's translation), or seeds of virtue. Another way to define these four *tuan* is to call them the fonts of virtue—the very essence, when fully cultivated, of what it means to be human. Because this is such an important aspect of his theory, it is worth quoting the crucial definitional passage:

> My reason for saying that no man is devoid of a heart sensitive to the suffering of others is this. Suppose a man were, all of a sudden, to see a young child on the verge of falling into a well. He would certainly be moved to compassion, not because he wanted to get in the good graces of the parents, nor because he wished to win praise of his fellow villagers or friends, nor yet because he disliked the cry of the child. From this it can be seen that whoever is devoid of the heart of compassion is not human, whoever is devoid of shame is not human, whoever is devoid of the heart of courtesy and modesty is not human, and whoever is devoid of the heart of right and wrong is not human. The heart of compassion is the germ of benevolence; the heart of shame, of dutifulness; the heart of courtesy and modesty, of observance of the rites; the heart of right and wrong, of wisdom. Man has these four germs just as he has four limbs. For a man possessing these four germs to deny his own potentialities is for him to cripple himself; for him to deny the potentialities of his prince is for him to

cripple his prince. If a man is able to develop all of these four germs that he possesses, it will be like a fire starting up or a spring coming through. When these are fully developed, he can tend the whole realm within the Four Seas, but if he fails to develop them, he will not be able even to serve his parents. (Mencius 1984:67–69)

In a later passage, Mencius tells us why it is so important to let these germs or sprouts come to fruition: Mencius said, "Benevolence is the heart of man, and rightness his road. Sad is it indeed when a man gives up the right road instead of following it and allows his heart to stray without enough sense to go after it. When his chickens and dogs stray, he has sense enough to go after them, but not when his heart strays. The sole concern of learning is to go after his strayed heart. That is all" (Mencius 1984: 235–237). Of course, the "that is all" encompasses a great range of teachings, actions, and dispositions, to say the least. As in so many other ways, Mencius' warning about the straying mind-heart sets the agenda for the tradition. From Mencius' time on, Confucians have sought to keep an eye on their mind-heart and not let it stray in odd or perverse ways.

The second method Mencius often uses to make his argument is to ask us to take part in a thought experiment. The most famous of these is the one just quoted in which the child is about to fall into a well. What Mencius asks us to contemplate is the fact that no one would be unmoved by such a sight. Mencius does not suggest that each and every one of us would then do the right thing or even a moral thing. We might make other decisions, and they could be bad or rash ones at that. Mencius' claim is much more modest. As P. J. Ivanhoe has noted, "At most he has shown that we have *some* moral sensitivity as part of our nature" (1993b:29).

The source of our sensitivity is, of course, the *hsin,* or mind-heart. Mencius believes that to manifest true virtue, a human being must cultivate the mind-heart. The mind-heart is able to do this because it can weigh and judge our actions and dispositions. Furthermore, the mind-heart has the power to change our actions and dispositions from the immoral or pre-moral into the moral because it can master what Mencius calls the "flood-like energy" (*hao-jan chih ch'i*). As Ivanhoe noted, this *ch'i,* another of those very crucial and pan-Chinese philosophical concepts, has a special kind of energy for Mencius that gives the mind-heart moral power. "It is the energy of moral courage; the power that enables one to perform difficult moral tasks" (Ivanhoe 1993b:31).

The mind-heart is the repository of all the emotions, passions, appetites, and even reflective abilities that can make us human if properly cultivated. The problem, as Mencius sees it, is that when we interact with our world without a properly cultivated mind-heart, this mind-heart is prone to wander about in all sorts of different directions. According to Mencius, there is nothing innately wrong with many of these emotions and passions, only that they can be misguided. Only the truly cultivated mind-heart can correctly guide these emotions and passions. This is why Mencius often used the image of the unmoved mind-heart to speak about the kind of mind-heart that responds to the four sprouts of human nature in order to control the passions and emotions. Hence, only the cultivated mind-heart can control both the senses and the *ch'i*, the matter-energy of the body.

Mencius rounds out the argument about the cultivation of the mind-heart and human nature by returning attention to the social dimension of Confucian thought. Accordingly, it is this mind-heart that, informed by the manifestation of the four sprouts of virtue, will recognize the rites as the right ways to act. And when these actions are the rites of a true king, the world will be well ordered. The final act of a cultivated mind-heart, the mind of the cultured person, will be a benevolent government. One of the key features of Mencius' image of good government is merit for all. A government is only legitimate if it serves the people. Mencius, like his master, believed that heaven hears as the people hear and speaks as the people speak and that any ruler would be foolish in the extreme not to listen assiduously to what the people hear and say.

Hsün Tzu and the Rational Defense of Ritual

As was the case in the period between Confucius and Mencius, much happened before Hsün Tzu, the third of the great classical masters, commenced his defense of Confucian tradition. Although the philosophical situation was even more complex because of the ongoing political, social, legal, technological, and intellectual debates between and among what the Chinese have called the Hundred Schools, this also meant that Hsün Tzu could make use of the thought of other thinkers in defense of the Confucian tradition. As with Confucius and Mencius, we are not sure about the precise dates for Hsün Tzu. John Knoblock (1988–1994) has dated him roughly from 310–211 B.C.E. Whatever the exact dates, it is clear from internal and external evidence that Hsün Tzu must have lived into his nineties.

Hsün Tzu's longevity allowed him to witness a momentous reorganization of the Chinese states. Politically, the struggle for the unification of the empire, anticipated by Mencius, proceeded apace. A number of great states, mostly on the edge of the traditional Chinese world, contested for supremacy. As the Warring States period came to an end (221 B.C.E.), it was the great western state of Ch'in that finally abolished the Chou and established a great new empire. The Ch'in ruler refused the old title of king and adopted the title of emperor. This became the designation for all the rulers of China who wanted to assume a universal rule until the end of the Ch'ing dynasty in 1911.

Although Hsün Tzu's genius as a Confucian thinker is recognized, he remains a controversial figure. This is so because he wrote one major essay wherein he argued, more rhetorically than anything else, that human nature was evil, directly contravening Mencius' position that human nature is good. Hsün Tzu probably knew exactly what he was doing when he criticized the Second Sage since he had a keen awareness of the development of the history not only of his own school but of the other intellectual currents of his time. He disagreed with Mencius' understanding of human nature even though his essay never posited a notion of total human depravity. On the contrary, no Confucian believed more in the possibilities of education and the civilizing effect of Confucian ritual and education than Hsün Tzu, although he was very aware that this was a difficult task for any normal human being to accomplish.

Besides having contradicted Mencius' teaching about human nature, Hsün Tzu also had the dubious distinction of having been the teacher of two of the great Legalist thinkers of the next generation. The first of these, Han Fei Tzu, was the greatest theoretician of Legalism, and the second, Li Ssu, although no philosopher, became the prime minister of the first emperor of the Ch'in. These were not the distinctions needed to cement Hsün Tzu's reputation as a great Confucian teacher. Many later Confucians argued that Hsün Tzu, however inadvertently, contributed to the growth of the pernicious Legalist school and the final demise of the beloved Chou dynasty.

The classical age was so vibrant because there were all kinds of philosophers at work beyond the great traditions of Confucianism, Taoism, Mohism, and Legalism. There were those who defended the role of logic (often called the School of Names); further, the great appendices of the *Book of Changes* and the *Kuan Tzu* arranged and commented on the life forces of the universe and medical theory; and finally, some thinkers even put in a good word for the simplicity of rural life. The scene was varied and argumentative. The intellectual life of the age was intimately connected to the political struggles that finally gave birth to the Ch'in empire. Whereas some Chinese intellectuals developed a taste for pure philosophical speculation, most of the major schools aimed at giving advice to the rulers about how to preserve and expand their powers. The great question of political philosophy was this: What would help an aspiring noble to hold on to his own state or to conquer other states? Most schools tried to provide rulers with a blueprint for creating an empire.

As it turns out, the most effective short-term advice for rulers came from what was later known as the Legalist School. This school traces its roots to the thinking of Lord Shang and ends in the brilliance of Han Fei Tzu, Hsün Tzu's onetime student at the famous Chi-hsia Academy in the state of Chi. What disturbed later Chinese thinkers about the Legalist solution was its raw appeal to consolidating power in the hands of the ruler and its ruthless pragmatism in the search for and protection of this power at the expense of anyone but the person of the ruler. All Legalist thinkers struggled to equip a ruler to rule and rule effectively. Hence, the great Legalist reforms of the state of Ch'in emphasized the role of the military and agricultural production at the expense of any other state aims.

The Legalists, of course, based these political, military, and economic reforms on a theory of human nature and social control. They argued that people were not motivated by noble ritual or fine ideals like humaneness, contrary to what the Confucians might say. In their view, the only thing that most people respond to is pleasure and pain. Therefore, the true ruler must hold the reigns of reward and punishment in his hands and govern the state, not by moral principle but by laws and regulations that carefully spell out the rewards for following the laws and the harsh punishments for failure or malfeasance. If Han Fei Tzu was uninterested in the inter-Confucian debate about the goodness or evil of human nature, it was because this ultimately did not concern him; he believed that whatever the correct philosophic answer might be, the ruler would be better advised to ignore it and to focus on rewards and punishments and the manipulation of power as the only truly effective ways to rule the empire.

As it turns out, Hsün Tzu could not disagree more with his Legalist students. Although he did not share Mencius' highly positive view of the innate goodness of human nature, Hsün Tzu nonetheless maintained that the empire could not be ruled the way the Legalists said it could. Even if human nature was not perfectly good, it still needed high ideals and a way to inculcate these ideals in order to achieve stability of government and general human flourishing. Many of his essays showed how the ruler could accomplish this feat.

Hsün Tzu had a superbly rational mind, and although he disliked disputation for its own sake, there was no alternative for someone living in his time but to embrace the arts of debate. He had to do intellectual battle with assorted Taoists, Mohists, Logicians, Legalists, and others—because all of these schools had learned how to debate effectively with each other. We find in many of Hsün Tzu's essays the tight kind of organization and argumentation that satisfies even the most stringent demands of modern Western philosophical tastes. Hsün Tzu's willingness to borrow ideas and logical methods from the Taoists, Logicians, and Mohists is nowhere more evident than in his essays on logical method and epistemology.

Hsün Tzu was also the great secularizer of the Confucian concept of Heaven. For him, the old Shang and early Chou notion of *t'ien* as some kind of sky divinity was replaced by a more philosophical reading of heaven as a name for the various natural processes of the Way, that is, nature itself. Hsün Tzu believed that the things of the world were created through the agency of yin-yang forces of the primal matter-energy. In his essay on *t'ien*/Heaven, he writes that "the course of Nature is constant: it does not survive because of the actions of a Yao; it does not perish because of the actions of a Jie . . . If you conform to the Way and are not of two minds, then Nature cannot bring about calamity" (Knoblock 1988–1994:3, 14). Or, as he says slightly later in the same essay, "The constellations follow their revolutions; the sun and moon alternately shine; the four seasons present themselves in succession; the Yin and Yang enlarge and transform; the wind and the rain spread out everywhere" (Knoblock 1988–1994:3, 15). As we shall note later, human beings are definitely part of nature. And although it is true that human beings have certain special or complex functions within the web of the Way, these functions still emerge out of the basic matter-energy of the cosmos.

However orderly Hsün Tzu's world is, he is no determinist. He is an inclusive humanist. As noted earlier, he believes that our successes and failures come from our own efforts. He rejects the notion that people can read the heavens for portents or interpret strange natural events for preknowledge about human life. Further, he discards the pseudosciences of his day such as physiognomy. Social decay and individual human failure, he contends, comes from three typical human errors: (1) the decline of agricultural production, (2) governmental interference in the economy, and (3) social disharmony or imbalance due to the neglect of proper ritual action and civility. Along with his reinterpretation of *t'ien*, he also offers an expanded interpretation of *li*, or ritual action. Hsün Tzu argues that ritual action is designed by the sages to legitimize social cohesion. "Heaven possesses a constant Way; Earth has an invariable size; the gentleman has constancy of deportment" (Knoblock 1988–1994:3, 17).

Hsün Tzu's epistemological stance is set within his view of the cosmos and humanity's place in it. For him, the reason one knows anything at all is because that is part of human nature, and what one knows is the pattern of things in the natural order. He starts his analysis of human understanding with sensation and then moves on to an analysis of the structure and function of the mind-heart. "Each of the myriad things has a form that is perceptible. Each being perceived can be assigned its proper place. Each, having been assigned its proper place, will not lose its proper position. Although a person sits in his own house, yet he can perceive all within the four seas" (Knoblock 1988–1994:3, 105). He goes on to point out that "as a general principle, the faculty of knowing belongs to the inborn nature of man. That things are knowable is part of the natural principle of the order of things" (Knoblock 1988–1994:3, 110).

Hsün Tzu maintained that the knowing power of the mind is the power to discriminate the proper order of the world and the things within the world and to notice the differences between things. In his view, the greatest obstacle on the road to knowledge is "one-sideness," an improper fixation with only one aspect of any situation, an inability to uncover the real differences between things. It is at this point that Hsün Tzu introduces his famous theory that the mind-heart is empty, unified, and still.

> I say by its emptiness, unity, and stillness. The mind never stops storing; nonetheless it possesses what is called emptiness, The mind never lacks duality; nonetheless it possesses what is called unity. The mind never stops moving; nonetheless it possesses what is called stillness. Men from birth have awareness. Having awareness, there is memory. Memories are what is stored, yet the mind has the property called emptiness. Not allowing what has previously been stored to interfere with what is being perceived in the mind is called emptiness. The mind from birth has awareness. Having awareness, there is perception of difference. Perception of difference consists in awareness of two aspects of things at the same time. Awareness of two aspects of things all at the same time entails duality, nonetheless the mind has the quality called unity. Not allowing one thing to interfere with the other is called unity. When the mind is asleep, it dreams. When it relaxes, it moves at its own accord. When it is employed in a task, it plans. Thus the mind never stops moving; nonetheless it possesses the quality called stillness. Not allowing dreams and fantasies to bring disorder to awareness is called stillness. (Knoblock 1988–1994:3, 104)

Hence, the mind-heart is empty of preconceptions and able to entertain both new theories and old theories, new sensory data, and old memories and to compare and contrast all of these while preserving their essential differences. Being unified or one means that the mind-heart can compare things without confusing their natures and aspects. And finally, being quiet or still means that the mind-heart can be calm, dispassionate, and not deluded by new data or dreams that affect the mind-heart in sleep or other mental states.

Along with analysis of the epistemological powers of the mind-heart, Hsün Tzu was fascinated by the arts of disputation, logic, and language. He was concerned with understanding the proper role of general ideas, the nature of cognitive discrimination, and the function of inference. For him, concept formation arose from the labeling of things or events in order to fit reality as conventionally defined. How do we know that this reality we perceive and the names we give it fit together? We make use of empirical observation of the nature of the objects named. Therefore, even if names are conventional, they are based on empirical observation and the similarities and differences of function and aspect. He clearly recognizes that names represent family types that are the same even if the individuals are unique. For example, in his essay on names, he notes that the greatest common name (*ta-kung-ming*) would be thing (*wu*). This indicated to him that the most general "thing," or *wu*, we can name is done so by the method of difference. Yet why do we use certain names and not others? Hsün Tzu observes that we use names because of general social agreement about their particulars over a long period of time.

Hsün Tzu made use of these epistemological claims in framing his complex and controversial theory of human nature. Like his theory of mind-heart, he begins with the analysis of the difference between nature as the constant flux of the yin-yang forces and the conscious nurture of the mind-heart controlled by responsible human activity. Although Hsün Tzu shocked other Confucians by stating that human nature is evil, this is a curious kind of definition if we remember the role of cultivation in the perfecting of the human person. What really makes us human is not our *hsing* per se but rather how the *hsing* acts in concert with the mind-heart. Here Hsün Tzu does have a quarrel with Mencius, but not the quarrel that he is supposed to have had with the Second Sage. I take it to be the case that Hsün Tzu is much less impressed with the innate, uncultivated aspects of the mind-heart and nature than is Mencius.

One of the best definitions of what it means to be human is found in Hsün Tzu's chapter 9, "On the Regulations of a King."

> Fire and water possess vital breath but have no life. Plant and trees possess life, but lack awareness. Birds and beasts have awareness, but lack a sense of morality and justice. Humans possess vital breath, life, and awareness, and add to them a sense of morality and justice. It is for this reason that they are the noblest beings in the world. In physical power they are not so good as an ox, in swiftness they do not equal the horse; yet the ox and horse can be put to use. Why is this? I say it is because humans alone form societies and animals cannot. Why can man form a society? I say it is due to the division of society into classes. How can social divisions be translated into behavior? I say it is because of humans' sense of morality and justice. (Knoblock 1988–1994:2, 103)

Along with his quarrel with Mencius about human nature and mind-heart and his proclivity for structured argument, Hsün Tzu is best remembered as the great defender of Confucian ritual. As he himself noted, "Rites trim what is too long, stretch out what is too short, eliminate excess, remedy deficiency, and extend cultivated forms that express love and respect so that they increase and complete the beauty of conduct according to one's duty" (Knoblock 1988–1994:3, 65). Or variously, "Ritual principles are the ridgepoles of the Way of Man" (Knoblock 1988–1994:3, 61). Ritual actions and the study of ritual action are one of the disciplines that refine the rough nature of humanity into the pattern of the sages. In his theory of ritual, Hsün Tzu displays both his love for rational discourse and his veneration of history: "One who is adept at study exhausts principles of rational order. One who is adept at putting things into practice examines problems" (Knoblock 1988–1994:3, 225).

All rites begin with coarseness, are brought to fulfillment with form, and end with pleasure and beauty. Rites reach their highest perfection when both emotion and form are fully realized and order and harmony prevail.

> *Through rites, Heaven and Earth are conjoined,*
> *the sun and moon shine brightly,*
> *the four seasons observe their natural precedence,*
> *the stars and planets move in ranks,*
> *the rivers and streams flow,*
> *and the myriad things prosper.*
> *Through them, love and hate are tempered,*
> *and joy and anger made to fit the occasion.*

> . . . Establish them and exalt them, make of them the ridgepole, and nothing in the world can add to or subtract from them. (Knoblock 1988–1994:3, 60)

Hsün Tzu, as is typical of his orderly way of defending the Confucian Tao, has a theory about how rituals came to be.

> How did ritual principles arise? I say that men are born with desires which, if not satisfied, cannot but lead men to seek to satisfy them. If in seeking to satisfy their desires men observe no measure and apportion things without limit, then it would be impossible for them not to contend over the means to satisfy their desires. Such contention leads to disorder. Disorder leads to poverty. The Ancient Kings abhorred such disorder; so they established the regulations contained within ritual and moral principles in order to apportion things, to nurture the desires of men, and to supply the means for their satisfaction. They so fashioned their regulations that desires should not want for the things which satisfy them and good would not be exhausted by the desires. In this way the two of them, desires and goods, sustained each other over the course of time. This is the origin of ritual principles. (Knoblock 1988–1994:3, 55)

It is often asserted that China, in distinction from other cultures, has very few creation myths and stories. It is somewhat ironic that Hsün Tzu, who himself has a very human view of *t'ien*, tells such a fascinating tale about the origin of ritual life.

Another thing that distinguished Hsün Tzu from his Legalist students is the final vision of a cultivated person living in a civilized society. For instance, Hsün Tzu believed in the virtue of *ch'eng*/integrity or the complete realization of human virtues. Knoblock translates *ch'eng* as "truthfulness," in the sense of being true to oneself and to the society as a whole. This is a fitting way to remember the third of the classical Confucian sages.

> For the gentleman to nurture his mind, nothing is more excellent than truthfulness.

If a man has attained perfection of truthfulness, he will have no other concern than to uphold the principle of humanity and to behave with justice. If with truthfulness of mind he upholds the principle of humanity, it will be given form.

Having been given form, it becomes intelligible. Having become intelligible, it can produce transmutation. If with truthfulness of mind he behaves with justice, it will accord with natural order. According with nature order, it will become clear. Having become clear, it can produce transformation.

To cause transmutation and transformation to flourish in succession is called the "Power of Nature." (Knoblock 1988–1994:1, 177–178)

Sadly for the Chinese people, things did not go the way Hsün Tzu would have liked after his death. Even though the Legalist advisers of the Ch'in first emperor were successful in ushering in a new phase of Chinese history, they failed to provide the empire with an ideology that would both work and satisfy the human need for meaning. The end of the Chou then takes us to the beginning of the Han dynasty and into a completely new world of Confucian thought.

The three great classical Confucian masters prescribed the philosophic agenda, provided the metaphors, and suggested future projects for the tradition. The disciples of these masters created works such as the *Great Learning* and the *Doctrine of the Mean* that organized, summarized, and extended the insights of their teachers. For instance, these two short works, originally incorporated in *Chou-li*, one of the larger ritual texts, were rediscovered by the great T'ang and Sung Neo-Confucians and were used to supplement the thought of Confucius, Mencius, and Hsün Tzu in innovative ways. However, from the tradition's point of view, all the texts of the disciples were valuable precisely because they relied on the original thought of the classical masters of Confucian discourse.

❀ 2 ❀

The Comments of the Han:
The Confucian Canon Defined

CHINESE PHILOSOPHY AND RELIGION owe an immense debt to the scholars of the Han dynasty that is only grudgingly acknowledged. The problem arises because the Han thinkers had the bad luck to come directly after the universally recognized brilliance of the Hundred Schools of the Spring and Autumn and Warring States periods of the Chou dynasty (722–221 B.C.E.). It proved impossible to compete with the legendary sages and the founding masters of Confucianism, Taoism, Mohism, Legalism, and all the other streams of thought that went into the creation of Chinese philosophy and religion. Nonetheless, it was the Han scholars who lovingly preserved, collected, and edited the texts of the Chinese tradition after the bibliographical disasters of the Ch'in dynasty and the great civil wars that finally led to the foundation of the Han dynasty.

No other imperial institution lasted as long or was as successful as the Chinese empire founded by the Han. A. C. Graham noticed that, like the rise of modern science, the invention of such an enduring political and social order happened only once in human history. And with the rise of modern industrial East Asia, who can say that the Chinese empire, at least in a modified form, is finished? Of course there were interregnums when no dynasty ruled all of China. These periods, such as the time between the fall of the Han and the rise of the T'ang and the fall of the T'ang and the rise of the Sung, are seen as aberrations. The Chinese imperial state—both the dream and the reality—probably produced the longest running set of political institutions in the history of the world. The Buddhist movement in China drastically transformed philosophy, religion, the arts, poetry, and education, but it did not alter the structure of the imperial state. The first real challenge to the post-Han imperial Chinese state came with the Western expansion into Asia in the nineteenth century.

It was because of the need to define and organize the chaotic classical material that great Han historians such as Ssu-ma T'an (d. 110 B.C.E.), Ssu-ma Ch'ien, and Pan Ku (32–92) invented the nomenclature that commonly applied to Chinese philosophy. According to Ssu-ma T'an, the six schools of the classical period are:

1. Yin-Yang school
2. Ju (Confucian)
3. Mohist
4. School of Law (Legalist)
5. School of Names (logicians and experts in disputation)
6. School of the Way (or School of the Way and Potency—Taoist)

Pan Ku's bibliographical chapter of the *Han Shu* modifies the classification of Ssu-ma T'an. The philosophical schools are considered the second genre of literature, following only the classics themselves in importance. Pan Ku lists the nine main schools of philosophy in the following order:

1. Ju (Confucians)
2. Taoist
3. Yin-Yang
4. Legalist
5. School of Names
6. Mohist
7. Verticalist and Horizontalist (as in Graham 1989:381; these thinkers represent various theorists of interstate diplomacy in both practical and moral terms)
8. Syncretist (such works as the *Huai-nan Tzu,* the *Kuan Tzu,* and the *Lü-shih ch'un-ch'iu*)
9. Farmers' school (these are mostly farming manuals)

A. C. Graham suggested, with his typical humor, that the Han scholars were able to distill "the Chinese secret of social immortality" by selectively collecting aspects from all of these schools

(From Confucianism). An ethic rooted, below the level of conscious reflection, in the most fundamental social bonds, kinship and custom which models the community on the family; relates ruler/subject to father/son and past/present to ancestor/descendant.

(From Legalism). A rational statescraft with the techniques to organise an empire of unprecedented size and partially homogenise custom throughout it.

(From Yin-Yang). A proto-science which models the cosmos on the community.

(From Taoism, reinforced by Buddhism). Personal philosophies relating individual directly to cosmos, allowing room within the social order for unassimilables which might disrupt the community.

(From Mo-tzu through the argumentation of the competing schools). A rationality confined to the useful, which leaves fundamental questions outside its range. (Graham 1989:373)

The problem the Han scholars faced was that the whole late Chou enterprise was chaotic since the transition to empire had been destructive not only of the lives of the people but also of the archives and written records of the philosophical schools. The most famous episode in this loss of material was the famous burning of prescribed books by the first Ch'in emperor. Along with the books confiscated, and suppressed, the Ch'in emperor also purportedly burned many scholars who defied his edicts about destroying these pernicious texts. In a society where books were hand copied and rare, such government orders greatly reduced the quantity of early texts. But what was even more damaging was the long civil war that followed the demise of the Ch'in state.

Philosophical Bases of Han Thought

Correlative Thinking and Cosmology

One of the main philosophical convictions of the Han, shared by all its schools and almost all its scholars, is called "correlative thinking." The appended commentaries of the *Classic of Changes* are paradigmatic exemplars of correlative thinking and were used as a warrant for claiming this style of discourse for the Confucian tradition. But mere eclecticism is not what makes correlative thinking unique. The paradigm of correlative systems is the ubiquitous pair, yin-yang. These two archetypal contrasting concepts stand for male and female, dark and light, the sun and moon, hot and cold, the sunny and dark side of a mountain, and so on. Although yin and yang as concepts can be found in the early philosophic texts, their true glory is derived from the various protosciences such as medicine and divination techniques of the court diviners. Perhaps the philosophical text that displays these features best is the *Kuan Tzu*, especially in the sections that deal with health and self-cultivation.

Correlative thinking and cosmology surely had been a part of pre-Han thought, though not a dominant metaphor of any of the major philosophical schools. Correlative thinking was the domain of diviners, physicians, astronomers, astrologers, and magic workers of all kinds. As Graham has noted, "The problem had been solved at the start (of the Han reconstruction) by the rapid adoption of the cosmology of the court astronomers and diviners, whom rulers must always have taken more seriously than the philosophers to whom they granted an occasional audience" (Graham 1989:314). The grand system provided a place for everything, and the Han thinkers tried to put everything in its proper place. The great historian of

Chinese science Joseph Needham has described the correlative system as something like one of those glorious and huge Victorian roller-top desks with a myriad of drawers. Each element of the correlative cosmology had its own drawer and hence reduced any disorder in the cosmos. Needham noted that the correlative system was probably too perfect an organizing system for its own good.

The tradition records that it was Tsou Yen (ca. 250 B.C.E.) who moved correlative thinking into the mainstream of Chou and Han thought. Tsou Yen was successful because he applied yin-yang and the five phases theory to the political scene, formulating a theory of the rise and fall of political power based on the correlation of the two forces and the five phases. For instance, the Chou ruled the empire because they possessed the power of the water element. The way Tsou worked the system was to suggest that one of the five different phases of the five processes would, in turn, dominate or conquer the others. So, for instance, the water symbol of the Chou conquered the fire of the Shang, and so on. The full range of this complicated interweaving of yin-yang and five phases theory is most fully recorded in the *Lü-shih ch'un-ch'iu.*

> Whenever emperor or king is about to arise, Heaven is sure to display a good omen beforehand to the people below. In the time of the Yellow Emperor, Heaven displayed beforehand big earthworms and big ants (creatures of the soil). The Yellow Emperor said, "The *ch'i* of soil had conquered." Because the *ch'i* of soil had conquered, as his colour he honoured yellow, for his affairs took soil as norm (that is, he chose the correlates of soil). (Graham 1989:329)

Another key conceptual cluster in the correlative cosmology of the Han was the notion of *wu-hsing*, variously translated as the "five powers," "five phases," "five elements," "five processes," and so forth. It was often assumed in early Western studies of Chinese thought that *wu-hsing* could be translated as the "five elements." This proved to be an inadequate rendering of the protean Chinese term. Traditionally the five phases are identified with fire, water, wood, metal, air, and earth. For this reason it is easy, but misleading, to see why the term was often translated as the five "elements." However, it is crucial to remember that these five *hsing* are not five separate substances; rather, each one is a special phase or process, a special manifestation of the primordial *ch'i*, or matter-energy itself. The five phases represent five typical or archetypal forms of the *ch'i*, as human beings perceive the spatial-temporal world through the senses. Along with yin-yang, the five phases became, as it were, the bedrock of early Chinese world building.

In many ways, *ch'i*, variously translated as "energy," "prime matter," "matter-energy," and so on, is a perfect candidate for a pan-Chinese metaphysical concept. It is hard, within Confucian thought at least, to recall any thinker who simply did not take *ch'i*, in one of its many modes, for granted. Because it was there for everyone to see, touch, think about, and dream in, everyone assumed that they knew what it meant. There is very little formal definition of just what *ch'i* is beyond noting its more special manifestations, such as *wu-hsing*, for instance. It is interesting to note that so far, no one has found an oracle bone graph for *ch'i*. But as Schwartz wrote concerning the relationship of *ch'i* as the vapor of clouds, "Even if the winds and clouds are divine, their manifestations suggest the formless and undivided 'substance' and 'energy'" (Schwartz 1985:180). The problem with identifying *ch'i* too closely with Western notions of matter is that although matter is the basis of all things material, it is too protean and dynamic simply to be matter conceived as something static and completely spatialized. As Schwartz has noted in his summary of the various classical uses of *ch'i*, it also encompasses "states of emotion, dispositions of sentiment, and attitudes" (Schwartz 1985:181). For example, this is the reason that Mencius can talk about learning to cultivate his vast flowing *ch'i* as if it were both some kind of great power and an emotional state.

The Role of the I-Ching: Unceasing Production and Reproduction

Whereas many texts made a contribution to the development of the Han Confucian cosmological synthesis, such as the *Kuan Tzu*, the *Lü-shih ch'un-ch'iu*, and the *Huai-nan Tzu*, their significance pales in comparison with the role of the *I-Ching*, or the *Classic of Changes*. As the first of the Confucian classics, the *Classic of Changes* has been a constant source of information and possibilities for constructive thought. The tradition tells us that Confucius so loved the *Classic of Changes* that he wore out the leather bindings of his copy. The story of the actual composition of the classic is complicated in the extreme. At one end, the earliest parts of the work are some of the oldest written texts still extant anywhere in the world, whereas some of the later sections of the book were probably written during the Han dynasty itself.

The Confucian tradition holds that Confucius himself venerated the classic and that ten commentaries or "wings" that form an integral part of the received text came from his hand. No one accepts the Confucian authorship of these sections of the classic anymore, although all recognize that there are strong Confucian elements in the text. Edward Shaughnessy (1996), in discussing the very early Mawangdui text of the *Changes*, has translated some very early commentaries that also purport to be the comments of Confucius concerning the enduring value of the book. Furthermore, as Richard John Lynn notes in his translation of the later received text of Wang Pi, "Only the Commentaries on the Judgments and

Commentaries on the Images, which for the most part seem to date from the sixth or fifth century B.C., appear to have been the direct product of Confucius' school, if not the work of Confucius himself" (Lynn 1994:3). The *Classic of Changes* became the common property of all Chinese intellectuals.

First and foremost, the *Classic of Changes* began life as a divination manual and has always retained that role within Chinese society. It provides a method for interpreting the flow of the cosmos. The later commentaries—the wings, as they are called—added their own philosophical interpretation of what was to be found when divination occurred. For the purposes of the history of the Confucian tradition, the most important commentary was the *Commentary on the Appended Phrases,* or, more simply, the Great Commentary. This commentary illustrates the early correlative cosmology of the late Chou and early Han and became the cultural property of all later Confucian cosmologists.

As the Great Commentary says,

> The *Changes* is a paradigm of Heaven and Earth, and so it shows how one can fill in and pull together the Dao of Heaven and Earth. Looking up, we use it to observe the configurations of Heaven, and, looking down, we use it to examine the patterns of Earth. Thus we understand the reasons underlying what is hidden and what is clear. We trace things back to their origins then turn back to their end. Thus we understand the axioms of life and death. (Lynn 1994:51)

As with all Chinese thought, there is a practical turn, even when searching for the beginnings and ends of things.

The *Changes*, like the entire Confucian canon, is the creation of the sages so that human beings can understand the Tao and act in a timely and appropriate fashion.

> The sages set down the hexagrams and observed the images. . . .
> Therefore what allows the noble man to find himself anywhere and yet remain secure are the sequences presented by the *Changes*. What he ponders with delight are the phases appended to the lines. Therefore, once the noble man finds himself in a situation, he observes its image and ponders the phases involved, and, once he takes action, he observes the change (of the lines) and ponders the prognostications involved. This is why since Heaven helps him, "it is auspicious" and "nothing will fail to be advantageous." (Lynn 1994:49–50)

Here again, we can see why Confucius was called the "timely" sage. I have also quoted this passage to demonstrate that the study of the changes of the cosmos was not a thankless or painful task. Rather, as the passage shows, true study and action are joyful activities.

Another aspect of the *Changes* is the role it gives to reason, conceived as the need to broadly understand the world.

> It is by means of the *Changes* that the sages plumb the utmost profundity and dig into the very incipience of things. It is profundity alone that thus allows one to generate the aspirations of all the people in the world; it is a grasp of incipience alone that thus allows one to accomplish the great affairs of the world; and it is the numinous alone that thus allows one to make quick progress without hurrying and reach goals without forcing one's way. (Lynn 1994:63)

Along with Hsün Tzu's essays on knowledge, disputation, and epistemology, the *Changes* warrants the intellectually attentive structuring of Confucian thought. Although this does not mean that Confucians were particularly interested in the kind of logic that finds its Western origins in Aristotle, it does mean that there is nothing within the Confucian tradition that would immediately disregard such interests if it could be shown how such philosophical techniques help the person dig into the very origins of things. What the Confucians stressed, however, was that such speculation must always be in service to the broader human issues of personal and social conduct.

The *I-Ching* provided the locus classicus for the Sung Neo-Confucian interest in speculative cosmology. It introduces the concept of the supreme ultimate, *t'ai-chi*, an idea that waits for its full flowering until the Northern Sung.

> Therefore, in change there is the great ultimate. This is what generates the two modes (the yin and yang). The two basic modes generate the four basic images, and the four basic images generate the eight trigrams (by adding first one unbroken [yang] line—to each, then one broken [yin] line). The eight trigrams determine good fortune and misfortune, and good fortune and misfortune generate the great enterprise. (Lynn 1994:65–66)

Although the authors of *Changes* probably did not anticipate the "great enterprise" of the Neo-Confucian movement, the Neo-Confucians were certainly aware of the debt they owed the *Changes* in providing them with the image of a creative cosmos.

The Great Commentary reconfirms the importance of the prime Confucian virtues within its correlative vision of the cosmos.

> The reciprocal process of yin and yang is called the Dao. That which allows the Dao to continue to operate is human goodness (*shan*), and that which allows it to bring things to completion is human nature (*hsing*). The benevolent see it and call it benevolence, and the wise (*zhi*) see it and call it wisdom. It functions for the common fold on a daily basis, yet they are unaware of it. This is why the Dao of the noble man is a rare thing! (Lynn 1994:53)

In this passage we perceive the characteristic marks of a Confucian view of human nature and morality. For instance, that we can be morally good is predicated on the fact that there is a fundamental goodness embedded in human nature. Nonetheless, only the truly benevolent, that is to say those who practice *jen* as the highest virtue, can manifest it, and then only when they apply wisdom to their self-cultivation. In fact, morality is the particular sphere of the human person in contradistinction to other spheres of the natural world.

The Great Synthesis of Tung Chung-shu

As tradition records, in the reign of the Han emperor Wu-ti (140–87 B.C.E.), the emperor made the momentous decision to adopt the suggestion of Tung Chung-shu that only the six classical disciplines, as interpreted by Confucius, were to be the basis for the future progress of the dynasty. What were the alternatives to the Confucian project? First, in terms of alternatives for running the imperial state, there was the structure of empire inherited from the Ch'in state, a form of government based on the Legalist theories of Lord Shang brought to a brilliant completion by Han Fei Tzu. In fact, a great deal of the actual mechanisms of the Han state simply incorporated Ch'in policy in terms of governance and law. However, because of all that had gone wrong with the Ch'in rule, the early Han rulers were not interested in simply taking over the form and practice of the Ch'in state. They were seeking something else to replace the discredited (yet often practical) Legalist ideology of the Ch'in rulers.

Second, there was the Huang-Lao tradition that functioned within the emerging Taoist world much like Tung Chung-shu's own thought did for the Confucians. Huang-Lao scholars presented the ruler with advice, tinged with the realism of Legalism, about how to rule. Those of us who view this as incongruous must remember that the *Lao Tzu* itself gives advice to rulers and thus represents a wing of the Taoist tradition that suggests how the empire ought to be ordered and ruled.

Contrary to alternative advice, Tung Chung-shu argued that if the emperor followed the six Confucian arts his rule would be successful. Although other schools might have some of the truth, only the Confucian tradition, because of its mastery of all the six arts, could provide the complete kit necessary for government. As Tung pointed out in a section of his surviving major work, the *Ch'un-ch'iu Fan-lu,*

> The prince knows that he who is in power cannot by evil methods make men submit to him. Therefore he chooses the Six Disciplines through which to develop the people. The *Shih* (Poetry) and *Shu* (History) make orderly their aims. The *Li* (Ritual) and *Yüeh* (Music) purify their five qualities. The *I* (Changes)

and *Ch'un-ch'iu* (Spring and Autumn) illumine their knowledge. These six teachings are all great, and at the same time each has that in which it stands pre-eminent. The *Shih* describes aims, and therefore is pre-eminent for its un-spoiled naturalness. The *Li* regulates distinctions, and therefore is pre-eminent in its decorative qualities. The *Yüeh* intones virtue, and therefore is pre-emi-nent in its influencing power. The *Shu* records achievements, and therefore is pre-eminent concerning events. The *I* takes Heaven and Earth as its bases, and therefore is pre-eminent in calculating probabilities. The *Ch'un-ch'iu* rectifies right and wrong, and therefore stands pre-eminent in ruling men. (Fung 1952–1953:1, 401–402)

Tung's summary is a perfect example of his teaching about the Confucian tradition as well as an exposition of this teaching interpreted as correlative cosmology. Both aspects need comment.

Furthermore, Tung Chung-shu also represented an interpretive tradition called the New Text school. The name refers to the fact that during his life-time, Tung had access to the reconstructed texts of the various Han schol-ars, compiled after the end of the Ch'in and the beginning of the Han dy-nasty. They were called the "new" texts because later in the Han dynasty, an even older set of the classics was purportedly found in the walls of a build-ing in Confucius' home, hence the name "old" text was applied to this al-ternative set of classics. The debate about which set of texts most accurately presents the true teaching of Confucius has raged ever since. Although the differences between the texts are not that great for general purposes, the way the two schools read their texts bears directly on Tung's great fascina-tion with the *Ch'un-ch'iu* as the basis for his philosophical system.

The key to Tung Chung-shu's veneration of the *Ch'un-ch'iu* stems from the fact that he believed that Confucius, who never claimed more for him-self than his love of study, was actually awarded the Mandate of Heaven as an uncrowned king shortly before his death. As Sarah Queen has noted, "But Tung Chung-shu maintained that, because Confucius has left his blue-print for the perfect state in the form of judgments purposely couched in an esoteric language, the salvific power of the *Spring and Autumn* was latent, contingent on the appropriate interpreter" (1996:232).

Like the other Han thinkers influenced by correlative modalities, Tung Chung-shu begins his account with speculation on the origins of all things, or what he calls the *yüan* of the cosmos. "What is called the single *Yüan* (Origin) is the great beginning. . . . It is only the sage who is capable of re-lating the many to the one, and thus linking them to *Yüan* . . . This *Yüan* is like a source. It[s] significance is that it permeates Heaven and Earth from beginning to end . . . Therefore *Yüan* is the root of all things, and in it lies man's own origin" (Fung 1952:2, 19–20). Whatever the true nature of this cosmic origin, Tung quickly moves to its actual manifestations. "Heaven,

Earth, the yin and yang, and wood, fire, earth, metal and water (the five phases), make nine; together with man, they make ten. Heaven's number is with this made complete" (Fung 1952:2, 19).

Tung Chung-shu's vision of the ceaseless interaction of the primal forces and the five phases is not mechanistic or merely spatial. It has a temporal dimension as well.

> Heaven sends forth yang to create warmth and thereby generates things. Earth sends forth yin to create coolness and thereby brings things to maturity. Without warmth there is no generation, and without coolness there is not maturation. Nevertheless, if you calculate the quantities of their apportionment, warmth and heat constitute one hundred, while coolness and cold constitute one. Virtue and education compare to penalties and punishments in the same way. Therefore the sage increases his love and decreases his sternness, extends his virtue and limits his punishment. He relies on this to be a counterpart to Heaven. (Queen 1996:95)

Of course, such attention to the nature of time is not just of philosophical interest, at least to the early Han rulers. If read correctly, the interaction of the yin-yang forces and the five phases can be used for changing the destiny of the state.

According to Tung Chung-shu, the human person is also an exemplar of the correlative forces of the universe. For instance, "Man has 360 joints, which matches the number of Heaven. His body, with its bones and flesh, matches the thickness of Earth. He has ears and eyes above, with their capacity for hearing and seeing, which correspond to the forms of the sun and moon" (Fung 1952:2, 30). The list can be extended over and over again, all calculated to show the grand design of the cosmos and how all things are interrelated to each other; or, Heaven, Earth, and man are the origin of all things. "Heaven gives them birth, Earth nourishes them, and man perfects them" (Fung 1952:2, 32).

Tung's Moral Anthropology

Tung Chung-shu's attempt to answer the question of the nature of human nature and the question of its nurture is both a continuation of the classical Confucian thinking about *hsing* and an amplification of it in terms of Han correlative cosmology. It is a continuation because it continues to ask, as did Mencius and Hsün Tzu, about the real nature of humanity as well as about how this can be manifested. It also seeks, through the application of yin-yang theory, to answer the question about whether human nature is good or evil. Tung makes the sensible, and as he notes, the empirical point that this is a complicated question because people are obviously capable of both good and evil actions and intentions.

Furthermore, Tung demonstrates the commentarial interest that now becomes so dominant in Han culture. For instance, Tung knows that he differs in his theory of human nature from Mencius.

> My way of evaluating the nature differs from that of Mencius. Mencius evaluates it in comparison with the doings of birds and beasts below, and therefore he calls the nature good itself. I evaluate it in comparison with the doings of the sages above, and therefore I say that the nature is no good. Goodness transcends the (ordinary) nature, just as the sage transcends (ordinary) goodness. (Fung 1952:2, 37)

Of course, Tung then argues that we need a method by which to manifest the goodness of human nature in the ordinary person.

In order to transform or reform human nature, we must learn to follow the teachings of the sages in terms of moral reform.

> Why have Heaven and Earth not yet responded and auspicious signs not yet appeared? It is because transformation through moral instruction has not been established and consequently the people are not yet rectified. The people continue to see profit as water naturally tends to flow downward. If you do not rely on transformation to dam up this (tendency), you will not be able to stop it. Hence, when moral instruction has been established, evil and corrupt practices cease because the dikes have been perfected. (Queen 1996:132)

Once the wisdom of moral reform has worked its way with the discernment of humaneness and righteous, then the person is ready to take part in the ordering of the larger social world.

Tung Chung-shu's political philosophy reinforces his view of human virtue and self-cultivation and, hence, the role of the king in educating people to become fully human. One can certainly see why this was such an appealing doctrine to the early Han rulers—because it gave moral sanction to their role as emperors and supreme educators of the empire. However, we must note that Tung stresses that government is for the good of the people even though it is not government by the people. As we have already seen, an emperor can lose the Mandate of Heaven if he does not attend to the prosperity of the people.

> Heaven has produced mankind with natures containing the "basic stuff" of goodness but unable to be good (in themselves). Therefore it has established kingship to make them good. This is Heaven's purpose. The people receive from Heaven this nature which is unable to be good (by itself) and, conversely, receive from the king the instruction which gives completeness to their nature. The king, following Heaven's purpose, accepts as his charge the task of giving completeness to the people's nature. (Fung 1952:2, 46)

But Tung was always careful to make sure to teach the king that he is only a true king when he has the welfare of all as his aim. And, of course, no one person can do all this himself. Tung urged the emperor to carefully select worthy Confucians to be ministers and to listen to their wise counsel for the benefit of all.

The Pursuit of the Classics:
Annotating the Tradition

The Han was an era that produced some of the most famous classical exegetes in Chinese history along with philosophers such as Tung Chung-shu. Perhaps the most famous of these exegetes was Cheng Hsüan (127–200), who sought not merely to master one of the classical texts but to comment on all of them in order to make them intelligible to his students. But there was also a philosophical agenda embedded in the exegetical and philological labors of Cheng, his teacher Ma Jung (79–166), and the great lexicographer Hsü Shen (fl. 110), author of the *Shuo-wen chieh-tzu*. Why were the classics so important to the Han scholars?

As with all terms, the early meaning of *ching* is shrouded in mystery. Tsai Yen-zen, through an examination of the use of *ching* and *chuan* in the Han period, provides a summary of what the Han scholars thought about their texts. Whatever else the term *ching* comes to mean, it certainly signifies a set of texts that are venerated as expressing the Way. It is for this reason that the Buddhists and Taoists also adopted the term *ching* for their later collections of canonical writings. The term *ching*, for instance was used by Mencius as meaning an unchanging standard, and in most senses this is an excellent way to look at what the classics came to mean for the Confucian tradition (Mencius 1984:305). As Tsai notes, the term can also mean a boundary and decisive political action to preserve the welfare of the state. The term *chuan*, always related to the scriptures in the Han, means a writing that carries forward the meaning or the message of the text. For example, the *Analects* and the *Hsiao Ching,* or the *Classic of Filial Piety,* are two very important examples of *chuan* that become practically more important than some of the five canonical Han classics.

Liu Hsiang (ca. 77–6 B.C.E.), as he did with so many other aspects of Chinese bibliography, began the process of sorting out the various genres of the classical texts. It was he who designated the Confucian classics as the Six Arts. Liu called these six texts *ching* in order to indicate that they were the most important and venerated texts. For the Confucian scholars, it was further assumed that Confucius had a role in the production of the six texts. Some thought he actually wrote them all; others held the more restrained view that Confucius' role was that of collector, arranger, and editor of the classics. This started a raging debate about just how heavy or light the final touch of the Master was on these texts. And it was at this time that the Six Arts became the Five Classics because of the loss of one of the texts, namely, the music classic.

Along with the use of the knowledge of the Confucian texts as a prerequisite for government service, Emperor Wu also recognized the use of these texts for religious ritual services. In that sense they embellished the luster of the empire. As noted earlier, the *ju* of classical China always played the role of ritual experts, and this role was continued and expanded in the Han period. It was to the *ju* experts that the emperors turned when they needed to master a particular rite or conduct a special religious service. From the Confucian side, this knowledge of ritual and religion was a useful pedagogic tool in the education of rulers. As early as Chia I (221–168 B.C.E.), this idea was clearly expressed in Confucian terms.

> As for human wisdom, it (always) sees what has taken place (but) is unable to see what will happen in the future. *Li* (rites, etiquette) are meant to prohibit what will happen and *fa* (laws, rules) are constituted to forbid what has happened, therefore the function of *fa* is conspicuous and yet what *li* will generate is hard to know ... (If the ruler) rules by *li* and *i* (righteousness), he accumulates *li* and *i*; (if he rules) by *hsing-fa* (punishments), he accumulates punishments. (Once) punishments would be piled up, the people would resent and revolt; (but once) *li* and *i* would be stored up, the people would become harmonious and amiable. (Tsai 1994:112)

It is not at all hard to see why a ruler would want a world ruled by rites, although the Han Confucians always recognized a proper, though philosophically limited, role for a good legal code. However, the main point is clear. It is only ritual action that can project a wise ruler into the future and hence both justify and extend the rule of any emperor.

The Han veneration of the *Hsiao Ching*, or *Classic of Filial Piety*, as a *ching*, or classic, is an excellent example of how the Han concern for commentary also contributes to the growth of the intellectual content of the Confucian tradition. Everyone has recognized the close fit between Confucian thought and the Chinese family system, but it was in the *Hsiao Ching* that generations of Confucians were first exposed to the particular Confucian virtue. Filial piety, because of the exegetes of the Han and their interest in the *Hsiao Ching* as a basic manual of Confucian ethics, takes its place along with the other five Confucian virtues in the broad range of Confucian civilized activity. Here again, the Confucian tradition would not be what it is without the creative energies of the Han scholars.

Political Debates on Iron and Salt

Although correlative cosmology and textual preservation and elaboration have been stressed thus far as Han Confucianism's two most important contributions, Confucians continued to play an active role in political life. Nowhere is that better seen than in the preserved records of a famous debate at the early Han court in 81 B.C.E. concerning what economic policies the Han state should follow. The actual text has been preserved by Huan K'uan (73–49 B.C.E.) from records of the debate over what is called the iron and salt debate.

The government's side was presented by Sang Hung-yang and was opposed by a group of Confucian scholars. Minister Sang defended an active role for the government in the generation of wealth. As we shall see, the Confucians were less sanguine about what the government could and ought to do. What is particularly appealing about the record of the debate is that the arguments of both sides are recorded equally, an evenhanded approach that allows us to see what the issues were and how they were debated in the early Han. The Confucians, simply put, attacked the government's attempt to monopolize the iron and salt industries. The government countered by pointing out that the monopoly actually increased the aggregate wealth of all the people and kept a few wealthy individuals from controlling the iron and salt industries for their private advantages. It is also tempting to see the debate as the perennial one between those who favor active state participation in the economy and those who believe that the economy ought to be left entirely in private hands. Whatever the intellectual outcome of the debate, history records that government's monopolistic polices stayed in place.

The crux of the Confucian argument is contained in the following passage.

> The Literati: Far-sighted and far-reaching in intent is your (the government's) policy but contiguous with profit for powerful families. The aim of your prohibitory laws is profound indeed, but manifestly leading you into the path of wild extravagance. Since the establishment of the Profit-and-Loss System and the initiation of the Three Enterprises, the privileged families throng the streets like drifting clouds, the hubs of their chariots knocking against one another on the road. Violating all public laws, they promote but their own interests; sitting astride mountains and marshes and monopolizing all offices and markets, they present a far greater problem than the feudal possessors of fisheries and salt-beds. They hold the state authority and travel around the Empire. (Gale 1973:55–56)

In this debate the Confucian longing for the strong virtues of the rural world is evident. The Confucians also disliked the notion of the government actively competing with the people for their livelihood.

> The government has entered into financial competition with the people, dissipating primordial candor and simplicity and sanctioning propensities to selfishness and greed. As a result, few among our people take up the fundamental pursuits of life, while many flock to the unessential. Now sturdy natural qualities decay as artificiality thrives and rural values decline when industrialism

flourishes ... We pray that the salt, iron and liquor monopolies and the system of *equable marketing* be abolished so that the rural pursuits may be encouraged, people be deterred from entering the secondary occupations, and national agriculture be materially and financially benefited. (Gale 1973:2–3)

The grand secretary was not always impressed with these Confucian arguments. He pointed out that all of this was well and good, but without sufficient revenue, how could goods be provided and the northern frontier defended against the Hsiung-nu hordes? If there was no funding, how could the government pay for soldiers and other essentials of good order? And so the debate raged. One also senses that the grand secretary was irritated by the moralistic discourse of the Confucians. The Confucians, for their part, were serenely self-assured because they were convinced that they were defending the ultimate well-being of the people, not to mention primordial virtue.

The grand secretary was not without an ethical appeal of his own:

The ancient founders of the Commonwealth made open the ways for both fundamental and branch industries and facilitated equitable distribution of goods. Markets and courts provided to harmonize various demands; there people of all classes gathered together and all goods collected, so that farmer, merchant, and worker could each obtain what he desired; the exchange completed, everyone went back to his occupation. ... Thus without artisans, the farmers will be deprived of the use of implements; without merchants, all prized commodities will be cut off. The former would lead to stoppage of grain production, the latter to exhaustion of wealth. It is clear that the salt and iron monopoly and the *equable marketing* are really intended for the circulation of amassed wealth and the regulation of the consumption according to the urgency of the need. It is inexpedient to abolish them. (Gale 1973:6)

This is an argument that invoked its own fundamental Confucian virtue: provisioning for the needs of the people. Also, the grand secretary notes, as did Mencius, that there needs to be a variety of different occupations for the social and economic welfare of all the people. As we shall see, this is a debate that goes on unabated between the Confucian purists and the government—which often also saw itself as following Confucian norms—for the rest of Chinese history.

After reading the record of the debate, one wonders if the grand secretary believed that his speech might be a good lesson for his Confucian critics. It is a paean to virtue that any good Confucian could have written, perhaps especially one who had to deal with the concrete complexities of national administration. The great Northern Sung Confucian statesman, Wang An-shih, would surely have felt an affinity with the arguments of the grand secretary when confronted by such pristine Confucian ethical purity.

Yang Hsiung (53 B.C.E.–18 C.E.) and the Search for a Correlative Synthesis

Yang Hsiung, considered the foremost Old Text scholar of his generation, gave a more humanistic and rational account of Confucius' life than did some of the more enthusiastic New Text conferees such as Tung Chung-shu. The New Text scholars, according to later tradition, went to extremes in postulating a divine or mystical role for the First Sage. Yang Hsiung and Wang Ch'ung took a more sober view of the First Sage and were respected for their attempt to both laud Confucius and recognize his humanity. Yang and Wang did not want to let the First Sage become some kind of mystagogic Taoist adept or semidivine character outside of real human history.

As Michael Nylan pointed out in the introduction to the *Canon of Supreme Mystery*, Yang "sees the Five Confucian Classics as an inexhaustible repository of cosmic wisdom:

> Among the explanations of Heaven, there is none more discerning in its language than that of the *Changes*. Among the explanations for events, there is none more discerning than that of the *Documents*. Among the explanations for the outward embodiment (for virtue), there is none more discerning than that of the *Rites*. Among the explanation of intent, there is none more discerning than that of the *Odes*. Among the explanations for inherent pattern, there is none more discerning than the *Chronicles*. Except in the case of these (Five Classics), discerning language is wasted upon petty subjects. (Yang 1993:4)

Nylan further concluded that Yang, although deeply committed to the Confucian project, departed from its early classic form in three ways. First, Yang was willing to defend the Confucian tradition by citing sources that most Confucians considered outside of the tradition, such as the *Lao Tzu*. Second, Yang also tried to explain his Confucian tradition in terms of the most modern Han theories of cosmology. In this regard, Yang is a fine example of Han correlative cosmology in the service of Confucian theories of virtue. Third, Yang made use of the literary conventions of distinctly Han genres such as the highly refined and structured long prose poems that were so popular in his time.

According to Yang, "The Mystery constitutes the course (*Tao*) of Heaven, the course of earth, and the course of man" (Fung 1953:2, 140). In a very potent sense, Mystery as the matrix of all spontaneity as the Tao of the world serves as an organizing first principle for the cosmos.

> The Mystery secretly permeates the myriad species (of creatures), yet its form is not visible. Does it, then, take sustenance from emptiness and nothingness, and produce life? (The reply is that) it manipulates the spiritual intelligence and so creates fixed forms. It links together past and present so as to thus give

free development to the various species of things. It extends and set[s] forth the yin and yang, and gives free reign to their ethers. (Fung 1953:2, 139–140)

The very reason that Yang writes his *Canon* is to explain the forms of the *Book of Changes* in order to defend the Confucian virtues as a coherent vision of human life and the cosmos by means of the most subtle Han correlative cosmological speculation.

The question of fate or the determination of the cosmos had always been a problem for the Confucian tradition. The question of fatalism was a contested issue in Chou and Han thought. For instance, Mo Tzu became a critic of the Confucian schools of his day because he believed that they were wedded to a strict form of determinism. Although Mencius and Hsün Tzu countered Mo Tzu's arguments about the correct interpretation of *ming*/fate, the issue was not closed, and Confucian philosophers continued to return to the debate about the nature of *ming* from time to time. No one did more in his time to clarify the meaning of *ming* than Yang Hsiung.

As Michael Nylan has written,

Among modern translators, no consensus exits about the proper definition of *ming*; the term is most often rendered as fate of Decree . . . but it is also translated variously as "duty," "destiny," "predestination," "causal connections and their possibilities," manifestation of Heaven's will," "the inevitable," "empirical facts," "created world," "lifespan," "objective circumstance," "circumstances beyond human control," and so on. (Yang 1993:35)

Nonetheless, the core meaning of the term, at least by Yang Hsiung's time, was focused on the notion of the Decree of Heaven as a form of covenant, that is to say, a bond of morality and mutual obligation for which each and every person bears responsibility and obligation. As Nylan noted, the concept of *t'ien-ming,* or the Mandate of Heaven, typical of Han thought, migrated socially beyond the relationship of the Chou king to the command or mandate of *t'ien* to include the whole range of correct conduct expected of the aristocracy and the common people as well. But this expansion of the range of the meaning of the term, of course, made it more difficult to understand in any univocal fashion.

In Yang Hsiung's hands, the notion of fate or destiny was linked to all the kinds of questions about human nature that had become so important to Confucians during the Chou and Han dynasties. Is there something like fate that controls and guides our lives? Is it fixed? Is there an individual fate or a common fate for all human beings? What makes for a good or evil fate? How does a person's fate relate to virtue and its cultivation?

Although Yang Hsiung did not specifically review and refute all the current theories about fate in the *Canon,* he offered his own elegant solution to the question of fate in a number of remarks scattered throughout the text.

> Someone asked about *ming*. I replied: "*Ming* refers to the decrees of Heaven. It has nothing to do with people's actions." "If people's actions do not constitute *ming*, I beg to ask what about people's actions?" I responded: "By (their actions) they may be preserved or lost; by them they may live or die. (Still,) that is not *ming*. *Ming* refers to what cannot be avoided. (Yang 1993:39)

Yang's position is more subtle than a simple determinism, even though it recognizes that we are subject to the constraints of circumstance. According to Yang, each person constructs a character based on four features, what he calls Virtue, Tools, Position, and Time. What is crucial in his discussion of human conduct is that only time and *ming* are linked in a technical sense.

Yang affirms that the cultivation of true virtue lies in the grasp of each person who has the will to try. The notion of Tools includes not just the technical features of the technology of a culture but also the various social institutions of society such as the arts and government itself. A person's home includes not only actual furniture but also the furniture of ritual action and social conventions. Nylan (1993:42–43) noted that Yang pointedly does not list the mystical arts of divination among the tools of a civilized person because there are enough practical, nonesoteric, arts of self-cultivation open to any person of virtue.

The notion of Position also has a dual meaning, indicating social rank and physical location. This means that a ruler will have all kinds of resources for doing good simply because of birth and that other people, of more humble origins, may also have things at hand simply because of the luck of time and place. For Yang, Time, the last of the four conditions of fate, refers not only to interlocking cycles of yin and yang but also to how this correlative cosmology of temporal cycles is applied to individuals. Time is a very important part of the grid that forms the boundaries of human life. What is particularly interesting is that Virtue and Time are linked or even mediated by their reciprocal relationship to Tools and Position in a balanced dance of human self-creation. "(Timely) opportunities come and go, the gap between them is finer than a hair" (Yang 1993:44).

Time, Yang clearly points out, is itself not something that can be completely calculated even by the most clever or wise sage. There is a pattern to Time governed by the alternation of yin-yang and the five phases, but by its very expanse, we cannot know what it held in the past and what it holds in the future for any individual. "What is (truly) great has no borders; what changes has no (set) time" (Yang 1993:45). Although Time as a cosmological category, and hence fate itself, lies beyond the possibility of comprehensive human knowledge and action, we must pay special attention to that part of our humanity that we can control, especially our cultivation of human virtue. What we can do is to create a virtuous society for all human beings, regardless of the uncertain and mysterious dictates of Time. Hence, we must, to use one of Yang's favorite phrases, learn "to love the days," to embrace the limited temporality of the finite and the incomplete. Only the proper understanding and use of time can offset the ravages of Time as Fate. In this appeal to virtue, Yang displays his Confucian roots. As Nylan has noted, "Yang Hsiung wants to direct human effort away from a detailed examination of the shifting phenomenal world and refocus attention upon the preservation of ritual norms and cultural patterns" (Yang 1993:54).

Huan T'an (43 B.C.E–28 C.E.)

Another influential Old Text scholar was Huan T'an, who, like so many other intellectuals of his day, was involved in the usurpation of Wang Mang (9–23) and the restoration of the later Han dynasty. Huan is well known for his broad range of practical experience and his attempt, like Yang Hsiung, to move away from some of the more extravagant speculations about the role of Confucius as an uncrowned king. The very title of his main philosophical work, *New Treatise*, explains that he wanted not so much to venerate history as to make use of history in order to explicate the present and to assist the emperor in providing good government. Huan, like other Old Text scholars, appreciated non-Confucian texts when they helped in understanding the world. Later Confucians might well privately have delighted in Chuang Tzu's wonderful stories, but this did not mean that they could confess like Huan T'an, that this material could be used in the proper defense of the Confucian way.

Nowhere is Huan T'an's rejection of the credulous nature of his age more evident than in his statement about the simple humanity of Confucius. Whereas others might be interested in seeking strange portents, Huan held that a critical mind and a willingness to look directly at the facts of the age would serve the purposes of good government much better: "Confucius was an ordinary man, but he became eminent and his hand became famous. When they come to his tomb, those of high-rank sacrifice beef, mutton, chicken and pork, while the lower people offer wine, dried meat and a cold repast. After paying their respects they leave" (Pokora 1975:67).

It is clear that to Huan T'an such dignified behavior was truly appropriate for the First Teacher. What is truly pertinent is to realize that Confucius sought the same things that any person does: good government and a civilized way of life guided by correct ritual. This kind of critical teaching inspired Huan's great student Wang Ch'ung to continue the critical tradition within the Confucian Old Text tradition.

Wang Ch'ung (27–ca. 100) and Critical Reason

Because of his critical and irenic spirit, there has been a great deal of debate about whether Wang Ch'ung can be included in the roster of Han Confucian thinkers. If we adopt, retroactively, the strict formulation of Confucian orthodoxy developed in the Sung dynasty, then it would be difficult to define Wang as a Confucian because of his obvious incorporation of Taoist materials, especially his linked notions of spontaneity and uncontrived action. However, if we focus on his approval of the critical and humanistic tendencies of the Old Text school of Han Confucian exegesis, then we can argue that Wang was part of the history of the Confucian Way. Because of his commitment to an inclusive use of Chou philosophic texts, the modern historian of Chinese thought Fung Yu-lan calls Wang a naturalistic Taoist. It is probably true that Wang himself was an independent spirit who tried to be as critical as possible of all traditions.

The basis for this critical viewpoint was Wang's unabashed naturalism. Basing his theory of the cosmos on the dual concepts of spontaneity and uncontrived action, or *wu-wei*, Wang criticized many of the commonplace beliefs of his day. Wang turned the critical eye of naturalism against all kinds of folk beliefs and religious convictions. He did not believe overly in ghosts or strange happenings. The world was not quite as correlative for him as it was for other Han thinkers. For instance, he did not believe in an afterlife at all.

> Human death is like the extinction of fire. When a fire is extinguished, its light does not shine any more, and when a man dies, his intellect does not comprehend any more. The actuality of both is the same. So if people nevertheless say that the dead have consciousness, they are mistaken. For what is the difference between a sick man about to die and a light about to go out? When a flame is extinguished, its radiation is dispersed and only its candle remains, and when a man dies, his vital essence is gone and the body alone remains. To assert that a man after death is still conscious is like saying that an extinguished flame may again have light. (Fung 1952–1953:2, 157)

It is this kind of critical commonsense view of a natural world that endeared Wang to later Confucian and modern philosophers as well.

The Late Han Reflections of Hsün Yüeh (148–209), Hsü Kan (170–217), and the Po Hu T'ung

As we move into the end of the Han dynasty, the tone of Confucian discourse changes. The later Han thinkers became more and more aware that they were living at the end of an era. The signs of dynastic, political, and social decay were evident for all to see. Thinkers such as Hsün Yüeh and Hsü Kan devoted their considerable talents to trying to understand what had gone wrong with the grand synthesis of Confucian thought and to suggest ways to elevate the distress of the anxious end of a great dynasty. In this kind of ethical discourse, they followed hallowed Confucian patterns of applying Confucian doctrine to the social realities of their times.

Although it has often been argued that the Neo-Taoist revival of the following Wei-Chin period (220–316) marks the end of the intellectual dominance of the Han Confucian movement, it is perhaps just as accurate to say that many late Han thinkers anticipated some of the intellectual and social concerns identified with the Neo-Taoists. For instance, a thinker such as Hsün Yüeh shows much more interest in the particular emotions, characteristics, and talents of the individual person and much less interest in the grand correlative cosmology of someone like Tung Chung-shu. Further, Hsün's slightly younger contemporary, Hsü Kan, returns Confucian discourse to an interest in the relationship of name and reality, mirroring a revival of interest in a topic important to the classical Confucians and to the post-Han Neo-Taoist thinkers.

Hsün Yüeh, in a most Confucian fashion, went about diagnosing the ills of his age by writing history and reflecting on the meaning of the history from a philosophical point of view. As with so many other Confucians, it is vital to remember that history really matters for someone like Hsün because it serves as a guide for action, edification, and correction.

> One must comprehend the law of nature and examine the nature of men; pursue the canonical classics and cross-examine (these against) the records of the past and the present events; take heed of the three different conditions of men and penetrate into their subtlest details; avoid the two extremes and grasp the mean; take reference from the Five Elements in their mutations; and place these in different combinations and sequences; then one may dimly envisage an approximation of truth. (Ch'en 1980:107)

This passage is revealing in that although Ch'en (1980) acknowledges the role of correlative cosmology as part of Hsün's integral worldview, he is more interested in the complex interaction of human nature and the changing circumstances of time and place. Although Hsün believed in the connection of humanity and destiny, he was more concerned with the cultivation of individual virtue than in trying to comprehend the vastness of the cosmos.

Hsün Yüeh, in another section of his discussions on history, wrote:

> The method of planning successful strategies consists of (the comprehension of) three important factors: first, *hsing* (the general conditions); second, *shih*

(specific situation); third, *ch'ing* (the conditions of men). *Hsing* means the overall favorable or unfavorable conditions; *shih* means that which is appropriate at the moment and makes a time propitious for advancing or retreating; *ch'ing* means the mind and intention (of men), which may or may not be appropriate (for the task). The same strategy adopted in similar tasks may produce different results. Why? (This is because in each case any of) the three factors involved may be different. (Ch'en 1980:81–82)

To base action merely on any one of these factors is flawed. And, of course, the only aspect that individuals really have effective control over is their own state of mind, the kind of character and intelligence they bring to the concrete situation. This is surely a direct extension of the claim that Confucius was, above all else, a timely sage. Furthermore, Hsün offers a method whereby a person can be prepared for this complicated analysis of character and situation.

The steadfast Confucian nature of his intellectual and moral commitment shines through the following series of comments about the cultivation of integrity, understanding, and determination in pursuit of what is proper for civilized conduct.

Man builds his virtue out of three things: first, integrity; second, understanding; and third, determination. Integrity is the essence (of virtue); understanding is (the means) by which to achieve it; and determination is (the power) to accomplish it. (He who possesses these) is a superior man. If a man is not able to possess all three (qualities) but only one of them, (let him seek) the most important: integrity.

Man achieves self-discipline in four (areas): sincerity of mind, uprightness of intention, truthfulness of action, and firmness in (adhering to) his assigned position. When his mind is sincere, even the Divine Spirit will respond to him, not to mention the myriad people. When he is upright in intention, even Heaven and Earth will be in harmony with him, not to mention the myriad things. When he is truthful in his actions, he will accomplish meritorious deeds. When he is firm in his position, he will not go astray. (Ch'en 1980:179–181)

The simplicity of the argument reminds the reader of an earlier era in Confucian thought and points toward later developments. Although the triad of integrity, understanding, and determination is not used by later Confucians in discussing the issue of self-cultivation, they are certainly still central themes for Confucian morality. Further, it is of primary importance to focus on the cultivation of the person and let questions of fate and cosmology take their proper place in human life. This does not mean that Hsün was uninterested in larger issues; rather, these larger cosmological issues must be understood in their proper place within the larger ambit of the Confucian Way.

Like Hsün Yüeh, Hsü Kan (170–217) returns to important classical Chou Confucian intellectual topics, specifically the relationship of name and actuality, and points in the direction of the debate with the Neo-Taoist thinkers of the third and fourth centuries. And as with so many other aspects of Confucian thought, Hsü's reflections on *ming*/name and *shih*/reality or actuality, is linked both to the Chinese philosophical tradition's interpretation of names and their relationship to reality and to the social context of his time. Hsü's argumentation was contained in the *Chung Lun*, or, as John Makeham translated the title, *Discourses That Hit the Mark*. "As a whole, the text can be best described as an inquiry into the causes of political and social breakdown and the presentation of various ethical and political remedies" (Makeham 1995:xi). This late Han work demonstrates that Confucian discourse never wanders far from what can be called social ethics and the axiology of normative thought even when it is pursing philosophical and epistemological questions, such as the relationship of names to what is named.

Hsü Kan's reflections on the proper relationship between name and actuality is interesting from yet another perspective. The Confucian tradition is often criticized for being needlessly traditionalistic, bound by the tradition itself, closed to any new or novel ideas. As we have already seen, this is a mistaken reading of the history of Confucianism. For instance, as Makeham (1995) has so cogently argued, when the majority of classical Confucian thinkers considered the question of the relationship of name to actuality, they held a "nominalist" view of the relationship. By contrast, Hsü—and this should not surprise us the end of our survey of Han Confucian thought—held a "correlative" interpretation. This is how Makeham sorted out the issues involved:

> I define a correlative theory of naming as the view that there is a proper or correct correlation between a given name and a given actuality, determined, variously, by what is ordained by "Heaven" (*tian*) or by what is "naturally so" itself (*zi ran*), and a nominalist theory of naming as the view that it is man who arbitrarily or conventionally determines which *ming* should apply to which *shi*. (Makeham 1995:9)

Or as Hsü wrote, "Names are bonded to actualities just as plants are bonded to the seasons. In spring, plants blossom into flower, in summer, they are covered in leaves, in autumn their foliage withers and falls, and in winter they produce seeds" (Makeham 1995:8). In short, Hsü applied the correlative cosmology so popular in Han thought to the vexing question of names and reality or actuality.

The question of the relationship of names and reality, of course, traces its lineage in Confucian discourse to Confucius' own epigram that government depends on the rectification of names. What Confucius meant was that if someone took the title of a king or a father, then that person would need to act in a fashion appropriate to what these names define. A king should try to act as the sage kings of antiquity did and a father should act in a way that shows love to his family. Not to be able to live up to the reality of the moral import of these names means that individuals so named would have to rectify their behavior in order to be a true father, mother, brother, sister, friend, or king.

The debate took on even more bite when someone asked Mencius, the Second Sage, about the death of a local ruler, framing the question in terms of the murder of a king. Mencius feigned surprise, and went on to say that he had never heard of the murder of a true king, though he allowed that he had heard of the execution of evil and immoral tyrants. Mencius thus gives clear approval of the right of regicide, a doctrine that made many later Chinese emperors nervous about including this text in the Confucian canon. Mencius stated that no real king—a king who loves virtue and the welfare of his people—will ever have to worry about such questions.

Sadly and correctly, Hsü sensed that the times were not with him and that names and actuality were falling apart both socially and cosmologically. The grand Han state, by the 190s, had fallen apart, and people wondered what would come next. Someone like Hsü hoped against hope that it would be a revived Confucianism. We now know that this was a forlorn hope, or at least one that would have to wait until the revival of the great Northern Sung masters to again fuse name and actuality into another integrated whole.

It may seem odd to end a chapter on Han thought by returning to a work that purportedly was written before the essays of Hsün Yüeh and Hsü Kan. In fact, there has been an almost endless debate about the dating of the *Po Hu T'ung* in critical Chinese and Western circles. Whenever the text itself was finally compiled, in its present form (perhaps as late as 240) it represents the kind of debate that went on in the later Han. The book itself claims to be a record of a great debate about the nature of the classics themselves that took place at the Po-hu Hall in 79 at the behest of the imperial court. The stated aim of the debate was to elucidate the nature of each of the classics. It was a timely discussion because, as already noted, there was a great deal of debate in this period between the Old and New Texts schools, a debate that continued throughout Confucian history.

According to the *Po Hu T'ung*, sages, although they are the most inspired of human beings, are still completely human in form and intelligence. As the text says, among good men there are ever more exemplary grades: the talented, the distinguished, the refined, the excellent, the worthy, and the hero: "(The best among) ten thousand men is called "hero," (the best among) ten thousand heroes is called "Sage" (Som 1973:2, 528). The text also gives an analytic definition of sage:

What is meant by a "Sage"? "Sage" means *t'ung* "to be in communication with," *tao* "the Way," *sheng* "sound." The way of a Sage is in communication with everything, his understanding illuminates everything, he knows the nature of everything the sound of which he hears.

His spiritual power is in harmony with (that of) Heaven and Earth, his lustre is in harmony with (that of) the sun and moon, his orderly procedure is in harmony with (that of) the four seasons, his relation to what is fortunate and what is calamitous is in harmony with the spirits. (Som 1973:2, 528)

Hence, the sage is a true hero who hears the Way, conforms to the patterns of Heaven and Earth, and is in harmony with all things and all peoples. Moreover, this sagely wisdom always manifests itself in the realm of human affairs.

Why is it that, though Lord and subject, father and son, husband and wife, make six people, we speak of the Three Major Relationships? "The alternation of the yin and yang is called the Way"; the yang completes itself by yin, the yin adapts itself to the yang, hard and soft supplement each other. Therefore the six people make up the Three Major Relationships. (Som 1973:2, 560)

It is crucial here to note the element of complementarity. Although it would be foolish to argue that the Confucian tradition was egalitarian in form, for it always and everywhere affirms a form of graded relationships, it would be equally mistaken to say that it is harsh or tyrannical teaching. What is so important to observe is the careful notion of balance and the way all individuals need the other to be complete.

This note of reciprocity as a key to human relationships is most clearly illustrated in the section on friendship.

What does *p'eng-yu* "friends" mean? *P'eng* means *tang* "associate," *yu* means *yu* "to have." The *Li chi* says: "One of the same school is called a *p'eng*; one of the same intention is called a *yu*." The association of friends (implies that) in each other's company they correct each other's words, and when they are separated they abstain from criticizing one another. When the one behaves well the other rejoices with him, when he behaves ill he grieves for him. Their property they share without reckoning. They share each other's distress and sorrow, mutually giving assistance. In life they do not hang on one another, at their death they do not burden each other. Therefore the *Lun yü* says: "Tay-lu said: I should like carriage and horses, and light fur dresses to wear them out for my friends." It also says, "If a friend has no (relations) to fall back on I shall provide for his home when he is alive, and for his burial when he dies." (Som 1973:2, 562)

I know of few better definitions of friendship. Although Confucians could be authoritarian, there is little warrant for viewing them as such when we look carefully at what the classical texts have to tell us. That there is a need for strictness and order, yes; for tyranny, no. The Confucians would need all the friends they could find to survive the next few centuries after the fall of the Han—when it seemed as though their world had been thrown into the outer darkness of decay and despair.

❀ 3 ❀

The Defense of the Faith from the Wei-Chin (220–420) to the T'ang (618–907): The Challenge of Taoism and Buddhism

THE CHALLENGES TO CONFUCIANISM posed by a revived Taoism and the arrival of Buddhism are the subject of this chapter. This was the longest single epoch in the development of the Confucian tradition. The Confucian response to Taoism and Buddhism runs from the end of the Han dynasty to the end of the T'ang, roughly from the third century to the beginning of the tenth century. It brackets the history of Confucianism between two of the most famous and successful dynasties, the Han and the T'ang. The very complexity of the era, or series of eras and dynasties, is mirrored in the fact that its list of dynasties takes up as much space as the rest of Chinese history put together.

This period was essentially composed of mini-eras during which intellectual currents were complex and eclectic. In fact, many of the greatest thinkers of this age were unapologetic about the multiple origins of their thought. For instance, the great Wei-Chin Confucian Fu Hsüan, although a staunch defender of the correctness of the Confucian Way, saw nothing wrong in making use of any technological innovation or theoretical construct if it would help in providing good government and promoting Confucian virtues. Nonetheless, Fu's willingness to read widely caused some later scholars to list him among eclectic rather than Confucian thinkers. Along with a love of metaphysical discourse, some of the thinkers of this age also exhibited a pragmatic spirit as they sought to pilot the Chinese world through troubled times.

The story is a drama in three parts. First, the post-Han Confucians came to grips with the collapse of their first great empire and the definitive end of the classical world. This denouement was truly shocking because the

Chinese had no indication that the Han empire, which seemed so strong, was so fragile. First, if the Han emperors and ministers had adopted Confucianism for their own, how could the empire fail to provide good government and security to the people? Second, the Confucians again confronted a Taoist tradition that was critical of Confucian standards and procedures. The Neo-Taoists were a moving target because they also saw themselves as the true heirs of the classical period and often happily acknowledged a debt and reverence for Confucius, if not the later Confucians. Third, the post-Han Confucians faced the awesome challenge, stimulation, and undoubted influence of one of the greatest missionary traditions the world has ever seen—Buddhism.

Politically and socially, after the rise of the T'ang in the seventh century, the Chinese people surveyed an ecumenically diverse culture that was the envy of the whole world. Who can argue, save for the most circumscribed of Confucian intellectuals, that this was not the very height of Chinese culture? Even the Confucians were in awe of the artistic achievements of the T'ang age. But the glory that was T'ang China is still centuries away from the battered Confucians of the third century of the Common Era.

The Question of Influence: Neo-Taoism and Buddhism

The fluidity of the patterns of Wei-Chin (220–420) to T'ang (618) thought are fascinating for the light they throw on what it means to be Confucian. As I have argued before, one practical key to understanding the self-definition of Chinese thinkers resides in their choice of a canon for study and self-cultivation, coupled with an ultimate existential appropriation of the ideals expressed in these classical texts. Confucians accept the Confucian canon as it came to be formally constituted by the Han scholars. Taoists likewise had a canon that included the *Lao Tzu*, the *Chuang Tzu*, the *Lieh Tzu*, and the *Huai-nan Tzu* as the core of their philosophical tradition. However, in the Wei-Chin period these boundaries, which are only lists of books, wavered. It was perfectly acceptable for a person to be interested equally in both Confucian and Taoist classics. And when a thinker was happy to embrace both sets of canonical texts as important, it is very hard to say whether we are dealing with a Taoist Confucian or a Confucian Taoist.

The arrival of Buddhism presented Chinese intellectuals with a threefold challenge. First, the Buddhists brought their own huge canon. Over the early centuries of Chinese Buddhism, from the second to the sixth centuries, one of the main tasks of scholarly Chinese and foreign missionaries was translating the vast range of Buddhist literature. There are more sutras, essays, and treatises in the Chinese Tripitaka than in any other set of canonical classics in any other tradition. The translation of Buddhist scriptures was one of the truly great ecumenical achievements of any culture. Second, the teachings of this vast array of texts challenged the classical and Han understanding of heaven, earth, and humanity. It took the best Chinese intellectuals centuries to come to grips with the foreign nature of Buddhism. But in the end, they enhanced and expanded the Buddha's dharma. Third, Buddhist missionaries introduced atypical forms of social organizations such as a celibate monastic system. There had never been anything like a celibate monastic system in China, where the world was dominated by the family and the state until the arrival of Buddhism, with its novel understanding of how people were to achieve liberation from the red dust of the mundane world.

In short, Buddhism contested Chinese worldviews in every way in which one tradition can engage another culture. No aspect of Chinese life escaped what scholars call the Buddhist conquest of China. But it was a remarkably benign and peaceful conquest, one carried out by lay merchants, monks, and nuns. In fact, it was a conquest joyfully accepted by the Chinese. Few missionary efforts cast more honor on both the missionaries and their audience in terms of mutual respect and transformation. Nor was the impact only on Confucians. Taoists also appropriated immense amounts of material from the Buddhists, including the formation of their own vast scriptural canon and the social structures of monasticism. Long after the arrival of Buddhism in China, the great Sung Neo-Confucian Chu Hsi would complain, only half joking, that every time he went to a beautiful and quiet place, the site was already taken by a Buddhist monastery or a Taoist temple.

Liu Shao and the Study of Human Abilities

The work of Liu Shao (fl. 196–250) has always been held in high regard because of Liu's reflections on what constitutes human ability. J. K. Shryock has noted that we are not sure exactly when Liu lived and died, but that his work on human abilities was probably written in 240–250, when he had already retired from public service. Liu's *Study of Human Abilities* is a fascinating work for a number of reasons. First, it is a subtle and systematic treatise that attempts to discuss the nature of human talent and ability. This is an important topic for any Confucian because such analysis is necessary for everything from the choosing of one's friends to the careful selection of government officials. Second, Liu anticipates many of the themes and the vocabulary of the later Sung dynasty Neo-Confucian revival.

Liu Shao had a definite view of the cosmos and human ability. He posited that there was an essential unity to the cosmos rooted in the *tao* of Heaven. But even more important to Liu was the notion that the unity of the cosmos was based on a principle of *li*/order, which Shryock called "law" and the Sung Neo-Confucians later called "principle." Of course, this principle only finds its place in a world of yin-yang forces. The unity of a human being is completed by the inclusion of a third element, the shape or form of the person, which depends on the interaction of the five phases.

The first chapter of the *Study of Human Abilities* outlines how human abilities and capacities are organized.

> The temperament and nature issue from the original endowment of men. The laws by which temperament and nature operate are subtle and profound. Who can investigate these things, unless he has the insight of a sage?
>
> All living beings contain a profound unity which gives them substance. The *Yin* and *Yang* (the principles forming the universe) endow them with natures. The five elements embody their form.
>
> If a thing possesses both form and substance, it is possible to investigate it. (Shryock 1937:95–96)

Within this world of order, principle, the yin-yang and five phases, and human nature, Liu entwines his analysis around two views of humanity that are different from the Western view of human ability and capacity. In the first instance, Liu uses the notion of *ts'ai,* or ability, and the allied notion of *neng,* or capacity. The abilities are those human traits that a person has within the self. The capacities are the ways in which various personal abilities are manifested in a world of occupations and social positions. Not everyone has a perfect balance of abilities and hence will have limited capacities as well: "A man of clear vision may understand the secret of action, yet be unable to think profoundly" (Shryock 1937:96). The ideal is still that of a sage who has all the native abilities and manifests them in the capacities to incite human flourishing.

Liu Shao recognized the complexity of human ability and its attendant capacities. His reason for exploring all of this is that abilities differ from person to person.

> Abilities are different, and so each differs in its capacity. There is the capacity for responsibility. There are capacities which can establish law and make others follow it. There are capacities which can adjust and defend. There are capacities for virtue, which are able to teach men . . .
>
> The capacities come from the innate abilities. Innate abilities differ in quantity. Therefore since innate abilities and capacities are different, so their proper employment in government is also different. (Shryock 1937:119–120)

Liu makes use of this device of differentiating ability and capacities to show how to judge and employ people for service to the state and family. The problem that we have in recognizing and making use of a person's talents, abilities, and capacities is that in judging others, all of us tend to be blinded by our own innate ability and the particular slant this gives to our understanding of others. Liu illustrates this point by showing the strengths and weaknesses of characteristic Chinese philosophical positions. "The legalist has conformity to a standard as his rule. Therefore he is able to recognize the standards by which squareness and uprightness are compared, but cannot value the strategy of transformation" (Shryock 1937:125). Ultimately, this is the case because human ability mirrors the fundamental nature of reality. "The changeableness of all phenomena, the filling and the emptying, the increasing and lessening, is the law of *Tao*" (Shryock 1937:112). The issues of human nature, talents, abilities, and capacities are themes that will return when the Sung Neo-Confucians frame their answers to the Neo-Taoist and Buddhist challenges to the Confucian Way.

Fu Hsüan (217–278) and the Fu Tzu

As Jordan Paper noted in his study and translation of the *Fu Tzu*, Fu Hsüan wrote the treatise for the most impeccable of Confucian reasons, namely, to give practical advice to his ruler about how to select officials of talent. "How is it that the duck has a membrane on its feet and the rooster has spurs? I do not know. How can I question Heaven and Earth?" (Paper 1987:28) Many other Han and post-Han thinkers not only put these kinds of questions to Heaven and Earth but elicited elaborate answers to them. Actually, Fu had a great interest in practical technology that could be of use to the state. Fu justified this technical interest as an example of the proper Confucian investigation of things. Because he saw the task of philosophy as raising itself above petty quarrels between major traditions, his work has often been classified as eclectic rather than Confucian. Yet surely his dedication to the twin virtues of humanity and justice place him squarely within the development of the Confucian Tao. Although Fu may not have been the most original of Confucians, he solidly defended the tradition in a time when it needed all the support it could receive.

Nowhere is the Confucian import of the *Fu Tzu* more evident than in Fu's analysis of the rectification of the mind-heart. This focus on self-cultivation based on Mencian themes goes directly to the center of the Confucian project.

> In antiquity, those who well understood governing, knew that the (mind-)heart is the ruler of the myriad affairs; and that if one acts without moderation, there will be disruption. Therefore, they placed priority in rectifying the (mind-)heart. After their hearts were upright, whether they acted or not, they were not in the wrong. By means of this (whether to act or not and not be in the wrong), they led the world, and afterwards, the world became upright and preserved its nature. Is that very far? Seek it in the (mind-)heart, that is all! (Paper 1987:41–42)

As we shall see, such a notion that the truth of the sages' wisdom is to be found in the human mind-heart was a favorite doctrine of Sung Neo-

Confucians. Fu continues the argument by writing about humanity, justice, and truthfulness:

> Imitate Heaven and pattern oneself on Earth, act truthfully and think reasonably in order to unite the world: this is the truthfulness of the kind. Rely on laws, support uprightness, act without vacillating: this is the truthfulness of the feudal lords. When words come from the mouth, they should be bound in the (mind-)heart, they should be kept unaltered in order to establish the character: this is truthfulness of the gentleman. Endeavor in truthfulness, cultivate righteousness, and the way of men will be established. (Paper 1987:45)

Of course, all of this is solid Confucian advice, but somehow it does not provide the kind of ontological and metaphysical answers or discourse that appealed to the Chinese of the post-Han world. It repeated the main points of the Confucian Way but did not provide a defense in terms of the more complicated dialects of the Neo-Taoists thinkers.

Neo-Taoism and Hsüan-hsüeh/The Dark Learning

The Precocious Genius of Wang Pi (226–249)

Wang Pi has to be one of the most precocious philosophical geniuses the world has ever seen. He made a lasting impact on Chinese thought before he reached age twenty-four, when he suddenly died. His biography reports cases of his early interviews with the prime minister, before he was even twenty, when this governmental worthy found it difficult to take one so young seriously. One wonders what Wang would have accomplished if he had lived for another four or five decades. In his short life, he wrote what would become two of the most definitive philosophical commentaries on the *Tao Te Ching* and the *I-Ching*. Not only did he contribute two commentaries that formed the basis for much future philosophical speculation, but he also helped to introduce conjecture on issues such as being and nonbeing into the mainstream of philosophical discourse. As we shall see, Wang Pi helped to provide the philosophical vocabulary for all later Chinese thought in his selection of terms for nonbeing, being, principle, and substance and function. Wang Pi's work is a perfect example of the thought of this era because it reveals the essential ambiguity about whether he was a Confucian, a Taoist, or something entirely different.

Beyond Wang Pi's terminological contributions, such as *li* as principle and *t'i-yung* as substance-function, it is also crucial to recognize that he was passionately committed to the ontological uncovering of the ultimate nature of things without embracing static, reified, or substance views of reality. Although other Chinese thinkers had dealt with these issues before, it was Wang who refined them and made these ontological terms important parts of the Chinese intellectual scene because of the impact of his great commentaries on the *Tao Te Ching* and *I-Ching*. In this way, Wang Pi prepared the way for Buddhist and Neo-Confucian speculations on the ultimate reasons for the cosmos.

Wang Pi reflected on the notion of *wu*/nonbeing because this is what Confucius embodied beyond words. "The sage embodied *wu*, and since *wu* cannot be taught, he therefore did not discuss it. Lao Tzu, however, remained on the level of "being" (*yu*); thus he constantly addressed the inadequacies of being" (Chan 1991:28). The debate concerning Wang's true opinions of Confucianism hangs on his ingenious way of stating Confucius' true intent. Wang plays on the fact that Confucius did not discuss metaphysical issues and, according to Lao-tzu himself, those who really know do not speak. Hence, since Confucius really knew about nonbeing as the source of all being, he was not constrained to talk about nonbeing in any formal way. This is a wonderful example of how Wang Pi creatively reinterpreted the Confucian tradition to include ontological questions that had not been such an important part of the tradition before that.

In Wang Pi's defense of the Confucian Way, we also need to remember his preservation of sagely emotion against his colleague Ho Yen. Ho Yen believed that a true sage was beyond mere emotion and that the sage, like nonbeing, had no emotional life like common women and men. Quite to the contrary, Wang Pi held that the sage, by truly embodying nonbeing and being, could harmonize all feelings in a timely fashion. As the story of the debate between these two friends records, "Nevertheless, while the feelings of the sage respond to things, they are not bound by things. Now, if one thinks that because the sage is not bound by things, he therefore does not respond to them, he indeed misses the mark" (Chan 1991:36).

On the contrary, Wang Pi was fascinated by the power of nonbeing to engender all the other mundane beings of the cosmos. In his commentary on the opening chapter of the *Lao Tzu*, Wang says, "All beings (*yu*) originated from non-being (*wu*)" (Chan 1991:47). For Wang, nonbeing signifies another name for the Way itself. However, what is engaging from a Confucian point of view is that Wang, along with all his talk about nonbeing, makes the case that nonbeing is implicated in the formation of the true principle of things. Although Alan Chan was careful to note that we cannot argue that Wang Pi was really a Neo-Confucian because of his use of the term "principle," nonetheless Wang defined a train of thought that was to bear fruit seven centuries later in the thought of Ch'eng I and Chu Hsi.

The Buddha's Dharma

No one is certain exactly when the first Buddhists arrived in China or whether they were missionaries in any formal sense of the term. It is probable that the first Buddhists to arrive in China were lay merchants from

Central Asia who were bent on trade but not averse to spreading the dharma when they had a chance. In future centuries, China began to receive a flow of actual Buddhist monks from Central Asia and in later periods, many famous monk-travelers were sent to India itself in search of authentic texts and teachings. However and whenever the first Buddhists disembarked, what happened next was truly, as Eric Zürcher (1959) has called it, the Buddhist conquest of China.

Along with the seismic shocks of the fall of the Han, which we must remember was as profound a disruption for educated Chinese as the fall of the Roman Empire was for Europeans, there was now the need to come to terms with the fact of Buddhism. Suddenly, from the Far West of China, there came stories of a learned man, the Buddha, and his message of liberation. Whatever else Buddhism was, it was complex and different. The main religious and intellectual story of the next few centuries was the gradual assimilation and transformation of Buddhism in China. By the end of the account, the Chinese had come to understand that Buddhism represented a completely different worldview, a philosophy that owed nothing to the wisdom of the Chinese sages.

During the long period between the fall of the Han and the rise of the T'ang, the Chinese were unable to bring order to the northern frontier. However, sometimes enterprising tribal chiefs were able to form powerful confederacies that sought not merely great tribute and booty but the actual conquest of all of China. However, from the third to the sixth centuries no great tribal leader was able to forge a confederacy that was able to overrun all of China. Nonetheless, there was a constant movement of non-Chinese tribal peoples into North China and the formation of mixed Sino-barbarian kingdoms. On the Chinese side, more and more Chinese moved south from the North China plain, beginning the great historic shift of the center of gravity of China from the north to the south. The tribal peoples discovered, as have most of China's foreign conquerors, that once you had gained supremacy by sword and horse, it was vital to find a way to rule the vast country you had just conquered. Part of the solution, of course, was to make use of Confucianism; but Buddhism became another popular way to cement the diverse world of North China together.

The introduction of Buddhism to China is one of the greatest stories of human discovery between cultures. As noted before, there was nothing in the Chinese intellectual tradition that prepared the Chinese for the emergence of an alternative worldview. In fact, at first many Chinese simply could not believe that Buddhism was a new or independent form of thought; one suggestion was that Buddhism was just a form of Taoism. Educated Chinese knew that Lao Tzu was purported to have left China for the West long ago. It was speculated that Lao Tzu had become a teacher of the Western barbarians and Buddhism was hence a form of Taoism as it had come to be understood in the mysterious world of the Chinese Far West. In short, the Chinese tried to fit Buddhism into their own intellectual world, and the only philosophical system that seemed at all convergent with Buddhism was Taoism. The constant interaction of Taoist and Buddhist intellectuals did nothing to discourage such speculation.

Buddhism disembarked in bits and pieces and was itself undergoing continual growth and transformation in India and Central Asia. It is hard to find just one image to describe its entrance into China. As we shall see, Buddhism during this period was in its golden age of territorial and intellectual growth throughout Asia. There were many different schools competing for their place in the Buddhist world and its universities in North India. There were also regional variations caused by the transmission of Buddhism from one area to another. For instance, the Buddhism of Central Asia differed from that of India, and even more so from the countries of South Asia. Buddhism did not come directly to China from India but was transmitted by way of Central Asia.

Another point to bear in mind is that Buddhist intellectuals, if they were well trained in the intricacies of Buddhist philosophy, addressed questions that had never been debated at such length and with such precision within Chinese philosophy. A good example of this is the perennial question, at least for Indo-European thinkers, of the nature of being itself, or what is called ontology in Western philosophy. This question concerns why there is anything at all rather than nothing at all—and only Wang Pi and the Neo-Taoists had shown much interest in this kind of speculation before Buddhism arrived in China. Because Buddhism developed in an Indian milieu and made use of the richness of the Pali and Sanskrit technical vocabularies of these ancient Indo-European languages, ontological queries such as these were part and parcel of the Indian philosophical background. The question of being and nonbeing was discussed as part of the philosophical task in ways it never would have been in classical China. Even though the Buddhist tradition rejects categorically any notion of one's "own nature" or the reality of ultimately self-referencing substances, Buddhist philosophers understood what was at stake in such debate.

A good example of the Chinese transformation of Indic and Central Asian Buddhism resides in the emergence of the more optimistic view of the world that all East Asian Buddhists brought to their mature interpretations of the Buddha's teaching. The development of the concept of the Buddha-nature in East Asia demonstrates how much more world affirming East Asian Buddhism had become. The Chinese were aware that they gave a characteristically different reading to Buddhism, and they reasoned that distant countries simply had different, though authentic, ways of presenting the dharma—some more positive and some more negative than others, though all agreeing on the essentials of the Buddha's path. Therefore, because the Indian sensibility is more world denying does not mean that it is a better approach to liberation than more optimistic Chinese views. The task, as the Chinese Buddhists saw it, was to use whatever expedient means, or *upaya,* were at hand to help sentient beings escape the illusion of error and uncover their Buddha-nature.

The Range of Mahayana Doctrine

In its most basic format, the Buddha taught, as the fourth of the Four Noble Truths, that there is an eightfold path that will lead to liberation from suffering and ignorance. The eightfold path is organized in three subdivisions: the path of proper conduct; practice or meditation; and wisdom or insight. The Buddha taught that all three elements are essential to liberation and cannot, in religious praxis, be separated. The fairly common Western notion that Buddhists lack a social ethics, or that ethics as a whole is subordinated to the concerns of compassion and wisdom, is just plain wrong. All three elements must be present for the full nature of the Buddha's teaching to be present and effective. However, for the purposes of this survey of Confucian thought, I will stress those key intellectual elements of Buddhism that continued to impact the development of Confucian thought.

As Paul Williams (1989) has so effectively argued in *Mahayana Buddhism: The Doctrinal Foundations,* the Buddha's teachings arrived in a continuous manner in medieval China. The great conceptual breaks and paradigm shifts that we now accord to terms such as Theravada or Hinayana or Mahayana meant much less in the second, third, and fourth centuries than they do now because far fewer people were aware that these terms marked radically different "turnings" of the wheel of the dharma. In fact, if Williams is correct, there were no radical breaks between what is now considered the Hinayana forms of teaching and the complex of ideas that we now call Mahayana. The process of the emergence of Mahayana was more gradual than dramatic. Medieval Chinese travelers, such as Fa-hsien and Hsüan-tsang, noticed that the proponents of both Hinayana and Mahayana schools taught side by side in these large Indian monastic universities.

From a philosophical point of view, there are five developments in Buddhist thought in India, Central Asia, and East Asia that had exceptional pertinence for the future revival of Confucian philosophy in the late T'ang (ninth century) and Sung dynasties (960–1279). First, there is the inspiring idea of the perfection of wisdom as one of the paths of liberation. Second, Nagarjuna (fl. second century C.E.) provided the underpinnings for the philosophy of the Middle Way, or emptiness, that had such a pivotal impact on Chinese cosmological theories. Third, there is reception of the other great

Mahayana school, Mind Only, which reinforced the Chinese predilection for emphasizing the role of the enlightenment of the mind-heart at the center of self-cultivation. Fourth, there is use of *tathagatagarbha,* or Buddha-essence/Buddha-nature theory and texts, in order to support the classical Chinese search for the definition and reality of human nature. Fifth, there was also the addition of the images of the great bodhisattva saints that so profoundly shaped the devotional piety of East Asian Buddhists. I have chosen these elements because they represent fundamental aspects of the transmission of Buddhism into China and themes of Mahayana that had great influence on the overall developmental patterns of later Confucian thinkers.

Nagarjuna is often called the second founder of Buddhism because of his brilliant logical explication of the doctrine of emptiness, the teaching that decisively differentiated Buddhism from the emerging Hindu intellectual world. In China, the philosophical doctrine of emptiness marked the separation of Buddhism from Taoism and, most keenly, from the later Confucians. Nagarjuna certainly must rank as one of the most brilliant philosophers the world has ever produced. His Middle Way school provides the intellectual background for all the future Indian and East Asian philosophical schools.

Nagarjuna crafted his doctrine of emptiness with a relentless logical assault on any suggestion that things have their own being or substance. He sought to reduce to silence or intellectual incoherence any pretensions of being so that people could let go of erroneous views that would bind them to the illusion of the substantial reality of the world. He did so by linking his theory of emptiness to the classical Buddhism doctrine of *pratityasamutpada,* or dependent or codependent origination: "It is dependent origination that we call emptiness" (Williams 1989:61). What we have, according to Nagarjuna, is not a world of things that interconnect because they already exist in some ontological or cosmological sense but rather a world of codependent things, including sentient beings, that exist provisionally because they are related. It is relationality that causes things to become, rather than the cause being due to some kind of essence for each thing.

However, there were those who believed that Nagarjuna had destroyed the hope of liberation through the austere logic of his doctrine of emptiness. Nagarjuna calmly pointed out that this was not the case and demonstrated that his critics did not understand yet another characteristic Middle Way doctrine, that of the Two Truths. In short, Nagarjuna argued that there are two truths, a conventional and an ultimate truth. The ultimate truth is, of course, that of emptiness. Nonetheless, there is the conventional truth of the world as well. Here again Nagarjuna, like most Buddhist teachers, points out that the ultimate truth of emptiness is based on sound everyday practice. In fact, without everyday, ordinary truth, there would be no ultimate truth. Because of the linkage of the ultimate and conventional truth, Nagarjuna asserted that he did not destroy the Buddhist religion.

There were later Buddhist scholars, including the Asanga (fl. fourth century), who, while appreciating Nagarjuna's dialectical brilliance, did not agree with his Middle Way school. Simply put, the Mind Only school agreed with Nagarjuna's critics that his attitude toward the Buddha's teaching was too negative. Although in Nagarjuna's capable hands the teaching of emptiness did not have to degenerate into nihilism, something more positive was needed for the less intellectually and spiritually advanced. No one would argue that reality lacks the marks of own being, but the Mind Only school was interested in proposing a more positive way of reviewing of the Buddha's dharma by stressing the role of consciousness, or mind, along with the doctrine of emptiness, as it would be translated in East Asia.

The Mind Only school taught that although the various objects and events of the world lack any ultimate substantial existence, there is always a flow of consciousness that subtends our awareness of these objects, or dharmas. Although there was a great deal of debate within the Mind Only school about how to describe this primordial flow of consciousness, there was a common agreement that consciousness was fundamental to any philosophical or religious analysis, and when freed of false doctrines and illusion, reality itself was beyond the subject-object dichotomies that infect mundane human perception. The Mind Only school asserted that all the world resides on or is perceived through consciousness itself. Hence, the school paid special attention to the role of mind-heart in Buddhist praxis and doctrine.

Of course, there were other Buddhists, especially in the Middle Way school and the later Ch'an/Zen schools, who took a dim view of this potentially misleading and positive interpretation of consciousness. They countered with an argument that Mind Only simply reinserts a concept of an enduring soul back into Buddhism. The Mind Only thinkers denied this: "The substratum consciousness is an ever-changing stream, no doubt an attempt to explain the evolution of the world from consciousness, and certain problems of personal identity, but in no way something to be grasped or attached to as a Self. According to Asanga and Vasubandhu, it 'ceases' at enlightenment" (Williams 1989:92).

Nonetheless, some Chinese Mind Only scholars, such as Hsüan-tsang, held that it was only the tainted aspects of consciousness that ceased; there was still the wondrous power of the pure or immaculate consciousness that provides for the act of liberation itself.

It is not hard to see why Hsüan-tsang's version of East Asian Mind Only was so appealing to the Chinese intellectual world, especially those who believed that the human person, however deluded and evil, contained the wherewithal to achieve real emancipation from error and false actions.

Confucians and Taoists had spent considerable intellectual energy during the classical period comprehending the nature and function of the mind-heart as the center of the living person. Thus, although the Mind Only school did not last very long in China, Korea, or Japan as an independent school, its contribution to the unique East Asian schools such as T'ien-t'ai, Hua-yen, and Ch'an/Zen was enormous. For example, the later Neo-Confucians would argue that the prime mistake of schools such as Mind Only was that they mistook the mind-heart as the seat of consciousness for human nature itself. According to the Neo-Confucians, Buddhists committed what is now called a category mistake in conflating consciousness, the mind-heart, and human nature.

The fourth trait of Buddhist doctrine is the concept of the *tathagatagarbha* or, as Williams (1989) has translated it, the Buddha-essence, or Buddha-nature. On the surface this again seems like a retrogressive idea when compared to Nagarjuna's resounding Middle Way rejection of any theory or notion of essential substance. How can the Buddha have something called an essence of nature if the truth is emptiness? The early Buddha sutras teach that "all living beings, though they are among the defilements of hatred, anger and ignorance, have the Buddha's wisdom, Buddha's Eye, Buddha's Body sitting in the form of meditation . . . they are possessed of the Matrix of the Tathagata (*tathagatagarbha*)" (Williams 1989:97). Although there is a great deal of debate about the ontological and cosmological status of this Buddha-nature within every sentient being, this teaching holds its doctrine as a way of affirming that it is this wonderful Buddha-nature that allows every sentient being to aspire to enlightenment. There is even a strong part of the tradition that holds that we are already enlightened but that we have forgotten our original pure nature. That is why the Buddha came to teach: to help us to uncover our true Buddha-nature.

The theme of the Buddha-nature is picked up in one of the most important of all East Asian scholastic treatises, *The Awakening of Faith in Mahayana*. The treatise claims an Indian origin, but no Sanskrit or Central Asian version has yet been found. *The Awakening of Faith* made the Buddha-nature theory into an organized cosmological theory of the way the world works. Rather like yin-yang correlative cosmology, *The Awakening of Faith* assumes that the Buddha-nature is the very basis and support for the world of samsara, or mundane illusion, and nirvana itself as the goal of final liberation. Because of this theory, the Buddha-nature, the true mind, and even the Dharmakaya, or the highest body of the ultimate Buddha, are all seen as unified in one grand cosmological synthesis.

Just as the Confucian tradition holds that each person ought to become a sage, the high Mahayana world of East Asia held that all sentient beings should model themselves on the path of the bodhisattva. As found in the Lotus Sutra, easily the most important devotional text in East Asia, we discover the world of the bodhisattvas and Buddhas who seek, through inconceivable epochs of time and infinite world and with incomparably skillful means, to save all sentient beings. The essence of the bodhisattva path is the vow to try to save all beings before the bodhisattva finally partakes of the last liberation and finds the bliss of nirvana. Because sentient beings are themselves infinite in number, the vows of the bodhisattavas and the Buddhas who teach them are infinite and all-encompassing.

Although I acknowledge the demonstrable impact of Buddhist teaching, I suggest that the Confucian tradition was not without its own internal philosophical resources for continued development, however much this growth was stimulated by the fructification of Buddhist nourishment. It is more likely that there was a combination of stimulus, response, and growth of the Confucian tradition in interaction with Buddhism. The obvious classical model is the symbiotic and fruitful relationship of Taoism and Confucianism. For instance, I do not believe that anyone can read Chang Tsai's eleventh-century "Western Inscription" without thinking of the bodhisattva's vow; but equally, no one can read Chang's hymn to Confucian concern and wisdom without remembering the *Doctrine of the Mean* and *Mencius* as well.

T'ang Confucianism

That Confucianism was never absent from Chinese culture during this long medieval period is nowhere better illustrated than in the lives and works of the founders of what the Chinese have called the "Glorious T'ang Dynasty." For instance, as Howard J. Wechsler (1985) has demonstrated in his *Offerings of Jade and Silk*, it was in the T'ang dynasty that certain very important points about the interpretation of ritual were decided. In fact, it is hard to think of any dynasty that did not pay more attention to the question of ritual.

For instance, David McMullen (1988) has pointed out that Confucian ritual education was expanded under T'ang patronage. Although what was taught might not have been to the taste of later ages, this does not mean that Confucianism did not continue its role as the foundational social philosophy in Chinese life, especially among many of the aristocratic civil servants of the T'ang empire. The early T'ang scholar-minister Wei Cheng (580–643) wrote about the necessity for Confucian education: "How great is Confucianism as a teaching; how copious the benefits it brings to living beings . . . It is the very root and course of good administration and moral reform; it is the ears and eyes of all humanity" (McMullen 1988:31). Minister Wei went on to make sure that Confucian education was expanded so that its benefits in the areas of good administration and moral reform could be appreciated by the whole realm.

Along with a concern for civil education and administration, the T'ang Confucians were famous for their dedication to establishing and commenting on the Confucian classics and for writing history. The T'ang state encouraged and financed great scholarly projects aimed at providing all scholars with a definitive version of the Confucian classics. For instance, a direct descendant of Confucius, K'ung Yin-ta (574–648), produced a series of commentaries on the Five Classics that became classics in their own right. The production of these texts and their commentaries were not the work of individual or isolated scholars; rather, they represented the best collaborative efforts of the T'ang Confucians working within large imperial commissions. The series became known as the *Wu Ching Cheng I,* or *The True Meaning of the Five Canons.* These cumulative works are invaluable even today for the careful scholarship that has been brought to key Confucian texts.

Along with canonical studies, the T'ang Confucians were also fascinated by China's imperial history, and most specifically by the Han dynasty. The T'ang saw themselves as restoring the glory of the Han and thought that there were many records available to T'ang historians in their pursuit of the lessons of Han history. The Confucian study of history was only second to the study of the canonical texts. As has already been noted, Confucianism is a resolutely historical tradition that affirms the importance for history for the cultivation of a just society and even for the nurture of a refined mind-heart. History is a mirror that the past holds up in order to remind us that we, too, will be judged worthy or at fault.

In addition to compiling various historical texts and archival records, the T'ang produced Confucians who articulated a philosophy of history. For instance, Liu Chih-chi (661–721) wrote the famous *Shih T'ung* as a comprehensive study of the role of the historian as responsible social critic. As well as contributing to the study of the range and scope of institutional historiography, Liu was acutely aware of the difficulties that Confucian historians had when they allowed themselves to be too influenced by questions of authority. Liu worried about whether scholar-officials could retain their objectivity in the face of imperial power and prestige. One of his great contributions was to call for what McMullen has described as a "boldness in demanding clarity and objectivity in history," even when this was risky business (McMullen 1988:178).

Although Liu Chih-chi was conservative in the sense that he believed in the great classical models of Han history, he defended the position that a historian must record how history changes from one era to the next. In this respect, Liu explored the history of institutional change. He stressed that over time the great imperial institution had changed dramatically. He included new topics such as genealogy, and he conducted studies of the various capital cities and investigated how the tribute system worked along the northern frontier. Liu also contributed various specialized essays about specific historical topics. He provided a model of what a serious Confucian scholar-historian ought to be.

Along with classical and historical studies, T'ang Confucians had great debates about literature. As with many literate aristocratic cultures, the gentleman of the T'ang dynasty placed a premium on the ability to express oneself in belles lettres and poetry. As we shall see, a number of the most famous late T'ang Confucians, especially Han Yü, were commemorated as great prose stylists. Furthermore, one of the truly greatest poets the world has ever seen—Tu Fu (712–770)—is counted as a Confucian when compared to his friend Li Po (699–762), the great free-spirited Taoist of the age. Tu, by contrast, was a worried soul, deeply concerned about the plight of the Chinese people. Any number of his poems reveal that concern, but the one that follows about his horse demonstrates the personal side of a Confucian gentleman-poet. Such work belies the temptation to think of Confucian sensibility as mere commentary and dry history, or even concern merely for the realm of humanity.

The Sick Horse

For so long I have ridden you,
Now on the frontier through bitter
Winter; you have worked long and well
And I am saddened that you are old and sick;
Only an ordinary horse, they would say,
Yet only I know how fine and loyal
You have been; just an animal, surely!
But to me a noble spirit, worthy of
This song of grief I sing. (Alley 1964:84)

The T'ang poets and painters loved, for instance, their great steeds from Central Asia. They also loved wine and the strange songs from barbarian lands. Whitehead once suggested that only a fairly conservative and successful orthodoxy can afford to be truly ecumenical and tolerant in spirit and taste. The aristocratic T'ang Confucians were all that in their receptivity to the new Buddhist faith and philosophies. The T'ang dynasty was an age of supreme Chinese self-assurance in religion, military success, art, food, music—this finds expression in the fact that the Chinese do not call themselves *Han-jen,* or people of the Han, but they often use the term *T'ang-jen,* or people of the T'ang.

What the T'ang rulers were able to do militarily in extending Chinese rule far into Central Asia they also duplicated in the glories of their culture. It was during the T'ang period that Chinese culture came to completely dominate the East Asian landscape. Korea and Japan copied T'ang court culture, religion, city planning, and architecture. Just as Chinese pilgrim-monks traveled to the far reaches of India in search of new or more accurate Buddhist texts, Koreans and Japanese modeled themselves on Chinese civilization. The spell was not broken until the nineteenth and twentieth centuries. To be a civilized person in East Asia from the T'ang period on was to be a recipient of a classical Chinese education. The Chinese language of the age became the intellectual lingua franca of the whole region. Generations of Korean, Japanese, and Vietnamese intellectuals wrote Chinese poetry and took part in the creative expansion of Confucianism.

From a philosophical point of view, the only thing that the T'ang lacked was a metaphysical appetite equal to that of their Sung successors. But as we shall see, just what counts for philosophy often resides in the eye of the beholder. It was in the T'ang that great Confucian polemicists such as Han Yü began a defense of Confucianism against Buddhism by means of apologetics as a creative approach to the revival of the Confucian tradition.

The Late T'ang Transition: The Reformation of "This Culture of Ours"

Historians of the T'ang traditionally use the year 755 to mark the great dividing point of the dynasty with the rebellion of An Lu-shan. For the purposes of this study of Confucianism, we need not follow the story of this great rebellion beyond noting that it marked the high point and subsequent decline of the dynasty itself. It also marked a period when some Confucian intellectuals began to counter Buddhism as the dominant intellectual force of the age. From the Buddhist point of view, equally important events occurred in 845, when the reigning T'ang emperor began the most serious persecution of members of the Buddhist tradition China had ever witnessed. Temples and monasteries were destroyed, their wealth confiscated and the monks and nuns scattered to the four winds and often forcibly returned to lay life and marriage.

Great religious persecutions like that of 845 are rare in Chinese history, and yet this one, like the rebellion of An Lu-shan, marks the end of a great era. Although Buddhism continued as a force in Chinese life, its creative period in terms of founding new schools was at an end. In fact, the forms of Buddhism that continued to flourish after 845 were those traditions that relied less on imperial patronage and the accumulated wealth of the huge monastic institutions and were more localized.

However, Confucian scholars such as Han Yü (768–824), Li Ao, (ca. 772–836) and Liu Tsung-yüan (773–819) began the serious Confucian rebuttal of Buddhist philosophy. It should be noted that this was a peaceful attack mounted by intellectuals based on scholarly debate and apologetics. The T'ang emperor who lashed out at Buddhism in 845 did so—if he can be considered sane at all—for reasons that he claimed were Taoist inspired. Confucian critics, by contrast, based their arguments on what they considered to be Confucian truth and Buddhist error.

Nonetheless, the world of China after 845 was in a profound state of transition, and this is why Peter Bol (1992) has been able to write so persuasively about the intellectual passage that took place between the late T'ang and the Northern Sung dynasties. This was also the end of the great aristocratic age in China. Powerful elite families surely reemerged in Sung times, but they had nothing like the power of the early T'ang Confucian aristocrats. The social world of the elite is one of the things that changed drastically in the late T'ang transition. Bol hypothesized that the pattern of the late T'ang transition is a move from the easy affirmation of the value of history toward an examination of the role of moral thought as the fundamental basis for the defense of "this culture of ours." The great late T'ang intellectuals were precisely the people who marked the beginning of the movement from the early T'ang reverence for history and ritual to the moral metaphysics of the Northern and Southern Sung. Because they represent a period of change, these intellectuals both synthesized what had come before and anticipated what would come later.

Liu Tsung-yüan

Along with his colleague Han Yü, Liu Tsung-yüan was one of the most famous scholars of his time. He is also interesting in that he reflects a different view of the revival of Confucianism than Han or Li Ao. In many respects, as Jo-shui Chen (1992) has demonstrated, Liu is a bridge from the intellectual concerns of the early and middle T'ang to those of Han and Li Ao as representatives of what can only be called Neo-Confucianism. Yet, although Liu shared many concerns with Han and Li, such as the use of the *ku-wen* literary style, he did not go as far as Han and Li in changing the direction of Confucian thought that would ripen in the Sung to become Neo-Confucianism.

Liu Tsung-yüan, along with Han Yü and Li Ao, represents a turn in classical studies that moved from a concern for studying the previous interpretations or commentaries on the classics to the classics themselves. Along with other notable mid- and late T'ang scholars, Liu became interested in what the principles of the classics were rather than in outlining previous textual interpretations. This kind of preoccupation with the principles of the classics drove Liu to try to express what he meant by the true nature of the Confucian Tao.

Another important point to remember about Liu Tsung-yüan's philosophy is that it was driven by active political engagement. Liu was personally involved in some of the most important late T'ang reform movements. For instance, he was a player in the abortive reform movement of 805 and suffered politically for his attempt to apply Confucian theory to political life for the rest of his life. One of the key points of Liu's doctrine was that Confucianism must be involved in the real political life of the country.

For Liu Tsung-yüan, Tao was identified with what he called "antiquity." This does not mean that Liu became some kind of disinterested historical antiquarian. According to Jo-shui Chen, "It is hence clear that in Liu's vocabulary 'antiquity' was synonymous with the Confucian ideal. In other words, 'antiquity' actually indicated, as he often termed it, 'The ancient *Tao*,' the *Tao* that was discovered, expressed, and realized [to] some extent in ancient times" (1992:84). If this Tao is to be found in the actions of the sages in ancient times, it is easy to see why Liu believed that one has to read the classics for their own true meanings rather than merely studying what the later commentators said about them. Liu's definition of the Tao was that "in their teachings, the sages established the Middle Way to show to the people in the subsequent ages. (The Way) refers to humanity, righteousness, propriety, wisdom, and trustworthiness. These are called the 'Five Constancies.' This means that these ideas can be constantly practiced" (Chen 1992:86).

Liu Tsung-yüan thought this ancient Tao was always part of public service and governmental policy. But even more than concern for public policy, Liu stressed the human nature of the Confucian Tao.

> Some people concentrate on talking about Heaven rather than about man. This is a misapprehension of the Way. Why do they not study the mind of the people then (try to) perfect their own (i.e., humans) Way? When our Way is fully realized, the people will be transformed (and civilized). Therefore we know that the blue (over our heads) cannot participate in our affairs and be capable of understanding them. (Chen 1992:95)

Parenthetically, Liu was also a most harsh critic of the superstitious ideas of his age. For him, the Confucian Way was in the world and not subject to supernatural forces.

However, Liu added another dimension of his thought that brought him into conflict with people like Han Yü. As Chen shows, Liu "firmly believed that there existed legitimate styles of life other than Confucian secular life. He had in mind, among other things, the searches for psychological tranquillity, spirituality, and wisdom based on philosophic Taoism and more important, Buddhist tenets" (1992:123). This was not a popular view with Han Yü, and it is another reason that Liu was not considered an orthodox Confucian.

Han Yü

The most famous of the late T'ang Confucian intellectuals is Han Yü. Han's intellectual range was enormous. If any Chinese intellectual merits an accolade for being a Renaissance man, Han does. Along with being a Confucian philosopher, he was also a noted essayist, an anti-Buddhist polemicist, a poet, and a national political figure. In fact, many later commentators thought more of his literary efforts than they did of his philosophical endeavors; but this is a mistake. One of the things that makes Han's work distinctive is that he saw a unity in all that he did. Han's search for unity was driven by his desire to protect and revive his Confucian culture. All of his efforts were directed to this task of reviving the Confucian tradition. In many ways, the intellectual interests of Han and his friends serve to define the trajectory of the Confucian project for the next thousand years. Han provides a map that later Confucians were to chart and inscribe with more detail, but we still must honor him and his friends for lighting a path for the Way.

One of the things that Han Yü is best known for is the formation of a literary movement called *ku-wen*. The most prosaic way to translate this concept is to call it ancient writing, but this hardly does justice to Han's attempt to restore Chinese prose to the pristine beauty of the classical authors such as Mencius. The *ku-wen* movement was much more than literary in any shallow sense. The true aim of Han Yü was not only to write with the precision and clarity of the classical Chou Confucians but also to return to the clarity of their ideas as well. Han Yü reasoned that the ideas of the Confucian tradition needed a form of Confucian discourse that would support their exposition. He did not want art for art's sake, because ideas always carried the burden of culture.

Han Yü's *ku-wen* movement can be seen as a necessary prologue to the return to Confucian values he so passionately defended in that it provided the literary format for expressing the "plain" truth of the Confucian tradition without superfluous literary adornment. In this regard, as in so many others, Han deserves to be called a Neo-Confucian not only because of the nature of his ideas but also by the means he chose to defend them via literary composition. As he so often remarked: Were there any previous Confucians who also did not write? No, and their style and content, according to Han, were intimately interconnected. One of the things that marks the late T'ang and Sung Neo-Confucian revivals was their commitment to communication. They had a message, and they wanted to make sure that as many people as possible could understand it.

One of the essential points of Han Yü's Neo-Confucian discourse was to re-stress the nature of the moral way as the proper path of self-cultivation and his reinvigoration of the ideal of the sage as the highest form of human aspirations. As Charles Hartman observed, "Yet the masterstroke of Han Yü's proposal in 'Essentials of the Moral Way' is not his condemnation of the Buddhist and Taoist cultivation of an inner spiritual life but rather his insistence that the cultivation of spirituality serve as a connecting link to integrate the private and public halves of Confucian life into a unified and holistic social order" (Hartman 1986:150). It is fascinating to see how Han proposes to go about this task. Like any good Confucian, he assumes that this moral way has been shown before in the writings of the classical sages, even if this message has been obscured for the present generation. In this regard, Han lifts up passages from the *Great Learning* to make his point.

Han Yü here makes an exegetical move via the definition of *jen*/humanity that opened him to the criticism of other Neo-Confucians concerning the nature of his sources. There is actually something ironic about this debate, because as Hartman (1986) has shown, it was Han and his colleagues, such as Li Ao, who actually formulated the concept of the "four books [*Doctrine of the Mean, The Great Learning, Analects, Mencius*]" as the epitome of the Confucian text—that is, the choice of these late T'ang scholars becomes the canon within a canon for the whole Neo-Confucian tradition. Han annoyed some other Confucians by linking Confucian humanity, at least verbally, with the Mohist notion of universal *po-ai*/love.

According to Hartman (1986), Han Yü's explanation of humanity connected the inner and outer lives of the student of the Way in service to the state:

> The unity of the state becomes the measure of the success of this extension of *jen* into the wider political sphere. Such is the real significance of Han Yü's definition of *jen* as *po-ai* "to love widely": the "superior man" who has perfected his own sense of humanity in his immediate surroundings has directly contributed to the health of the state and thus enhanced the possibilities of a wider diffusion of such love. There is no distinction between private moral and public political action. (Hartman 1986:152)

Although both Han and Mo Tzu use the term *po-ai*, Han gave it the perfectly good Confucian definition "to love widely" rather than "to love universally," as Mo Tzu understood it. Han stubbornly defended his ability to make use of any good ideas that came his way, but always with the intent of supporting the Confucian vision of an ordered world.

> Those in the Confucian tradition and Mo-tzu alike endorse Yao and Shu, and alike condemn Chieh and Chou. We alike cultivate our individual persons and set our minds right for the purpose of regulating the empire and state. Should we both not delight in what we have in common? I believe these discords have arisen through pedantry and through each side striving to see its master's doctrines, not through anything essentially inherent in the Ways of the two masters.
> Confucians should make use of Mo-tzu, and Mohists should make use of Confucius; otherwise they are not worthy of these names. (Hartman 1986:153)

There is an openness that is refreshing in Han's willingness to admire Mo Tzu. We need to remember that Han Yü might just be right. As modern scholarship has shown, Mo Tzu began life as a Confucian, but one whose heart was broken by what he saw the Confucians of his day doing with the teaching of the sages. Han's definition of humanity is actually this: "A man who has a sense of the humane strengthens others through his wish to strengthen himself and perfect others through his wish to perfect himself. The ability to draw analogies from what is close at hand can be said to constitute the way of the humane" (Hartman 1986:154).

Han Yü suggests that one of the key ways by which we can assist the Confucian project is to achieve a better understanding of the Confucian sage. Here again, Han makes creative use of the materials of his age, somewhat to the constant consternation of the Sung purist Neo-Confucians. "He applied the Buddhist definition of the Sage as metaphysical Absolute to the old Confucian definition of the Sage as worldly and practical man of action" (Hartman 1986:186). In terms of his own classical references, Han makes use of material from the *Doctrine of the Mean*, the *Great Learning*, and the *Analects*. Han fuses public and private concerns into a unity of cosmos and humanity. From the Neo-Confucian perspective, Han now makes a very important claim about how this is to be done. The key phrase Han cites to point out the nature of the absolute Confucian concern for sageliness is *ch'iung-li chin-hsing,* or "to develop one's nature to perfection through the understanding of Principle." As I shall argue, we see here a characteristic Confucian commitment to the fusion of moral life and critical reason that is congruent with the entire development of Neo-Confucian thought.

Han Yü's image of the sage comes across in the following passage taken from a discussion of the *Analects* in his answer to a question in the palace examination of 794.

> *Answer:* The sage embraces integrity (*ch'eng*) and enlightenment (*ming*) as his true nature (*cheng hsing*); he takes as his base the perfect virtue; this is equilibrium and harmony (*chung yung*). He generates (*fa*) these inside and gives them form outside; they do not proceed from thought, yet all is in order. Thus a mind set on evil has no way to develop within him, and preferable behavior cannot be applied to him; so only the Sage commits no errors. (Hartman 1986:201)

As is so typical of Han Yü, we find the enunciation of themes that will resound throughout the entire history of the Neo-Confucian movement. Han goes on to praise Yen Hui, Confucius' best disciple, as someone who worked to achieve this kind of balance. As we shall see, Yen Hui became something of a patron saint for those Confucians who strove to achieve integrity and humanity.

It is not surprising that Han Yü also developed his own theory of the mind-heart and human nature, two key concepts for the generation of a full-blown Neo-Confucian moral metaphysics. In his writings on the mind-heart, Han's work is linked closely to that of Li Ao, as we shall see in the following section. Han stressed the need for the cultivation of the mind-heart in order to achieve sageliness. Han balanced the tranquillity of the sagely mind with its necessary action in the world. Of course, the perfection of the mind-heart can be achieved only through the investigation of things because Han affirmed the reality of the world in contrast with Buddhist and Taoist doctrines of emptiness and nonbeing.

> When one is tranquil, one knows that the mind is without thought, and this is "fasting." But to know that the mind is in essence without thought that it is separated from both movement and tranquillity, that is absolutely still and un-moving—this is Perfect Integrity (*chih ch'eng*). The *Mean* says, "From integrity there is enlightenment." The *Changes* say, "All movement under Heaven is regulated by unity." (Hartman 1986:204)

Han Yü linked the cultivation of the mind-heart to his doctrine of human nature. According to the common interpretation, Han Yü defends the notion that human nature is born in us at birth and contains five parts: "A sense of humanity (*jen*), propriety (*li*), trustworthiness (*hsin*), justice (*i*), and wisdom (*chih*)—the so called Five Norms (*wu-ch'ang*)" (Hartman 1986:205). According to Hartman, Han demonstrated how human nature plays out in three different grades and how the five norms are balanced in individuals. Hartman argued that the treatise on the origins of human nature is not one of Han's better essays. The contradiction is that Han affirmed that human nature is ultimately good but at the same time, he defined it in terms of the three grades of moral excellence, with the higher and lower of these three grades fixed in status and scope. Han wanted to maintain, and this can be inferred from other texts on human nature, that we have a variable nature and an essential human nature that is identical to *t'ien-tao*, or the Way of Heaven. Han stressed that the task of returning our mundane nature to the Way of Heaven is very difficult indeed. Nonetheless, here again Han anticipates and begins the extended Neo-Confucian debate about the nature of human nature.

Li Ao

If Han Yü's reputation is that of staunch Confucian, Li Ao's place in Confucian history is more suspect. Li is perceived as someone who incorporated too much Buddhist and Taoist material into his thought to warrant thoroughgoing recognition as a true Confucian. As T. H. Barrett has noted, "As a result Li is praised warmly for having at least tried to be Confucian in an age when it was obviously impossible" (1992:31). Barrett's assessment of how we need to read Li's most famous work, the *Fu-hsing shu,* or the *Book on Returning to Nature,* provides us with a different slant on what Li tried to accomplish: "If the *Fu-hsing shu* is judged as an exercise in the 'rectification of names' it emerges as something of a sustained *tour de force.* Far from incorporating Buddhist elements into Neo-Confucianism, Li was creating a Neo-Confucianism by extricating it from the syncretistic discourse of his age" (Barrett 1992:137).

According to Barrett, Li Ao was caught between his friend Han Yü who denounced Buddhism and those wealthy aristocrats who functioned as Li's patrons and who, contrary to Han, approved of the syncretism of the age. Nonetheless, Li did manage to provide a study of human nature that restated what he took to be the Confucian position. We must not judge Li by the later standards of Sung and Ming orthodoxy.

Li Ao began his essay on returning to the true human nature with the following statement of purpose: "That whereby a man may be a sage is his true nature; that whereby he may be deluded as to this nature is emotion. Joy, anger, sorrow, fear, love, hate, and desire—these seven are the workings of emotion. When the emotions have become darkened, the nature is hidden, but this is through no shortcoming of the nature: these seven follow one another in constant succession, so that the nature cannot achieve its fullness" (Barrett 1992:94). The Confucian philosophical point is clear and differentiates this kind of approach from Buddhism. Li Ao defended the notion of a true nature, no matter how hard it is for us to uncover or return to it, as his metaphor for the process suggests. The nature is true and not an illusion, and hence, it makes all the sense in the world to link Li with that great chain of Confucians all the way back to Mencius and Confucius. It is Li's second move that complicates the matter. Li is of the opinion that we must master the emotions and, in fact, must somehow get the emotions "not to work" in order for the true nature to shine forth. "If the emotions are not working, then the nature achieves fullness" (Barrett 1992:95).

The later Sung interpretation is that there is nothing inherently wrong with the feelings and emotions qua human sensibility; they agree with Li Ao that the passions need to be controlled for a person to be able to return to the true nature. For instance, Li says that "Neither the nature nor the emotions exist independently of one another. Nonetheless, without the nature the emotions would have nowhere to be born from . . . The nature is not a nature itself but shows its brightness through the emotions" (Barrett 1992:96). In fact, Li goes on to say that "the nature is the decree of Heaven: the sage is he who obtains it and is not deluded" (Barrett 1992:97). The real argument is about how we manifest the true nature.

What distinguishes the sage from an ordinary person is that the sage manifests true nature; all people have the true nature, but only the sage can return to it. "Therefore the sage is he who is the first of men to be awakened" (Barrett 1992:101). Again, Li Ao really does not say anything un-Confucian, even if he uses the notion of awakening, a term clearly drawn from Buddhist discourse. It is Li's desire to link the return to true nature in the sage to a kind of quiescence of spirit that irritates the Sung Neo-Confucians.

> Therefore it is sincerity that the sage takes as his nature, absolutely still and without movement, vast and great, clear and bright, shining on Heaven and Earth. When stimulated he can then penetrate all things in the world. In action or in rest, in speech or silence, he always remains in the ultimate. It is returning to his true nature that the worthy man follows without ceasing. If he follows it without ceasing he is enabled to get back to the source. (Barrett 1992:102)

With Li Ao's arguments about the quiet moment of the spirit, we have reached the end of the great medieval period of Confucian thought. The interregnum between the fall of the T'ang and the founding of the Sung in 960 was much shorter than the period between the Han and the T'ang. With the Sung dynasty, we move into another world altogether, the world of the great Neo-Confucianism revival. Many late T'ang thinkers can be called Neo-Confucians. However, we can only use that name retrospectively, because the Confucian revolution, begun in the late T'ang, ascended to new heights in the Northern Sung dynasty. It is to this second golden age of Confucian thought that we now turn.

❀ 4 ❀

The Renaissance of the Sung:
The Second Golden Age

THE SUNG DYNASTY'S CONFUCIAN revival announced the second golden age of the tradition. The great names of the Sung Confucian philosophical renaissance rank in stature and importance with those of Confucius, Mencius, and Hsün Tzu and the great Han and T'ang masters like Tung Chung-shu and Han Yü. Some praise the brave new Confucian world of the Sung as second only to the great classical founders in its innovative historical, political, social, artistic, and moral metaphysics. Others critically see the revival as a subtle or misguided abandonment of what ought to be any proper defense of the Confucian Way, that is, concrete study of ritual and service to the nation.

If there were any lingering doubts that Confucianism developed a philosophy with a fully expressed vision of the world, surely the work of Chu Hsi (1130–1200) as the great synthesizer and organizer of Sung thought, the elaborations of his disciples, and the countermoves of his critics demonstrated that Confucianism is a comprehensive worldview encompassing as much of human reality as any finite system of thought can achieve within the constraints of a particular time, place, and culture. If scholars still want to argue, often cogently, that there is nothing like Western metaphysics or comprehensive cosmology in Confucianism, the Sung achievement proves otherwise. The Sung Neo-Confucian movement organizes the world in terms of principles and insights taken from its reading of classical Confucianism and modified by its response to the Buddhist challenge.

The Sung revivalists explained that all they were doing was returning to the true teachings of the classical sages. They devised a plethora of ways to accomplish their ends, from governmental reform programs to the establishment of private schools and family charitable estates to new programs in self-cultivation, from the revival of literature and the arts to the refinement of commentaries on the true meaning of the classics; the list can be expanded almost at will because of the fecundity of the cultural and social refinement during the Sung period.

Sung intellectuals sought the intellectual coherence of a return to fundamentals but were not fundamentalists in the modern Christian or Islamic sense of the term. Kai-wing Chow (1995) has suggested a much better term to describe the Sung sense of return to classical values: purism. *"Purism* here designated an intellectual impulse that demands the recovery of the 'original' or 'pure' Confucian norms and language" (Chow 1995:8). Although Chow is writing specifically about the great ritual scholars of a later age, what he says about the Sung quest for the roots of tradition rings true. Someone who seeks purity of vision does not always need to be entranced completely by old forms but might often be willing to be creative in terms of a new age. This is precisely what the Sung Confucians were about.

Historically, the Sung dynasty marks a sociological and historical watershed in the development of Chinese culture that had begun in the late T'ang. One could simplistically call this the move to the south, a theory based on the recognition that the locus of Chinese intellectual culture was transferred from its classic heartland in North China to Central and South China by the Sung period. In fact, many historians of Chinese history argue that Sung culture marks the beginning of modern Chinese history. The Sung is an era when great social change was conjoined with equally dramatic intellectual transformation. It was a daring epoch when intellectuals argued that they, unlike anyone since the classical period of the Chou, truly understood the Confucian Way. This is an audacious claim, to say the least.

A major canonical and philosophical illustration of radical purism is illustrated by the way Chu Hsi radically and definitively reordered Confucian education and even modified the nature of the canon. Up to the Sung, Confucian scholars had worked with the various texts known as the Confucian classics—beginning with a core of five that had grown to thirteen in the Sung. Chu selected four texts from within the entire canon and called them the Four Books. After having selected these four texts, namely the *Great Learning*, the *Doctrine of the Mean*, the *Analects*, and the *Mencius*, Chu wrote a series of philosophical commentaries on these texts that later became the basis not only of the interpretation of his own students and school but of the entire Chinese examination system after 1313. What began as a specific reinterpretation of the textual foundation of the tradition by Chu Hsi became the common defining property of all later Confucian orthodoxy. And as if this were not enough, Chu Hsi even took it upon himself to insert Sung material into one of the texts, the *Great Learning*, in order to show what it should have said according to his reading of his Northern Sung teachers. Needless to say, in a tradition that prides itself on commentary and history, such a major reorientation did not go unnoticed or unchallenged.

Although the Sung dynasty was never militarily as strong as the Han, T'ang, Ming, or Ch'ing, it is remembered for its philosophical and poetic achievements; even its ceramics are revered as unrivaled for good taste. The world continues to stand in awe of the luminous landscape paintings and miniatures created by Sung artists. If Chu Hsi was famous as a philosopher, the Sung ruling house itself even produced a famous and literate emperor, Hui-tsung, more renowned for his painting of beautiful birds than for his genius as a politician or warrior. All in all, the Sung dynasty provides the general sense of a world of high culture, refinement, and even civility of government rarely matched in Chinese history. It was an age culturally awaiting a great revival of Confucian learning.

The Diversity and Richness of the Neo-Confucian Revival

The striking aspect of all of the great Sung Confucian thinkers was their willingness to innovate, to create a form of Confucianism unlike anything that had gone before—and in the case of a scholar-official like Wang An-shih (1021–1086), even an eagerness to reform the whole Chinese government so that it would itself serve this Confucian "culture of ours." The great modern Confucian scholar, Mou Tsung-san, uses the term "moral metaphysics" to describe the particular form of discourse that became the hallmark of all the major Sung thinkers on the philosophical side of the renovation.

The great political leader and sometimes prime minister Wang An-shih, although often in conflict with many of the leading Northern Sung systematic and moral philosophers, also shared their passion to revive the Confucian Way through governmental reform, scholarship, and education. Like Chu Hsi later in the Southern Sung, Wang wrote a set of commentaries on the ritual classics in order to help reform the educational process. A great activist, Wang tried to establish public schools throughout China in order to inculcate this new vision of an empire dominated by Confucian learning. Along with its moral character, another thing that distinguishes the Sung effort was its attempt to be comprehensive in ordering every aspect of life. It truly was a vast reasserting of Confucian philosophical speculation, aimed not only at satisfying internal Confucian dynamics but also at definitively answering to Buddhist and Taoist speculations.

However, for the sake of simplicity, we will follow the development of the Confucian Way primarily through the eyes of the founders and critics of Wang An-shih's reforms and the particular group of thinkers who later chose the name *tao-hsüeh,* or "study of the Way," as their rallying call. In order to honor their own self-designation, we will hereafter label this specific group the Tao philosophers, the Tao school, or the Tao schoolmen.

This new philosophy armed itself with a careful selection of classical ideas refitted for service in a new day. All the great ideas of the classical Chou, Han, and T'ang thinkers find their way into the work of various Sung thinkers. We find speculation on the nature of the mind-heart, human nature, the Mandate of Heaven, the role of language, yin-yang, institutional and social history, literary and artistic theory, the Tao, and all of the ethical virtues. Yet these ideas are joined in novel ways to emphasize new or previously underutilized terms such as principle, matter-energy, and the Supreme Ultimate. But even if the Neo-Confucians did not directly borrow their ideas from the Buddhists and Taoists, they were assuredly stimulated to discover Confucian responses to the challenges of Buddhist and Taoist thought.

The Founding Sung Confucian Intellectuals and Reformers

China of the 1020s was a transitional period for the Sung political and intellectual elite. Emperor Chen-tsung died in 1022, and this allowed the various factions at court to put forward their proposals for reform to the young emperor. One such figure was Fan Chung-yen (989–1052). Peter Bol has shown that the court did not follow Fan's advice on governmental policy, though Fan was very successful in attracting the admiration and support of a group of younger scholars who played a role in the reformation of Chinese thought. The linchpin of Fan's endeavor was a call to return to the true source of the Tao, a true teaching that had been obscured but could be revived by rightly educated and motivated Confucian scholars and officials.

Because of Fan Chung-yen's ability to capture the spirit of reform that was so much in the air, he and his followers began to bombard the court with all kinds of ideas for the reform of everything from the fundamental nature of the civil service examinations to the foundations of public education. They did so with a view toward activist government reform, a veritable Confucian study of the way of government based on their understanding of the way of the sage. Bol has outlined the early proposals of Fan and his supporters, pointing out four fundamental orientations: (1) they sought an active government that would benefit the people; (2) they sought to find ways to combat the purely self-seeking nature of the typical Sung bureaucrat; (3) they strenuously denounced what they saw as the pernicious influence of Buddhist and Taoist teachings at all levels of society, but particularly among the *shih,* or intellectual and governing class; and (4) they sought a return to the true moral and practical learning of the early sages in contradistinction to the mere pedantry of commentary scholasticism and the rote learning necessary to pass the civil service examinations (1992:170).

Along with Fan Chung-yen's government reform policies, he was also instrumental in framing a very influential set of rules for the charitable estate of his extended clan. Fan, to borrow a phrase from a completely different thought-world, thought nationally and acted locally. According to Fan, it was not merely enough to reform the national government, even though that was a very important part of his Confucian plan because he believed that if and only if the national government were an instrument of sage policies would the Sung flourish. Fan also pursued his goals at a local level by organizing a charitable estate for members of his clan, an estate that would help the state by producing the kind of men who would serve the state as scholars and moral leaders.

Fan Chung-yen's clan protocols of 1050 illustrate very well the moral and practical nature of the Confucian reform movement. Denis Twitchett (1959) recorded that we know a great deal about this particular venture not only because it came from the pen of a famous Sung scholar but because the estate itself lasted for centuries and actually achieved many of the estimable goals that Fan envisioned for it. The protocols were actually very simple and were designed to provide a social net for all worthy to be members of the clan. There were also grants to be given to needy members of the clan so that they could continue to practice the virtues appropriate to the *shih* class of literati dedicated to service to self, family, community, region, and, finally, the nation as a whole.

Ou-yang Hsiu and the Classical Tradition

With Ou-yang Hsiu (1007–1072) we see the new Confucians of the Sung as scholars of great intellectual range, ambition, and diverse interest. As James T. C. Liu has noted, Ou-yang was "a classicist, a historian, an archaeologist, a statesman, a political theorist, and above all an essayist and a poet" (Liu 1967:1). Moreover, in the generation of younger scholars who followed Fan Chung-yan's lead in reviving Confucian social theory and praxis, Ou-yang embodied all the major concerns of the new tradition. As Liu chronicled Ou-yang's life and thought, Ou-yang was concerned with four main areas of Confucian life: (1) what Liu calls "ethical fundamentalism," or what I call "ethical purism"; (2) restorationism; (2) historical-mindedness; and (4) humanism (Liu 1967:18). According to Liu, the restorationist inclination of these scholars was embedded in the belief that through their efforts at restoring the true nature of the Confucian Way, the golden age of the great sage emperors could be redeveloped in Sung China. This was certainly a utopian view but one that seems to have characterized the early generations of Northern Sung reformers. They did what they did because they truly believed that they might just be able to revive the Confucian world.

Ou-yang Hsiu tried to achieve his goals by framing new public social policy. First, his arguments were always based on his historical studies, for which he was justly famous. Second, Ou-yang tried very hard to be realistic about how power and public policy were actually made in traditional China. He noted that at one level, all human life was dominated by what could be called "factions." Even the family and extended clan formed something like a faction. The real key to the issue was not that there were factions but rather the ethical and social sense of public service that any group of scholars sought to apply to the civil service.

Along with his commitment to reform, Ou-yang was also known as a fine classicist, historian, and master of Sung literature. Regarding his classical scholarship, he combined an interest in the whole range of the classical canon with a firm belief in the ultimate rationality of the classics as records of human wisdom and conduct. He believed that there was a *li*/rational principle to be found in all the canonical texts. "Their language is simple and straightforward; it is the commentaries that make novel and unusual points" (Liu 1967:92). Ou-yang theorized that the real problem of interpretation had to do with finding this pragmatic and rational principle for the classics; the other side of the coin was the fact that scholars now needed to weed out all the extraneous non-Confucian accretions that had affixed themselves over the centuries to the original texts. In order to do this, Ou-yang applied his belief in the essential rationality of the canon to all the classical texts. Ou-yang even had the courage, somewhat rare in the Sung, to raise questions about the authenticity of all the material assembled in the Thirteen Classics. If something was irrational, Ou-yang then reasoned that it was not Confucian. Of course, the key question in all such debates is this: What is the rational?

Ou-yang Hsiu was quite realistic about the fact that reason would not always be successful in history:

> It is not that heaven does not prefer what is good; heaven probably cannot always prevail on human beings, mixed as they are. This is the rational meaning of the cardinal principle that governs the relationship between heaven and human beings . . . Knowing this principle, one understands rather than feels surprised by the fortune or misfortune, the success or failure, that the sages and the good people in history may or may not encounter. (Liu 1967:94)

Ou-yang believed there was always going to be a tension between reason and history precisely because he was such an astute historian. Part of his fame rests on his composition of *New History of the Five Dynasties* and for his work on the *New T'ang History*.

Along with Ou-yang's reputation as a political reformer and theorist, classicist, and historian, there is also his fame as a literary figure. As should be clear by now, there was a great deal of interest in Confucian circles not only about the correctness of principles themselves but also about how they were to be presented. Although most Neo-Confucians would argue that it is better to get the idea right at the expense of literary flair, they agreed that the best result would be the elegant expression of true doctrine, history, and commentary. Along with his philosophical acumen, Ou-yang was remembered and anthologized as a great poet and essayist. But here again, the Sung literati often broke with old convention. In his youth, Ou-yang was enchanted by the songs he learned from educated courtesans and made use of their phrasing in many of his own poems. And as if this were not bad enough, many of these early poems lingered over the emotions of love. Women, wine, and song were not always considered the proper genre for a Confucian gentleman.

Wang An-shih and the Case for Radical Reform

The later scholarly tradition has never been able to decide about the role and stature of Wang An-shih (1021–1086), objectively the greatest statesman and reformer of the Northern Sung. Was he a genius unappreciated for his vision and scholarship, or merely another in a long line of haughty prime ministers bent on using Confucian ideology for the crafty purposes of personal and state power? The debate about Wang has raged on ever since his dramatic rise to power in the 1060s. Although Wang's career began rather uneventfully, it was transformed into the arena of high drama after he finally agreed to leave local service and return to the capital in the 1060s, and especially after he began his appeal for massive reforms in 1067. After his return, nothing was quite the same. His policies, historically referred to as the New Policies, helped to divide the new Neo-Confucian movement between those who supported Wang and those who rejected some or all of his reforms.

Wang An-shih, writing and ruling in the heady times when the Northern Confucians believed that they could reform society, had an agenda for his fellow Confucians. He asked them to ponder antiquity in order to, as Bol puts it, "uncover a universal program, whose elements are coherently connected as root to branch (*pen mo*), thus revealing those that are basic to others, and for which there is a logical sequence of steps from first to last for establishing the basis" (Bol 1992:213). Once Confucians had crafted this careful work, Wang was sure that they would agree with the logic and Confucian nature of his reforms. And make no mistake, these were a major set of reforms that were designed to transform all levels of Chinese society from local schools to the national examination system.

Much of the debate was focused on which classic text provided the best model for framing the reform of Sung society. Wang held that one of the ritual texts, the *Chou-li*, best served these purposes. As Wang put it, "The best time in history was the reign of Ch'eng-wang in the Chou dynasty. Its regulating systems, that which can be applied in succeeding generations, and its records, that which is transmitted in words, are most found in the *Chou-li*" (Liu 1959:43). In choosing the *Chou-li,* Wang believed he had found the key not only to moral values but also to pragmatic and useful polices that would benefit all people. It was Wang's programmatic turn that often caused conflict with other, more idealistic, Confucian scholars, even when they also supported the positive nature of the reforms based on the *Chou-li.*

The philosophical issue that divided Wang An-shih from the *tao-hsüeh* masters of the Northern and Southern Sung had to do with the interpretation of human nature. The Tao philosophers held their version of the Mencian position that human nature, however flawed it may be in actual practice, was essentially and fundamentally good. Wang demurred from this philosophical consensus and held that human nature was neither essentially good nor evil but rather was inextricably linked to the vagaries of human emotion. "Human nature is the substance of human emotions and the human emotions are the functioning of human nature" (Liu 1959:41).

Because of this view of human nature, Wang believed that more stress had to be placed on the role of social custom and positive law in order to induce good actions and politics for people. Because of Wang's theory of human nature, we can see some of the reasons for his holding a more activist view of society when compared and contrasted to his colleagues who believed in essential human goodness. Those, as we shall see, who believed in the goodness of human nature often put their reforming emphasis not on public law and institutions but on the moral reform of the individual human mind-heart. They were often more conservative as well about the nature of institutions per se, believing that there was only so much that institutions could do for the reform process. The debate was one that would be continued throughout the entire record of the Neo-Confucian phase of Confucian history.

Ssu-ma Kuang and the Debate over Reform

Ssu-ma Kuang (1019–1086) was Wang An-shih's great opponent in the political and intellectual arena of their generation. Although they shared the general cultural dispositions of Northern Sung culture, they arrived at competing visions of what this culture should look like and how it should function. For instance, although both men sought to reform the Sung state, Ssu-ma's proposal was based on a different image of the world. In his "The Five Guidelines," Ssu-ma offered an arresting image of the dynastic institutions being something like a great house of state and the task of the reform being, as Bol has written, "simply like preserving a great house," wherein it is necessary for the ruler to "solidify the foundation, fortify the pillars, strengthen the beams, reinforce the roof, raise the walls, and tighten the lock. Once it is finished, he must also choose a good descendant and have him diligently maintain it" (Bol 1992:220).

In fact, Ssu-ma Kuang is most often remembered as a historian with a theoretical and philosophical agenda. Along with some friends, he completed one of the truly grand historical treatises of his or any time, the justly famous *The Comprehensive Mirror for the Aid in Government,* a study of dynastic rule from 403 B.C.E.–959 C.E. It is important to note that, as was the case with so many of his contemporaries, he was not merely interested in history as a scholarly craft but was also engaged in the creation of a Confucian philosophy of history as a means for moral and social reform.

Ssu-ma Kuang's views on Confucianism were certainly different from those of the Tao philosophers who were often his supporters in his political struggles with Wang An-shih. For instance, Ssu-ma believed that Hsün Tzu and Yang Hsiung were the only two former scholars who understood the "correct methods of the tao of the Former Kings" (Bol 1992:234). In contradistinction to what would become "orthodox" Neo-Confucianism, he did not believe that Mencius was the most important classical Confucian thinker, because Mencius did not have a proper appreciation of the role of hierarchy that was so necessary for effective rule. However, Ssu-ma did share the common Neo-Confucian conviction that there were common moral principles that could be found through the careful study of history.

Ssu-ma Kuang derived the philosophic point from history that "there are necessary principles, but that human action is also constrained by circumstances" (Bol 1992:237). To Ssu-ma, this meant that there was only so much that even the most principled reformer could accomplish when constrained by the circumstances of history. Ssu-ma believed that the ruler must rely on Confucian ritual in order to bring as much success as possible to social formation. He asserted that the ruler must take his principles from the very nature of the cosmos and that the natural order of this for human life would be a hierarchical system regulated by ritual. It is easy to see why Ssu-ma thought that Hsün Tzu was partially correct in his classical appeal to authority and ritual.

Su Shih and the Defense of Culture

Su Shih (1037–1101) is a very appealing thinker because of his understanding of the complexity of human life and his defense of the role of art and literature as part of any civilization worthy of the name. In the midst of the search for government reform and the renewal of society and its concomitant quest for general moral principles, Su defended the place of literature as an expression of the Tao. As Bol wrote about Su, we find a "portrait that emerges of a man who is opposed to a dogmatism in any form, who treasures flexibility, diversity, and individuality, yet who is consumed by the search for unifying values" (Bol 1992:258). Su was convinced that this was the case because it was clear to him that human beings would always face an imperfect world and hence it was probably impossible to find a perfect set of rules because there was no such final perfection to be found. But, of course, this did not mean that Su did not try to find what rules might still apply to a less than perfect reality.

Su Shih was definite about the nature of his search: "I have held that the real problem in learning is to be free of partiality and that the real problem in being free of partiality is to comprehend the inherent patterns of all things. . . . I fully exhaust the inherent patterns of their being so-by-themselves, and I judge them in my mind" (Bol 1992:260). Su's credo is noteworthy for his awareness of the epistemological problems of finding principles. In his statement, we can see the kind of commitment that was common to the ethical and cosmological search of the Sung Confucians. They wanted to develop both moral awareness and a cosmological sympathy for the way things really are. In searching for this pattern of the cosmos, Su sought the *tzu-jan*/thus-so of things; but in Su's case this is not the pure spontaneity that the classical Taoists meant by the term—rather, it was the selflessness of the things as expressing pattern.

According to Su, there is a mystery to the world balanced by what he calls moral principle. What is needed is a way to live between the mystery of the empirical world and the moral patterns that are essential to a civilized life. Therefore, with this talk of mystery and pattern, it is not surprising that Su Shih wrote extensively on the *I-Ching* as representing that classical Confucian vision that tried to explain the mystery of the world and moral principle. Along with his commentary on the *I-Ching*, Su also wrote on the model of benevolent government found in the *Documents*. In writing about these two sources of the tradition, Su illustrated the balancing of good government with the diversity of human flourishing, very much including the beauty of the fine arts.

Su Shih, as a great essayist, is capable of picturing what he meant by this kind of principled and spontaneous creativity:

My *wen* (or culture) is like a spring with a ten-thousand-gallon flow. It does not care where; it can come forth any place. On the flatland spreading and rolling, even a thousand miles a day give it no difficulty; when it twists and turns about mountain boulders, it takes shape according to the thing encountered—but it cannot be known. What can be known is that it will always go where it ought to go and stop where it cannot but stop, that is all. Even I am not able to understand the rest. (Bol 1992:297)

In the Sung Neo-Confucian world, such a freedom of spirit is a welcome respite from some of the intense moral fervor and purism of the day. Like Confucius long before, we can see here that part of the Confucian spirit that, from time to time in appropriate circumstances, takes time for poetry, painting, and maybe even a glass of wine with good friends.

Ronald Egan, in his masterful study of the various elements of Su Shih's varied achievements, has told a story of one of Su's characteristic encounters with Ch'eng I (known for his lack of humor) during the funeral rites for Ssu-ma Kuang.

> One day Su Shih and other officials attended a state ceremony in the Hall of Brightness to celebrate the recent accession of the new emperor. Music was a part of the ceremony. Later, Su went to where Ssu-ma Kuang was laid out to mourn for him. Ch'eng I tried to stop him from entering the room, citing the observation in the *Analects* that on the day he mourned the Master never sang. Shu Shih ignored him and observed, as he proceeded inside, that he had heard of not singing after you mourn, but had never heard of not mourning after you sing. Everyone laughed at Ch'eng I. (Egan 1994:94)

It is hard not to sympathize with Su Shih, who surely responded appropriately to the death of Ssu-ma Kuang while still taking part in his official government duties.

Yet another reason that Su Shih has not always been accepted as a completely reputable Sung philosopher is that he always acknowledged his debt to Buddhist doctrine and practice. In terms of praxis, Su wrote movingly against the rural custom of infanticide, citing both Confucian and Buddhist reasons for doing away with what Su believed to be a terrible crime against humanity. Regarding theory, Su recognized that Buddhism contributed a great deal to Chinese thought through its emphasis on compassion. But it is hard to place Su within any rigid understanding of the sectarian nature of Sung Buddhist schools. Above all else, Su was irenic. Take, for instance, these lines from a prayer that Su offered for his mother at a Buddhist monastery.

> *My mother and father*
> *Together with all living beings*
> *Reside in the Western Regions*
> *Knowing supreme joy in all they meet. (Egan 1994:145)*

Is this a Buddhist or a Confucian poem? It is precisely the kind of borrowing and acceptance of truth from wherever it may come that tended to drive more orthodox Confucians wild when they read it, not to mention Western scholars who have been taught to believe that a person of good faith can only embrace one religion at a time.

Su Shih's wonderfully evocative "Rhapsody on Red Cliff" captures the fleeing truths of the world better than dry commentary on ancient texts. While looking down at the river from the cliffs, Su mused,

> Do you not know about the river and the moon? The former flows on and on but never departs. The later waxes and wanes but never grows or shrinks. If you look at the things from the viewpoint of the changes they undergo, noth-

ing in Heaven or Earth lasts longer than the blink of an eye. But if you look at them from the viewpoint of their changeless traits, neither the objects of the world nor we ever come to an end. What is there to envy? . . . We're not prohibited from taking these for our own, and we can use them without exhausting them. They are, in fact, the Transformer's inexhaustible treasuries, given freely for us to jointly consume. (Egan 1994:223)

This is a beautiful image and bespeaks of the civility and culture of the Northern Sung age. But we now need to turn to another group of scholars, those I have chosen to call Tao school philosophers, to see what they make of the things that change and the principles that do not.

The Philosophers of the Tao School

The Northern Sung leaders of the Tao school were Shao Yung (1011–1077), Chou Tun-i (1017–1073), Chang Tsai (1020–1077), Ch'eng Hao (1032–1085), and Ch'eng I (1033–1107). In Hoyt Tillman's felicitous phrase, these thinkers were a true fellowship dedicated to the elaboration and exploration of their special vision of the Confucian Way.

The nature of their fellowship and the seriousness of the conversations and debates, in addition to the conviction, so typical of all revivalists and reformers anywhere, that what they were really doing was simply uncovering the real meaning of the early Confucian tradition, gave them confidence in their project. In their own eyes, they were about the foundational task of explaining to a new age the timeless truths of the early sages. They were fired by the confidence that if this could be done in a clear prose form, then the Sung could be reformed and the Confucian Way revived.

Shao Yung and the Search for Order

Shao Yung (1011–1077) has consistently been a difficult thinker to interpret within the Sung-Ming tradition of Tao school philosophy because of the special nature of his character and his thought. Clearly, Shao shared all of the typical concerns of the Sung revival noted earlier. For instance, Don Wyatt (1996) has demonstrated that Shao was as committed to ethical discourse and practice as any of his friends and rivals. Nonetheless, he was considered somewhat eccentric because he did not seek a place in the civil service and because he sought to discover the true order of the universe in terms of a numerological bent—actually, an interest in what is called images and numbers in Chinese, a science more of iconic meaning and symbols than of concern for numbers alone—that set him apart from his friends in the revival movement.

In short, Shao Yung appears to be a rare bird, a man committed to reflection on the cosmos and moral issues; in Western terms, he could be considered a pure philosopher or public intellectual and not a typical Confucian scholar-official, as so many of the other moral philosophers of his day were. Because of this unique set of philosophical and personal concerns, Chu Hsi—the person most responsible for the standard interpretation of the rise of Tao school philosophy—had a perplexing time placing Shao Yung in his rendition of Sung thought. In terms of Sung scholarship, Shao was identified with what was called *I-Ching* learning because he based his own systematic reflections on the *Book of Changes*.

As Anne Birdwhistell has noted, "Shao Yung was, above all, concerned with the problem of change and activity in the universe" (1989:15). Of course, Tung Chung-shu was equally interested in change per se, but there is a second aspect of Shao's consideration that distinguishes his thought from other Confucians both before and after him. Shao was convinced that there was an essential pattern to all the changes found in the cosmos. Therefore, Shao linked the Sung fascination with order with the earlier correlative thinking especially identified with the *Book of Changes* and its commentaries.

Shao Yung expressed this fascination with change and its pattern in the title of his magnum opus, the *Huang-chi Ching-shih*, or *Supreme Principles That Rule the World*, an appellation worthy of Gottfried Leibniz (1646–1716) in the West as regards what it promises to tell us about the cosmos. The *Supreme Principles That Rule the World* is a huge and daunting work wherein Shao attempts to answer all of his questions about the nature of the cosmos as well as outlining the role of the worthy person within the matrix of change that defines the world and humanity. Along with this large treatise, Shao also wrote other essays (although some scholars attribute these essays to Shao's students) such as the shorter *Dialogue Between a Fisherman and a Woodcutter*. This essay summarizes neatly most of Shao's concerns about the world and the sage and illustrates again why Shao was such a recalcitrant "Neo-Confucian." The very title of the essay indicates that Shao is going to make use of classical Taoist material taken from the *Chuang Tzu*. However, Shao does so from a very Confucian point of view, albeit not a very "orthodox" one.

Shao Yung sought to both describe and explain the world: He sought to understand the flux of things as well as the subtle and changing patterns that were manifested in the things and events of the cosmos. According to Birdwhistell, in order to carry out his descriptive and explanatory task, Shao relied on a set of three crucial assumptions about how the world works. First and foremost, Shao considered the world to have a pattern or order to it. Further, the order of the world could be ascertained by careful attention to the images, numbers, and the various permutations of the trigrams and hexagrams of the *I-Ching*.

Second, Shao Yung believed that there were two levels of perception: One was the perceived reality of the physical; the other was an unperceived level of the same physical reality as understood as a manifestation of pattern. As Birdwhistell has noted, the favored image of roots and branches expresses the common assumption that Shao takes to be the unperceived nature of physical reality. Just as we commonly perceive the branches of a plant, we usually do not perceive the roots of the plant, even though we make the assumption that the branches must be supported and nourished by the roots. In fact, the root of the branches may be deemed the foundation of the entire plant system. Related to the second assumption about what is perceived and unperceived is Shao's conviction that the cosmos is made up of two kinds of things or events: There are those events or things that are finite, and there is the infinite reality of the ultimate itself. For instance, we can give fixed names to the finite things precisely because they are finite and limited; but no one can give a simple or fixed name to the ultimate because it is the whole of which the finite things are parts, or the field wherein the focus on finite things finds its resolution.

Third, Shao Yung was aware of another problem that his fascination with a creative and changing cosmos forced upon him. If everything was changing, how could anyone find an objective standpoint from which to observe and describe change itself? Shao reached the conclusion that in the last instance, one simply could not find such an unchanging epistemological vantage point, though this did not cause him to give up hope that he could provide a stable epistemology sufficient to warrant this processive view of the universe. Shao believed that all this change was part of the network of structure and pattern that he called the Supreme Ultimate.

Shao Yung held that there were three types of knowledge about the organization of the world. The first was contained in words and their proper definition; the second had to do with actions, as one would expect for a Confucian; and third, there was the knowledge that existed in one's consciousness. Perhaps stimulated by great T'ang Buddhist thinkers such as Chi-tsang (549–623) of the San-lun school or Chih-i (538–597) of the T'ien-t'ai school, Shao was convinced that it was the knowledge embedded in human consciousness that was the highest form of possible insight into the nature of things and events: "Therefore, one knows that saying it with the mouth is not as good as performing it with the body, and performing it with the body is not as good as completely understanding it with the mind" (Birdwhistell 1989:165).

Shao Yung's method of broad comprehension is as detailed as his cosmology, yet it revolved around the notion of *kuan.* Shao is even more specific in that he calls this method that of *fan-kuan,* or "reflective perception," in Birdwhistell's translation. By this, Shao meant that we not only reflect on what the eyes or other senses give us but reflect on these perceptions with the consciousness of the mind-heart itself such that we can understand the connections and patterns of things. The first stage is indeed sense experience, but one never stops there. The second stage is where one begins to try to link the things or events perceived in sense perception to find out how they are related or patterned in the larger sensorium. At the third stage, the pretense of any ultimate object-subject split is rejected in favor of a unified comprehension of the total relationality of the things and events perceived during the first two stages.

In Shao Yung's essay (or essay from a disciple) on the woodcutter and the fisherman, we read the following summary of his epistemology:

> It is not with the eyes that we observe things, not even with the mind. We must observe them according to their principle (*li*). All things in the world have principle, nature and destiny, don't they? As to principle, we know it after having scrutinized it. We understood the nature of things when we have penetrated it. Finally, if we exert ourselves we realize what their destiny is. These three kinds of knowledge make up the true knowledge of the universe. Even the sages could not get further. He who goes beyond that cannot be called as sage. . . .
>
> To observe in a reversed manner (*fan-kuan*) means not to regard the things from one's own point of view. Not to regard things from one's own point of view means to regard them from their own point of view. But if I regard the things from the point of view of the things, where am I? So, I know that I am a man and man is me, I and every thing are things.
>
> Therefore, using the eyes of the universe as if they were one's own eyes, there is nothing which is not seen. Using the ears of the universe as if they were one's own ears, there is nothing which is not heard. Using the mouths of the universe as if they were one's own mouth, there is nothing which is not proclaimed. Using all the minds of the universe as if they were one's own mind, there is nothing that is not pondered. (Shao 1986:26)

One hears echoes of Chuang-tzu and Hsün Tzu in Shao Yung's concern for a proper perspective and doing the best that one can in a changing world. If the rest of the Tao school philosophers did not follow Shao's theories in detail, they did follow his lead in trying to figure out how to understand and then describe and explain the world and its ordering patterns.

Chou Tun-i and the Cosmological Outlines of the World

Chou Tun-i (1017–1073) has always been commemorated as the founder of Sung Tao school cosmology. This recognition rests on his authorship of the document deemed to be *the* manifesto of Sung cosmology and metaphysics. Chou's concise *Diagram of the Supreme Ultimate Explained* outlines the basic elements of the shared cosmological vision of the Sung moral philosophers. Like all founding texts, it is terse enough to invite explanation and ambiguous enough to allow for multiple interpretations.

Chou Tun-i wove together a great deal of suggestive material in the space of a very short document and diagram. The opening sentence of the explanation is one of the most famous lines in all Chinese philosophy, probably second only to the equally enigmatic beginning of the *Lao Tzu*; one is reminded, in terms of hermeneutic fecundity and complexity, of the great opening stanzas of Genesis or the Gospel of St. John within the Western tradition. There is no consensus on how to read this line, and it thus forces the reader to make an interpretive choice. The Chinese is short: *Wu-chi er t'ai-chi.*

Fung Yu-lan, for instance, has translated the sentence as "The Ultimateless! And yet also the Supreme Ultimate!" (Fung 1952–1953:2, 435). However, Wing-tsit Chan offered the following rendition: "The Ultimate of Nonbeing and also the Great Ultimate!" (Chu and Lü 1967:5). Or Carsun Chang has suggested this reading: "The Ultimate of Nothingness, but in turn the Supreme Ultimate!" (1957–1962, 1:142). These three readings illustrate the problem that students have had with the text from the inception of the Neo-Confucian movement. In the first place, there is the problem of translating the term *wu-chi*, a term that many Confucians believed belongs more to the world of Taoist speculation than to the Confucian world of moral philosophy. The reader will notice that although there is an accepted English translation for *t'ai-chi* as the Supreme Ultimate, a perfectly good concept taken impeccably from the *Book of Changes*, there is no agreement about how to read *wu-chi*. Is it a concept for nothingness out of which something comes, or is it simply used to explain that we cannot perfectly define, as finite beings, the infinite reality of the all that is, was, or will be?

From the perspective of the emerging Neo-Confucian discourse, grave issues are at stake here. For instance, does this sentence mean that there is a kind of "dual origin" theory involved in the formation of the world? Does something come from nothing, and does this mean that nothing, hence, is ontologically and cosmological prior to being? Most Confucians are very uncomfortable with such a reading of the text because it would suggest a rupture in their correlative and totalistic interpretation of the cosmos. But if Chou Tun-i was not making us aware of the separation of being and nonbeing, why did he introduce the strange notion of *wu-chi* at the beginning of his diagram and explanation? Or is Chou merely trying, rather like Shao Yung as well, to show that we live in a world of ceaseless change? Is Chou assuming that all things and events emerge out of the ultimate flux of change itself such that we cannot give a definite final reason or definition of ultimate reality, classically called the Supreme Ultimate in the Confucian tradition following the *Book of Changes*? In any event, as Carsun Chang noted, "The Diagram and its explanation are a Chinese version of the theory of the creation and evolution of the universe" (1957–1962, 2:143).

In terms of Chou Tun-i's explanation of the diagram, after we have moved from the origination of the cosmos in its most primal forms, we prescind to the generation of movement itself represented as *yang*. And of course, movement is always linked to tranquillity or rest in an unending alternating rhythm of becoming as the Supreme Ultimate: "So when movement and tranquillity alternate and become the root of each other, giving rise to the distinction of yin and yang, and the two modes are established" (Chan 1963:463). The Supreme Ultimate is also taken to be principle itself, the icon of order for the Sung Tao school philosophers. In this they all agree from Shao Yung right down to Chu Hsi.

The Tao school philosophers suggest that Chou Tun-i is setting up an explanatory contrast between the formal trait of principle and the dynamic trait of *ch'i*. Hence, the alternation of yin and yang as well as the various permutations of the five phases are taken by Chou to illustrate the fluctuations of the primal *ch'i*/matter-energy. However, Chou, true to the emerging tradition, stresses that the principle and the dynamic traits are never separated but are always and everywhere one. It will take a few generations for Chu Hsi to propose the final narrative of this cosmological drama begun with Chou's diagram and text.

Most expositions of Chou Tun-i focus on the cosmologically formative diagram and its appended texts and explanations because it was considered such an important treatise for the emerging moral philosophical tradition. But Chou wrote other works, including the longer *T'ung-shu,* or the *Penetrating the Book of Changes*. This important work lifted up Chou's characteristic moral concerns, the most important of which is the highlighting of the concept of *ch'eng*/sincerity or self-realization. Here again we can see the art of the moral philosophers at work. If one expects some kind of novel invention of new language, one will be disappointed. But if we can learn to see the uncommon ways someone like Chou manipulates his inherited vocabulary in order to give old terms new meanings, then we can begin to catch a glimmer of why this new philosophy was so powerful.

Consider the use of *ch'eng*, a term of considerable import in the classical period in *Doctrine of the Mean*. It is generally translated as sincerity, integrity, and the lack of any kind of duplicity and is mostly part of the moral vocabulary of the tradition. However, in Chou's reading, which includes all the overtones of the classical period, *ch'eng* comes to mean something more, something of fundamental importance for the cultivation of sagehood. In *Penetrating the Book of Changes,* Chou devotes the first three chapters to a discussion of the role of *ch'eng* as it pertains to the role of the sage as one of the agents of the cosmic drama of change. Furthermore, the classical Confucian tradition talked about the triad of heaven, earth, and humanity playing cocreative roles in the governance of the cosmos.

Chou Tun-i's introduction of the notion of self-realization, or *ch'eng,* is as abrupt as was the opening sentence of the diagram of the Supreme Ultimate, and just as dramatic. Chou states that "*Ch'eng* is the root of the sage." Wing-tsit Chan has translated the phrase as "sincerity is the foundation of the sage" (1963:465). I have chosen to take *pen* as "root" because the balance between root and branch is so important to the moral philosophers. Chou concluded that the very fundamental root of the sage is sincerity as the completion of the person and hence of all things as well; "Sagehood is nothing but Sincerity" (Chan 1963:466). Chou argues that it is this sincerity that gives substance and actuality to all the other cardinal virtues. If the sage does not have sincerity, then there will be depravity in deed and thought.

In his exposition of *ch'eng,* Chou Tun-i adds another important element in the creation of Sung Tao school philosophy. He took a classical moral term, retained its original ethical denotations, and expanded its original intent toward a general axiology wherein the ethical becomes the cosmological. It is also where the later Confucians have problems with Chou because he seems to speak of sincerity as being overidentified with the tranquil aspects of yin and hence is perhaps too close to Taoist and Buddhist forms of quietisms. As with all other forms of Northern Sung Tao school discourse, the legacy of the early masters is both fruitful and ambiguous.

Chang Tsai and the Dynamics of Ch'i

Chang Tsai (1020–1077) is the premier philosopher of *ch'i,* matter-energy or vital force—or a whole host of other English paraphrases of the most difficult to translate of all Chinese philosophical terms. If there were ever a truly "metaphysical" term in Chinese thought, surely *ch'i* would be the most likely candidate. As Whitehead once said, the problem with metaphysical concepts is that they never take a holiday. What Whitehead meant was that we can never think of a situation in which the concept does not obtain. This pervasiveness makes it difficult for us to identify it, because it is never absent from our purview. Whitehead argued that we learn by the method of difference: We compare and contrast what we find with what is absent and draw our knowledge from this interchange of presence and absence. But when something is never absent, then we cannot properly compare it or get a purchase on just what is compared to everything else that we know. *Ch'i* is like this because it informs everything that is for the Sung Neo-Confucians. It was Chang Tsai who most cogently tried to make the case for *ch'i* as a crucial part of Confucian discourse.

As we shall see, Chang Tsai actually contributed more than just reflections on the nature of *ch'i* theory to the ensemble of Sung Tao school philosophy. His "Western Inscription" is a defining statement of Neo-

Confucian spirituality, and no document is more quoted when scholars seek to prove that there is indeed a religious dimension to the Confucian tradition. Furthermore, Chang Tsai's definition of the mind-heart as that aspect of the person that unifies principle and dynamics was also a signal offering to Sung, Ming, and Ch'ing thought.

If one of the defining characteristics of Sung Tao school philosophy was its search for order and principle, Chang Tsai went at the common problem of these thinkers from a distinctive direction. Chang was convinced that matter-energy was the matrix out of which all things and events emerge. Without matter-energy, there would be nothing at all, not even principle itself because principle must adhere in some thing or event; without matter-energy there could be no patterns or principles at all. In this regard, Chang Tsai, even though he talked about matter-energy in terms such as the Great Vacuity, defended the realist inclinations of the Confucian tradition against Taoists and Buddhists who argued for nothingness and emptiness as that which is primordial before and beyond any of the things or events of the world.

According to Chang Tsai, there is nothing senseless or meaningless about the operation of change and its manifestations of things and events within the great *ch'i*. There have been some Western and Marxist historians who have argued that Chang Tsai's thought, because of his emphasis upon the reality of matter-energy, should be considered a form of materialism. This is much too reductionist a reading to encompass the complexity of Chang Tsai's thought. For instance, Chang is responsible for the orthodox interpretation of spirits (*kuei-shen*) as manifestations of matter-energy, certainly not a very materialist way of looking at the world. The point is that matter-energy is really everything that is material, in addition to what counts as spiritual, such as the spirits and ghosts and other wonderful inhabitants of traditional Chinese cosmological speculation.

Along with all the other Sung *tao-hsüeh* philosophers, Chang believed that there is an order to be discovered in the cosmos. "The nature and the Way of Heaven are but Change" (Chan 1963:506). Although change, by its very protean nature, is difficult to comprehend, this is precisely what sages do when they are in tune with the great patterns of matter-energy: "No two of the products of creation are alike. From this we know that although the number of things is infinite, at bottom there is nothing without yin and yang (which differentiate them). From this we know also that the transformations and changes in the universe are due to these two fundamental forces" (Chan 1963:506). Although there is nothing static about the nature of the cosmos, if we attend the pattern, or patterns, of the changes of the cosmos, then we will begin to understand how it operates. There is still a pattern to be seen even if it is complicated and infinite in its ongoing ramifications. Chang argues that if we can understand the principle of heaven (*t'ien-li*), then we understand the nature of change; if we fail in this understanding of principle, then we will be hopelessly lost in the swirl of things and events. This inattentive sense of being lost without understanding how the cosmos works is the basis for human finitude, ignorance, and error.

Nowhere is Chang Tsai's vision or hope for the Confucian fiduciary community better expressed than in the famous "Western Inscription." Along with providing an overview of the concern that a Confucian should have for the world, it illustrates the spiritual dimension of the Confucian tradition. Terms like "spirituality," "religiousness," and "mysticism" are notoriously hard to define but often easy to recognize when we see them. Although we may not be able to give a perfect cross-cultural definition of religion or spirituality, there is no doubt that the "Western Inscription" inscribes within the Sung Tao school philosophy that particular expansiveness of concern and desire for public and cosmic service that are the hallmarks of Confucian religiosity.

The opening verses of the inscription set the tone for the whole document and are worth reviewing now:

> Heaven is my father and Earth is my mother, and even such a small creature as I finds an intimate place in their midst.
>
> Therefore that which fills the universe I regard as my body and that which directs the universe I consider my nature.
>
> All people are my brothers and sisters, and all things are my companions. (Chan 1963:497)

Chang then goes on to explain how this is the case by means of appealing to the need to respond correctly and compassionately to the mandate of Heaven and to manifest one's true nature. "But he who puts his moral nature into practice and brings his physical existence into complete fulfillment can match (Heaven and Earth)" (Chan 1963:497). Many scholars have found in Chang's admonition to try to serve heaven, earth, and humanity a Confucian counterpart to the Buddhist bodhisattva ideal of wisdom and compassion. This is perfectly true; the Confucian also adds the absolute necessity to strive to serve human social needs by means of perfecting the self.

Chang Tsai notes that one's own fate is not as important as the effort to serve humanity. A true Confucian should not worry overly much about being rich or poor, humble or elevated in social status. "In life I follow and serve (Heaven and Earth). In death I will be at peace" (Chan 1963:498). Although the Confucian path is strenuous and there is no guarantee that it will end in success, there is a blessing in knowing that you have fought the good fight and run the good race. If you have done that, then Chang Tsai promises that there is a contentment to life that is beyond the mere vicissitudes of fate or fame. There is peace within the Tao.

The Ch'eng Brothers and the Patterns of Principle

With the remarkable careers of the two most famous brothers of the Sung philosophical revival, we reach the end of the great period of creativity in the Northern Sung. Although it is true that many other Northern Sung thinkers, from Shao Yung on, were enthralled with finding and describing the fundamental order of the universe, it was the Ch'eng brothers who canonized the concept of principle as the key to the philosophical puzzle of cosmic order. With the Ch'eng brothers' exposition of principle, all the pieces that were to form the mature Sung moral philosophy of the Tao school were in place.

There has been a great deal of debate about just how much the two brothers shared philosophically. The technical details of this complicated controversy need not detain us here, for it is clear that both brothers where interested in principle as a philosophical concept. Whether Ch'eng Hao (1032–1085) would have agreed with the developments of his younger brother's philosophy of principle if he had lived longer is a moot point. However, it is noteworthy that even if the brothers tended to agree philosophically, they had very different personalities. On the one hand, Ch'eng Hao was universally respected and revered as a kind, wise, friendly, and even humorous person. Ch'eng I (1033–1107), on the other hand, was seen as something of marionette, a punctilious stickler for all the minor rules of behavior that could be dredged up from the classical ritual texts. It was not that Ch'eng I was not a decent person, it was just that he lacked the flair of his older brother.

The two Ch'eng brothers focused attention on the concept of *li*, or principle, as the definitive formal trait of everything that is. Although it is a tricky business to try to separate the thought of the two brothers on this fundamental issue, it is helpful to note that they went about explaining their philosophies in different ways. Ch'eng Hao, for instance, is remembered as taking more time to focus on questions of moral cultivation and sagehood than in presenting a detailed rational explanation of principle. Ch'eng Hao counseled that one must begin with the cultivation of the virtue of humanity. "(One's duty) is to understand this principle (*li*) and preserve *jen* with sincerity and seriousness (*ching*), that is all" (Chan 1963:523). In another famous passage, Ch'eng Hao likened the lack of humanity to being paralyzed; there is a physical paralysis and a concomitant moral paralysis that infects a person who lacks humanity. It was left to his younger brother to bring out the uniqueness of their doctrine of just what principle really is.

A. C. Graham began his exemplary study of Ch'eng I's notion of principle by reviewing what the Sung scholars thought principle meant. The word was used both as a verb and a noun; the noun form meant the patterns or veins in a piece of jade and the verb meant to dress or finish a piece of jade. In the thinking of the Ch'eng brothers, principle is both a cosmological and an ethical principle: "All things have principles, for example *that by which* (*so-yi*) fire is hot and that by which water is cold" (Graham 1992a:8). Everything in the world has a principle, a pattern, or a formal trait that makes it what it is and how it comes to be, that determines how it manifests itself and how it is to act: "If we exhaust the principles in the things of the world, it will be found that a thing must have a reason why it is and a rule to which it should conform, which is what is meant by 'principle'" (Graham 1992a:8).

Graham suggested that we need to take the metaphor of veins in a piece of jade seriously when we try to figure out what the Ch'engs meant by principle. First of all, Graham argues that the Ch'engs never anticipated a theory of universals or one universal such as the perfect, unchanging good as suggested by Plato's theory of forms. There are many principles; in fact, there are as many principles as there are things and events.

> Principle seems to be conceived as a network of veins; however much they diverge from each other, the veins prove when we "extend" them to be one; on the other hand we can also go on indefinitely making finer and finer distinctions among them, finding as we proceed that not only classes by individuals and parts of individuals have *li* which distinguish them from each other. (Graham 1992a:13)

The Tao school philosophers never tired of stating that principle is one, but its manifestations are many.

For the Ch'engs, principle became the way they encompassed all the other concepts of the Confucian tradition. Thus, human nature became the principle by which people ought to act. The Mandate of Heaven became the principle of how things are given their natures or principle. For that matter, once having given pride of place to principle, the Ch'engs showed how such terms as heaven, mandate, and even the Way itself were just alternative specifications of principle itself. For instance, "What is called heaven is self-dependent (*tzu-jan*) principle" (Graham 1992a:23). Even the Way of Heaven itself is simply the principle of Heaven's way. This kind of reading allowed the Ch'engs to state that human nature is really principle as well. Hence, if principle is followed, then good will result; however, if principle is not followed, then evil will arise.

With the death of Ch'eng I in 1107, the great era of Northern Sung philosophy came to an end. In fact, though it could not have been foreseen, the dynasty was thrown into turmoil by a devastating war with northern neighbors that brought an end to the Northern Sung completely. Yet the legacy of this group of remarkable men continues to live on in Neo-Confucianism.

The Transition to the Southern Sung

In the 1120s, the Sung dynasty allied itself to a proto-Manchu tribal con-
federation in the hope of regaining land lost in North China to the Liao dynasty during the wars of the early 1120s. Unfortunately, the new
Manchurian Chin dynasty was successful in destroying the older Liao along
the northern frontier. The Sung were less successful and lost the battles on
the southern front. The Chin, who saw no reason to stop in North China,
tried to conquer the rest of Sung China and were successful in capturing
most of North China down to the Huai River.

The loss of North China was a devastating blow to Chinese self-esteem.
But oddly enough, it had a smaller impact on the development of Chinese
philosophy. As has been noted in previous chapters, ever since the middle
of the T'ang dynasty the center of Chinese intellectual gravity had been
shifting to the south. By the Southern Sung, the shift had been completed.
The great northern capital of K'ai-feng was lost, but a new capital, always
considered a temporary one until the recapture of the North, was established at Hang-chou. In its more chaotic, less organized way, Hang-chou
continued to be the center of a remarkable cultural world.

The most fruitful way to look at the change from the Northern to
Southern Sung has been outlined by James T. C. Liu (1988) in *China
Turning Inward*. Liu demonstrated that the remarkable confident, open
quality that marked the renewal of Confucian thought from the late T'ang
to the middle of the Sung was tempered and then abandoned for a more in-
ward-looking cultural sensibility. Chinese intellectuals looked within in order to seek the reasons for the fall of the Northern Sung, and became more
cautious and introspective than their immediate predecessors.

For instance, if the Sung had really been a Confucian dynasty, what had
gone wrong and caused the fiasco of the loss of the North? Was it the fault
of men of like Wang An-shih, who were too bold in changing honored tradition and not disciplined enough by intense moral self-cultivation? These
were the kind of questions that the Southern Sung philosophers grappled
with, along with all the other unexplored intellectual pathways of the
Northern Sung Confucian revival. Maybe, some Confucians hypothesized,
they had not gotten it just right, and the failure of the dynasty was due to
faulty Confucian discourse. Hence, it was up to the Southern Sung thinkers
to try to figure out what had gone wrong and to rectify any mistakes they
discovered.

Chu Hsi: The Grand Southern Sung Synthesis

Waiting in the wings to carry out the task of a comprehensive synthesis of
the Northern Sung achievement was one of the most remarkable philoso-

phers of China's long history, Chu Hsi (1130–1200). In terms of impact on the history of Chinese thought, Chu is second only to Confucius and Mencius as a Confucian thinker. Chu is often compared to St. Aquinas in the West, and here again, there is a great deal of merit in the comparison. Chinese thought would never be the same after Chu Hsi reworked and arranged the records of his beloved Northern Sung masters.

Although his final achievement was all-encompassing, the route to Chu's mature vision of the Confucian Tao took time. He had always been recognized as a philosophical genius, but it was not until his late thirties and early forties that he arrived at the philosophical conclusions that made him so famous. Rather like Kant's reading of Hume, Chu only began to doubt the teaching of his early teachers, who had been disciples of the great Ch'eng I, after a set of debates with some good friends about the nature of the mind-heart. But once the seeds of doubt about his own teachers' precise understandings of the Confucian Tao had been planted, Chu began a remarkable five- or six-year quest for a better position. And once he found it, he elaborated it for the rest of his life in an almost endless series of essays, commentaries, and letters.

There is an almost immeasurable list of Chu Hsi's accomplishments. We will focus here on only two in order to give some background to Chu's systematic philosophical position. First, Chu redefined the core of the Confucian canon. Second, he recast the family rituals expressive of the proper conduct of Confucian life and society. Both were remarkable achievements. For instance, by creating the new compilation of what is called the Four Books—the *Great Learning, Analects, Mencius,* and *Doctrine of the Mean*—and writing commentaries on them, Chu set the standard by which all educated Chinese would study Confucianism from 1313, when the Mongol Yüan dynasty made his commentaries definitive for the imperial examinations, right down to 1905, when the examinations were finally abolished. Chu Hsi himself would have been aghast to think that his work replaced study of the other thirteen classics; he saw his work as a way to introduce students to the richness of the tradition by setting them on the correct path that they needed to follow as far as they could.

The other project, a work titled *Master Chu's Family Rituals,* was just as ambitious and revolutionary. Building on the work of other Sung experts in ritual lore, Chu Hsi collected, corrected, and even emended a variety of ceremonies dealing with human life from birth to death and tried to explain them in simple language that any literate person could understand. What comes through the discussion of ritual is a style typical of the Tao school philosophers: Above all else, they saw themselves as educators and not pedants. That Chu Hsi wrote much of his material, including this famous work on ritual for family life, in a Sung vernacular designed to be easy to read, speaks volumes about the Confucian desire to reform society in the light of their understanding of the proper Way. Whereas the usefulness of the imperial examinations has long since disappeared, it is reported that many modern Chinese continue to this day to refer to Chu's ritual manual when they are planning ceremonies for their families.

Chu Hsi did even more than reform the family life of China and establish the curriculum for the whole civil service elite of the empire, as if that were not enough for one scholar. Chu Hsi tried to explain the philosophical vision that governed the whole structure of the Confucian way, from birth rituals and marriage ceremonies to speculation on the ultimate nature of the cosmos. For instance, in seeking to introduce young scholars to the study of the Confucian classics as exemplified by the Four Books, he and his good friend Lü Tsu-ch'ien composed the famous anthology *Reflections on Things at Hand*. This work became the ladder by which successive generations of aspiring youth gained their first access to the moral philosophy of the Sung reformers. It included all the major topics of Chu Hsi's curriculum of study and reflection necessary to encompass the Confucian vision of humanity, society, and the cosmos.

In many respects, like all great philosophers, Chu Hsi produced a vision of reality that has a simple elegance. But again like all great philosophers, this initial simplicity can and does give rise to a baroque set of ramifications that extends to all facets of human civilization and the natural order. Nor does this mean a mechanical rigidity of thought. One of the things that fascinates the student of Sung thought is the willingness of these great thinkers to debate and even modify their ideas in dialogue with their friends and colleagues. Chu Hsi also exemplifies this kind of intellectually open stance.

For example, Chu Hsi began his great adventure by reexamining his theory of human nature and the mind-heart. Once his friends had made it clear that his teacher Li T'ung (1093–1163), a follower of Ch'eng I, had not solved all the problems of Sung moral philosophy and cosmology, Chu Hsi embarked on a complete reevaluation of his thought. He discovered a key organizing insight when he reviewed Chang Tsai's theory of the mind-heart, wherein Chang asserted that the mind-heart controlled and unified human nature and emotions. This was the philosophical key that allowed Chu to apply the principle-oriented theory of Ch'eng I, the cosmology of Chou Tun-i, and the *ch'i* theory of Chang Tsai to the puzzles of human nature and action.

To greatly simplify Chu Hsi's great synthesis, Chu saw Chang's notion of the mind-heart as pointing to how the world of human emotion, the domain of *ch'i* as the dynamic element of reality, was linked to the world of human nature, the world of principle as explained by Ch'eng I. Chu assumed that the dynamic world of matter-energy was always conjoined with a principle that gave definiteness to all the things and events of the cosmos. Therefore, the world could be explained as the ceaseless unification of principle with matter-energy in some definite event or thing. For instance, in humans it is the role of the mind-heart to unify its nature qua ethical principles and virtues with the dynamic power of matter-energy as passion or emotion.

Regarding the cosmos, this meant the constant manifestation of principle in *ch'i* itself. For instance, Chu Hsi stipulated that this is what Chou Tun-i really meant when Chou talked about the Supreme Ultimate being the name of ultimate principle within the totality of matter-energy. This definition of the Supreme Ultimate allowed Chu to make sense of all kinds of inherited dyads such as yin and yang in terms of how the creative balance of principle and matter-energy always came together in some specific object-event. Of course, Chu did not imply that this always worked in a harmonious fashion. In fact, the theory allowed Chu to explain how evil and error enter the world. This, too, was initially simple: Sometimes Chu noted that principle did not win the struggle with matter-energy and was not perfectly manifested. For example, in human beings, even those rightly guided by the teachings of the sages, sometimes the emotions, as the dynamic of matter-energy, were not patterned on principle. Therefore people often gave in to their emotions when they should have been following their principle.

Chu Hsi made the point about the unity of principle and matter-energy by stating: "The beginning of (anything) is the beginning of (its) energy. The birth (of anything) is the beginning of (its) form" (Wittenborn 1991:60). For human beings, the key for the birth and beginning is the role of the mind-heart: "Someone asked what distinguished mind, nature, and feeling. Master Chu said: Master Ch'eng (Yi) said that the mind is like the seed of a grain. The principle of generation is contained in its nature. At the point where the energy of Yang occurs, it is feelings. By inference we can say that all things are like this" (Wittenborn 1991:66).

As always, Chu saw the world as a constantly changing pattern of the integration of the dynamics of matter-energy, the form of principle, and their ceaseless unification, which in the case of human beings was accomplished by the functions of the mind-heart.

In order to learn about the proper relationship of principle and matter-energy, Chu Hsi was everywhere clear that one must begin serious study through the investigation of things, the famous doctrine of *ko-wu*. "Master Chu said: Investigating the phenomena of things is the beginning of knowledge. Keeping out thoughts sincere is the beginning of practice" (Wittenborn 1991:89). The reason we need this kind of careful attention to the details of the world is that, as we have seen before, there is nothing in the world, however small or trivial at first glance, that does not have a principle, a reason, a form of definiteness that allows us to grasp its place in the Way: "Master Chu said: There is not one thing in the universe however great or small, obscure, that is without principle. There has never been anything lacking principle, nor has there ever been a principle not in something. We cannot speak of inner and outer. If there is anything that cannot be reasoned out, then how could it mean principle?" (Wittenborn 1991:88).

Chu was at pains to balance the world of inner self-cultivation with the need for serious study of the external world. He always wanted to make sure that the student linked ethical concerns with the examination of things.

Lu Hsiang-shan and Unity of the Mind and Nature

Of course, not everyone agreed with Chu Hsi. As the modern New Confucian Mou Tsung-san has magisterially demonstrated, there were whole schools of now neglected scholars, such as those in the Hu school, that did not agree with Chu's highly rationalistic view of Confucian discourse. The most famous challenger to Chu in his day was Lu Hsiang-shan (1139–1193). It is illustrative of the collaborative nature of Sung philosophy that both Lu and Chu thought highly of each other and that Chu invited Lu to give major lectures at Chu's famous White Deer Academy. For that matter, Chu even had Lu's words placed over the entrance of the school—because he prized Lu's pedagogy, even if he disagreed with Lu's philosophical stance.

Lu disagreed with Chu about the nature of the mind-heart and how it ought to be cultivated. This disagreement sprang from the fact that Lu's theory of cultivation was focused more on internal reflection than on the external examination of things. Here is a translation of Lu's typical response to Chu Hsi's theory of *ko-wu*:

> Po-min asked: How is one to investigate things (*ko-wu*)?
> The teacher (Lu Hsiang-shan) said: Investigate the principle of things.
> Po-min said: The ten thousand things under Heaven are extremely multitudinous; how, then, can we investigate all of them exhaustively?
> The teacher replied: The ten thousand things are already complete in us. It is only necessary to apprehend their principle. (Huang 1977:31)

Lu shared Chu's fascination with uncovering the principle of the Way and the principles of the things found in the Way. However, he believed that the best way to do this was through the moral rectification of the self. On another occasion, Lu was reported to have replied that even the Confucian classics were merely footnotes to his own mind-heart, strengthening the conviction of the priority of moral cultivation of the mind-heart over any external form of hermeneutic art.

Because of this emphasis on the moral cultivation of the mind-heart, Lu Hsiang-shan is later given the title of the founder of the School of Mind, in contradistinction to Chu's School of Principle. However, it is clear that both Lu and Chu were passionately concerned with principle and the mind-heart. The argument was over the methods needed for self-cultivation rather than about whether principle and the mind-heart were essential to Confucian philosophy. Lu sought the correct place to start the investigation of things. Because the world was such a confusing place, Lu believed that we have to secure correctly the principle of our own mind-heart, our heavenly endowed human nature as principle, before we merrily go our way among the object-events of the world. According to Lu, until and unless we are able to get the principle of the mind-heart in a firm grasp, all other efforts become futile, and perhaps even dangerously misleading.

Ch'en Liang and Public Interest and Policy

Another side of the reaction to Chu Hsi's synthesis is found in the work of the less-well-known critic, Ch'en Liang (1143–1194). Whereas Lu Hsiang-shan was worried that Chu Hsi did not pay enough attention to the specific cultivation and illumination of the mind-heart, Ch'en Liang was concerned that Chu was not enmeshed enough in the practical nature of social governance and public policy. In this regard, Ch'en presents the pragmatic Sung Confucian appeal to concrete results. If, as we shall see, Lu presages the introspective philosophy of Wang Yang-ming, the argument can be made that Ch'en prefigures the practical concerns of the great Ch'ing evidential research scholars who turned their attention to the application of Confucian theory to governmental reform.

Ch'en Liang was passionately committed to trying to find a way to win back North China from the barbarian Chin empire. Ch'en became more and more convinced that Confucian scholars needed to be serious about the results of their theories. Moral self-cultivation was fine if and only if it served some concrete social goal. To this end, Ch'en tried to demonstrate that the great Han and T'ang rulers were not to be denigrated because they were not paragons of moral or intellectual virtue; on the contrary, the Han and T'ang had many successful features that the Sung state should emulate if it was to be a defender of the public good. For instance, Ch'en concluded that carefully crafted law, something most Confucian found distasteful, had real merit. "The human mind-heart (*hsin*) is mostly self-regarding, but laws and regulations (*fa*) can be used to make it public-minded (*kung*) . . . Law and regulations comprise the collective or commonweal principle (*kung li*)" (Tillman 1994:16). Ch'en took his history as seriously as Chu Hsi but reached radically different conclusions. For Ch'en, the world is a more complex, complicated, and morally messy place than it is for Chu as Ch'en sees it. "I simply don't agree with (your) joining together principles and (complex) affairs (as neatly and artificially) as if they were barrel hoops" (Tillman 1994:52).

However, the grand debates about the ultimate nature of nature, the moral mind-heart, human passions, the laws, and all the other ideas and concepts of the Southern Sung would have to wait for further discussion. Out on the northern steppes, another great storm was rising, and this one would make the two previous storms look like child's play. While the Southern Sung philosophers argued about the best way to cultivate virtue and find the principles of all things, the Mongols were busily conquering the world. The Sung resisted the Mongol advance for a time, but they, too, finally fell in 1279 to the great Kublai Khan. However, the work initiated by the Northern and Southern Sung masters flourished in new ways in the Yüan and the revived Chinese Ming dynasty.

❀ 5 ❀

The Flourishing of the Yüan and Ming

THE STORY OF CONFUCIANISM in the Yüan and Ming dynasties is both simple and complex, simple because the Confucianism of these two Chinese dynasties continues the development of various strains of Sung Neo-Confucian thought but increasingly complex due to the internationalization of the tradition in Korea and Japan. It was not until the Ming period (1368–1644) that Confucianism became creatively independent from Buddhism in both Korea and Japan. By the middle of the Ming period, there were many intellectuals in both Korea and Japan who had come to identify themselves with the Confucian Way. As we shall see in Chapter 6, some of the most interesting elaborations and expansions of the Confucian Way took place after the sixteenth century, first in Korea and then in seventeenth-century Japan.

It is also in the late Ming that we have the first sustained glimpse into the world of women as Confucian scholars. Throughout Chinese history there were occasional great female historians, artists, and poets, but their records are so scanty that these remarkable women are more exceptions than the rule when it comes to charting the tradition. But in the sixteenth century, the screen of silence is drawn back and we have records of what Dorothy Ko (1994) has called "the teachers of the inner chambers." Along with the general explosion of diverse cultural interests that marks the world of Ming China after Wang Yang-ming, we find educated Chinese women writing as Confucian intellectuals and arguing for their proper place as teachers of the tradition for their sons and daughters and for other women as well.

Although it is true that all Confucians longed to serve a proper prince and to bring prosperity and justice the world, the philosophers of the Sung also taught a form of self-cultivation that could be practiced in difficult times. Reflection on the role of the mind-heart and its proper cultivation was one of the continuing puzzles of the Sung legacy. If a scholar could not spend a great deal of time writing memorials to a receptive emperor under the early Mongol Yüan dynasty, the scholar could still reflect on the philo-sophical aspects of Chu Hsi's thought and his arguments with people like Lu Hsiang-shan and Ch'en Liang.

The Turn Toward the Mind

A pertinent example of the perennial concern of Neo-Confucianism for the mind-heart that had a major impact in the Yüan period found paradigmatic expression in Chen Te-hsiu's (1178–1235) *Classic of the Mind-Heart*. This concise compilation of passages from the classics and commentaries of the Sung masters expresses Chen's interpretation of Chu's teachings on the matter of the mind-heart, with special concern for the issues of reverence or seriousness as keys to the cultivation of the person. Although Chen was fa-mous for his defense of the notion of the transmission of the teaching of the Way as defined by Chu Hsi, it was his work on the mind-heart that became important not just for later Chinese scholars but also for Korean and Japanese Confucians in their turn.

Chen makes it clear that a correct understanding of the mind-heart lies at the foundation of the Confucian Way: "When one has committed himself to this Way, to what should he then devote his practice of it? If we look to remote antiquity, we can see that in the one word 'reverence,' as passed down through a hundred sages, is presented their real method of the mind-and-heart (*hsin-fa*)" (de Bary 1989:47). In Chen's own mind, this teaching was linked to the theory of the transmission of the Way as guided by the method of the mind-heart itself.

The problem, as Chen saw it, was that we have two minds, the first be-ing the normal human mind-heart that is directly related to our specific en-dowment of matter-energy. The second aspect of our mind-heart is more precarious and is identified as the mind-heart of the Way itself, the aspect of the mind-heart that provides us access, when properly cultivated, to the normative principles of the cosmos. What we need to do is to find the proper way to refine this physical mind-heart so that the normative mind-heart of the Way can become a template for all our actions and thoughts. This is why it is so important to discover and cultivate the notions of rev-erence and willingness to find the correct way to be single-minded about the mind-heart.

Wm. Theodore de Bary (1981) has observed that Chen Te-hsiu's thought can be interpreted as a form of moral rigorism in that Chen was highly mo-tivated to control the human passions through moral and spiritual self-cul-tivation. Nonetheless, Chen maintained a strong link to another aspect of Chu's heritage through an emphasis on empirical learning as well. According to Chen, the reason for this is simple. Principles are without form; only concrete things embody form such that we can learn about it, from the sublime to the mundane: "If you set aside implements and search for principles, you cannot escape empty theorizing, which is not the real, practical learning of our Confucian school . . . Scholars should have the solid ground of reality on which to exert their efforts and not let their minds chase off into realms of empty nothingness" (de Bary 1981:105).

The Confucian Way Under Mongol Rule

The Mongol Yüan dynasty was so much involved with its world empire that China, albeit a major part of the empire, was only one part of a more complicated pattern of rule. Although the Mongols took a great deal of economic and political interest in the Chinese part of their empire, they were always innately suspicious of the Chinese because China was the last major part of Asia to be added to the Mongol domains; the Chinese were also not going to be digested and made part of any steppe empire on its own terms.

Yüan cultural life flourished in ways that compensated for the fall from grace of the Neo-Confucians as confidants of the emperor and his court. For instance, theater developed rapidly in China during the Yüan dynasty. In fact, some plays like *The Romance of the Western Chamber* become part of China's classical repertoire. If the literati could not comment to the emperor directly, they could write plays that, carefully constructed so as not to give direct offense to the Mongol elite, spoke about their views on the social problems of the day. With their mixture of social criticism, love stories, music, poetry, and dance, these plays were a heady mixture of popular and literati culture.

Painting was another famous cultural arena for the Yüan. As Conrad Schirokauer points out, later Chinese art historians are unanimous about the beauty and pathos of Yüan painting. In his cultural history of China, Schirokauer (1991:177) has reproduced Kung K'ai's (1222–1307) poignant painting of an emaciated horse. Kung was famous for his love of horses, and this particular painting shows a tired and hungry horse, head down, no doubt representing the crushed feelings of the Chinese elite at the sorrow of losing their country to the Mongols. Yet there is still something noble in the suffering of the horse that must have served to inspire the Confucian literati in their time of trial. At least this horse, even at a great sacrifice, managed to stay out of the imperial war stables of the Mongol armies.

Wu Ch'eng and the Preservation of Learning

Nonetheless, there were many creative and industrious Chinese scholars who not only preserved but also increased the deposit of the tradition in difficult times. An outstanding example is Wu Ch'eng (1249–1333), justly remembered as the most influential of the Confucian scholars of the Yüan dynasty. Wu is particularly fascinating because his main intellectual task, namely, the comparison and evaluation of the competing legacies of Chu Hsi and Lu Hsiang-shan, prefigured the grand debates of the Ming dynasty and Wang Yang-ming and his followers.

In order to cultivate and perfect his scholarship, Wu Ch'eng attempted to master not only the canonical tradition but also the emerging scholarship of the Sung Neo-Confucian movement. This approach demanded that he reflect on Chu Hsi's system and also on Lu Hsiang-shan's challenge to it. For instance, there was the problem of how to balance the external concerns for the facts of any given situation with the intense cultivation of the mind-heart, an endeavor more in line with some Buddhist meditation practices than with the typical social orientation of classical Confucianism. What was instructive about Wu's way of dealing with the issue was his attempt to preserve a basic fidelity both to the study of the external world and to the cultivation of human nature as represented by the fundamental mind-heart of humanity.

Another problem that occupied Wu was the question of the relationship of principle and the mind-heart, or the passions. As he put it, if principle is something abstract and the mind-heart is something very much alive, how can the abstract dominate the living reality of the mind-heart? Wu worried about the fact that he perceived a tendency to identify principle as taught by Ch'eng I and Chu Hsi with a kind of dry, intense scholasticism that missed the point that any study ought to be in service to a living morality. Hence, Wu wanted to remind scholars that Chu Hsi was committed to the cultivation of virtue and scholarship and that the two could never be separated in theory or praxis. In this respect, Wu put his finger on a question that generations of Confucians were to raise about the Chu Hsi school, that is, the existential import of principles as the norms of all that can be. As someone like Wu Ch'eng asks, is principle merely abstract and formal, or is there something living within principle that allows it to be a true moral norm, something alive enough to command attention and respect within the mind-heart? As we shall see, this was a question that came to the fore with a group of brilliant Korean Confucian thinkers during the sixteenth century.

The Ming Transition

The transition to the Ming was a return to Chinese rule in 1368, the formation of a highly successful dynastic polity, and a story of the continuing success and growth of the Confucian tradition. Although he was a great general and a self-educated politician, Chu Yüan-chang, known to history as Ming T'ai-tsu, was also a difficult and often ruthless authoritarian monarch. But he was a clever man and realized that he would need to make use of the Chinese Confucian elite to restore China to the glories of the imperial past. The question was, however, what would be the pattern of restoration and the Confucian contribution to that restoration of Chinese rule?

John Dardess's study of the founding of the Ming dynasty suggests that we must expand our vision of the Confucian elite to include the idea of a profession, a group of people who understand that their own learning allows them to form a special component within society as a whole. This formulation would have struck the Confucians as odd because it smacked of the kind of technical professionalization of the Confucian tradition that they would have found ideologically distasteful. Had not Confucius taught that the scholar was not a utensil to be used as a mere tool for the powerful? Would the formation of a professional status undermine the Confucian desire somehow to remain amateur civil servants? Nonetheless, Dardess's suggestion has a great deal of merit in terms of the sociology of knowledge, not to mention imperial power.

In his perceptive study of the "trouble" with Confucianism, de Bary (1991a) has pointed out that the ability of autocratic rulers to play upon the Confucian conviction that they were not mere utensils for common use precluded the formation of mediating social and political institutions in the Western sense. Mediating institutions are groups such as organized religions, medical guilds, and business corporations that stand between the individual and the government. Dardess's thesis is that the Confucians as a group played this role in traditional China. It was their sense of professionalism that allowed Confucians, in the words of the Quakers, to speak truth to power, often at great risk to them. Although the Confucians did not want to form factions because this would impede their claim to impartiality, their linkages of scholarly friendship and their schools helped to give them a sense that they were not just part of the court aristocracy. The Confucians were a proud and separate guild of educated public intellectuals.

Another interpretation of the relationship of Ming T'ai-tsu and his Confucian advisers is to address the issue raised by Thomas Metzger (1977) in his study of the Confucian "escape from predicament." Metzger began his study of China's political culture by revisiting Max Weber's thesis that Confucianism did not have a transcendent vision that would allow Confucians to effectively critique the government. There was, Weber believed, not enough tension between the notion of what ought to be and the description of what is to give Confucianism a prophetic voice in countering the problems of the age. Of course, Weber had in mind the Protestant Reformations as counterexamples of religious and social movements that provided the emerging middle and professional classes of Europe and England with just such a purchase on reality. Weber theorized that even concerned Confucians lacked a way to escape from the predicament of being compromised by the imperial power that they were to serve and, they hoped, to correct. There was no Confucian version of Weber's inner-world asceticism to help the Confucian in times of trouble.

Metzger's research led him to the conclusion that the Neo-Confucian philosophies of Chu Hsi and Wang Yang-ming provided the Confucians with both a profound sense of the predicament and woes of the world and a suggested way or ways out of the predicament. Or even if one could not escape the problems of the times, the Neo-Confucian path furnished a way to live with integrity. This philosophy ultimately affirmed the possibility of human goodness, but only at the end of a long and arduous path of self-cultivation. Nor was the outcome for any particular Confucian guaranteed to be successful; every Confucian had the image of Confucius himself as a political failure as a reminder and consolation if things did not work out, and sometimes in Ming China, they definitely did not work out. Unlike the gentle Sung rulers, Ming emperors could and did flog their ministers if their advice did not coincide with the opinion of the emperor. Nonetheless, the moral philosophy of Chu Hsi and Wang Yang-ming provided a way to deal with the tension of trying to hold high ideals in a less than perfect world. The Confucians were painfully aware that the mind of the Tao was not always the mind of mortal humanity.

Teachers of the Early Ming

The early Ming scholars were solid if not innovative guardians of the Confucian moral philosophy. But before we go racing on to Wang Yang-ming, we need to pause to review the work of three representative thinkers of the early Ming: Wu Yü-pi (1397–1469), Hu Chü-jen (1434–1484), and Ch'en Hsien-chang (1428–1500).

Our view of the early Ming scholars is now irrevocably shaped by Huang Tsung-hsi's epic history of Confucian thought, *The Records of Ming Scholars*. This grand history of philosophy summarizes the life of each individual and also gives us a brief, and sometimes fairly long, evaluation of his thought. Huang's work became the standard format for recording the words and deeds of the Confucian teachers from the Ming to the Ch'ing dynasty. Like the official imperial histories, later scholars honored and extended Huang's work in chronicling the development of the Confucian Way.

Huang begins by stating that Wu Yü-pi's "learning is not derived from any known master, although he was the first person in Ming times to seek the Way" (Huang 1987:73). This is a rather startling statement by Huang, if for no other reason than because he told the story of Confucian thought in terms of its schools and lineages. Yet there were times, such as during the beginning of the Ming, when worthy scholars such as Wu literally reinvigorated the study of the Way even if they did not have a living teacher. Of course, as Huang shows, Wu did have plenty of texts to study and this was how he was able to search for the Confucian Tao.

It is also important to read Huang's summary of Wu Yü-pi's teachings because it gives a synoptic account of many of the themes that dominated Ming philosophy and spiritual cultivation later on. Huang acknowledges that Wu faithfully transmits the teachings of the Sung masters:

> Speaking of the mind (*hsin*), he regards consciousness (*chih-chueh*) and principle (*li*) as two things. Speaking of the method (of spiritual cultivation) (*kung-fu*), he counsels preserving (mind) and nurturing (nature) in tranquillity and watching over oneself in activity. Hence, only when reverence and righteousness serve as mainstays (for action), when understanding and sincerity advance together (in the mind), could the effort of learning become complete. (Huang 1987:70)

As we have already seen, there is a turn inward in Ming thought that does not precisely mirror the Sung masters, though there were solid reasons for each of Wu's points. Nonetheless, one wonders if Chu Hsi would not have thought this a bit too subjective in spirit and lacking the proper balance of inner cultivation and external observation and study.

One of Wu Yü-pi's disciples, Hu Chü-jen, continued the work of his master by raising another characteristic debating point within Ming Confucian philosophy, namely, the question of its relationship to Buddhism. Hu is of the opinion that although the schools may verbally seem similar, there is nothing fundamentally linking the two traditions. Hu argued against the Buddhists because they "empty the mind, kill the mind, and manipulate the mind" (Huang 1987:78). Hu argued that the Buddhists are truly expert at emptying their minds and achieving states of wondrous clarity of thought, but this is only a mental trick and not what constitutes the real Confucian Way because it does not relate the mind-heart back to principle.

Hu Chü-jen, like his master Wu, lived the life he commended to others, refused to take the civil service examinations, and showed every indication of being perfectly at peace in a life of relative poverty. What Hu sought was wisdom, not the benefits of imperial patronage. Hu believed we really need to cultivate true seriousness in order to recover principle. According to Hu, the mind-heart encompasses all principle but cannot be understood without seriousness because without seriousness we are needlessly distracted both intellectually and materially by the larger world. Only through seriousness can we become intelligent and achieve the clarity of mind necessary to comprehend principle as truth. As with so many other Ming thinkers, Hu's commitment to seriousness as a way to cultivate the mind-heart took precedence over even the extension of knowledge through the examination of things. Hu reversed

Chu Hsi's suggestions about the order of learning itself. Nonetheless, the ultimate goal of reflection is, as for Chu, to seek principle. "The mark of the Confucian is to handle affairs, not by intellectual calculations, but by following the true pattern of Heaven" (Cleary 1991:7). Hu's disagreement with Chu is revealed when he talks about the order of teaching.

> Full knowledge of the true pattern does not have a single starting point, and it is not attained in only one way. Some get it from the books they read. Some get it from lectures. Some get it while thinking and pondering. Some get it while doing things. Though many get it from reading books, to get it from lectures is faster, to get it by thinking and pondering is deeper, and to get it by doing things is the most genuine. (Cleary 1991:5)

There is always a practical edge to the most idealistic Confucian. There is likewise the mark of a persistent realism in affirming that the world and its things are genuine and that Confucians had better find a way to comprehend the grand pattern of it all.

Ch'en Hsien-chang is the third of our early Ming thinkers. Although following in the footsteps of Wu and Hu, he made a mark as a Confucian intellectual with his philosophy of the natural. Like many Ming thinkers, Ch'en began his journey by struggling with Chu Hsi's rigorous curriculum and discovered that it was too much for him. Nonetheless, Ch'en persevered and found a form of enlightenment through reflecting on the mind-heart in great seriousness, uncovering what Jen Yu-wen in his fine study of Ch'en called a mind-heart that "was the master of everything, even of the universe" (Jen 1970:57). After his realization of the goal of mind-heart cultivation, Ch'en's reputation as a teacher grew steadily, and many students came to study with him. Ch'en, in deference to the classics, even included the physical training necessary to become proficient in archery. Like many scholars of his ilk, Ch'en had only marginal success in the standard imperial examination system, even though many friends recognized his talents and sought to find ways to facilitate his entrance into the civil service. Actually, once Ch'en was admitted to the civil service by means of some special examinations, he diligently discharged his assigned duties, as one would expect of such a cultivated gentleman.

Ch'en never broke formally with Chu Hsi's teaching, even if he found Chu to be overintellectual. In contradistinction, as Ch'en said, "My learning is based on the natural" (Jen 1970:64). Ch'en was referring to the return to the natural mind-heart of Mencius, as when the Second Sage urged us neither to forget the mind-heart nor to cultivate it too much. Ch'en also appealed to Ch'eng Hao's ideal of the "intuitive experience of the natural" or *ming-chiao tzu-jan* (Jen 1970:65). Ch'en was somewhat daring in making the natural a central part of his philosophy because this idea was so closely linked to Chuang Tzu's Taoist philosophy. He likened the natural to the cosmic generativity of the Tao. But unlike the Taoists, Ch'en found a great deal of pattern in the natural.

Ch'en Hsien-chang linked his natural principle to a special form of study. He argued that one must emphasize personal experience of principle within a mind that did not rely on too much external study. Nonetheless, principle was not really principle until and unless it was personally realized. As he put it in one of his poems, "Is there any idea not in one's own mind? / Why is it necessary to copy the ancient?" (Jen 1970:74). In order to realize this state of the mind-heart, Ch'en emphasized emptiness and quiescence. By emptiness, Ch'en meant something more like Hsün Tzu's notion that the mind must not be obscured than that it be truly empty of anything at all, which would have moved Ch'en more closely to Buddhist theories of cultivation. The mind-heart, according to Ch'en, must be empty in order to be filled with natural principle rather than mere nothingness. In this regard, Ch'en encouraged his students to practice quiet-sitting as a way to empty the mind-mind heart and make it quiet in order to comprehend principle.

This was a truly joyous teaching according to Ch'en. Once one really gets natural principle for oneself, one experiences the joy of spiritual satisfaction: "The joy of the natural is the real joy" (Jen 1970:83). Ch'en calls this process "self-acquisition": "Scholars today, each boasting of the school he belongs to, do not seek self-acquisition. Even though there may be a great deal of reading and talking, nevertheless they are merely shadows and echoes" (Jen 1970:82). Or as he put in an epigram, "What is nearest at hand is most divine" (Jen 1970:84). Once one has achieved the really natural, the natural principle becomes the true guide for moral conduct and the joyful embrace of life in all its rich details. Nor is it surprising that Ch'en taught that it was possible for a person to achieve a true union with the universe as the end of spiritual cultivation. Echoing Chang Tsai's insight into the unity of life, Ch'en wrote, "Different bodies are all my bone-and-flesh kinsmen / All living creatures are my companions" (Jen 1970:85).

Wang Yang-ming

The story of Wang Yang-ming's (1472–1529) philosophy is also the tale of his life. In no Confucian philosopher is the mixture or texture of the life and the search for wisdom as interwoven with such remarkable results. What started as a youthful investigation of principle became a lifelong engagement with the fundamental mind-heart. Wang was by turns a brilliant poet, philosopher, civil servant, and successful general. He was also the greatest challenger to Chu Hsi in the history of Confucian thought, so much so that later generations separate the history of Neo-Confucianism between Chu's School of Principle and Wang's School of the Mind-heart.

Although both Chu and Wang wrote a great deal on the two concepts of principle and mind-heart, the designations do suggest the profound difference between the two men.

There is a story about how his "wild ardor" for wisdom drove Wang to a passionate and perhaps naive reading of Chu Hsi. The crux of Chu's method was held to reside in the maxim *ko-wu,* or the investigation of things. Wang knew this, but he thought that one must learn what this meant in practice. When he was about twenty, he challenged a friend named Ch'ien to go into a pavilion and investigate the nature of some bamboo growing there. Wang assumed that if he and his friend were sincere enough, patient enough, and sat long enough, they would be able to discover the true principle of the bamboo. Wang reported that his friend spent three full days in front of the bamboo before he gave up. Not to be outdone, Wang wrote, "So I myself proceed to this investigation, working day and night without reaching the principle, until I also fell ill through mental exhaustion on the seventh day. So we lamented that sagehood is unattainable" (Ching 1976:29). One wonders what Wang would have made of the fact that even the high God of Jews and Christians had to rest on the seventh day.

While Wang was continuing his quest for enlightenment, he passed the imperial *chin-shih* examination in 1499 and was assigned a number of official appointments. Because of his fearless nature and love of justice, he tried to intervene in the case of some officials unjustly punished by the palace eunuchs. Wang wrote a memorial denouncing these crimes and was given a humiliating public flogging for his attempt to speak truth to the power of the throne. On top of the flogging, Wang was then banished to the Far South of China, to an area where the Miao tribesmen did not even speak Chinese. His life, which had shown such promise, had all the marks of a complete disaster in full making.

During his exile in the South, Wang was so desperate that he is reported to have fashioned a stone coffin for himself and spent a great deal of time sitting in front of it trying to figure out how things had gone so wrong. This odd form of quiet-sitting seems to have brought him some peace of mind. But one night, in a story of enlightenment that is reminiscent of St. Augustine long ago and in an intellectual tradition worlds apart, it suddenly occurred to Wang that he had been going about the investigation of things completely wrongly. It was revealed to him that he needed to look within the mind-heart rather than to external things for real principles. As Tu Wei-ming told the exciting story, sometime around midnight Wang felt that he heard a voice calling out to him about the method of investigating things: "For the first time Yang-ming came to the realization that 'My own nature is, of course, sufficient for me to attain sagehood. And I have been mistaken in searching for the *li* in external things and affairs' (*shih-wu*)" (Tu 1976:120).

The rest, as the learned rabbis are fond of saying, is commentary. After he thought about this realization, Wang decided that what he had just realized was completely in accord with the record of the sages. Canon and self-realization were in harmony, at least for the moment, and the enlightenment experience launched Wang onto the path of becoming the most important philosopher since Chu Hsi.

The starting point for Wang was the notion of the mind-heart. Wang Yang-ming realized that sagehood was not some distant goal, some object of study and reflection far outside the person, but rather something that could be experienced in the mind-heart and that was in fact located precisely in the person's own mind-heart and nowhere else. Wang also recognized that the form of Ch'eng-Chu philosophy that he had grappled with allowed for the possibility of sagehood for all people but that it was such a difficult task that few, if any, had a real chance of realizing sagehood. If that were the case for the Ch'eng-Chu method, then so much the worse for this method—because rather than promoting Confucian realization, it actually acted as a barrier in that it emphasized an eager and endless scholasticism based on the external reading of texts. The mind-heart and its proper content, Wang believed, were needlessly separated in Ch'eng-Chu orthodoxy.

Wang Yang-ming, not without a genuine and sincere attempt to understand what Chu Hsi really taught, came to his own formulation of the proper way to view the issue of the mind-heart. Wang's thesis was that the mind-heart is really principle, whereas he asserted that Chu Hsi had, however inadvertently, divided the mind-heart from principle; Wang wanted to put them back together, as he believed that was the real teaching of Confucius and Mencius. All principles are in the mind-heart, not outside of it and requiring that they be discovered by the investigation of things. Wang said that "*hsin chi li* (the mind-heart is principle): Is there any affair (*shih*) in the world which is outside (the realm of) *hsin*? Is there any virtue (*li*) which is outside (the realm of) *hsin*?" (Ching 1976:58). But we must not think that Wang was proposing some kind of pure idealism in which all a person had to do was reflect on the mind-heart. Wang wanted to urge us to find the roots of morality within our mind-heart as we go about our daily lives. Hence, we learn how to be filial to our parents by actually being filial to them and cultivate the filial virtues thus manifested in the mind-heart.

Wang's reflections on the centrality of the mind-heart in action in the world introduced him to another key principle, that of the unity of knowledge and action. Wang liked to draw an analogy about gaining moral knowledge from sense experience; once one feels pain, one then knows pain because the experience is immediate. The same thing obtains for moral knowledge; it is only real knowledge when it is immediate and something that happens in action. For Wang, virtue and action are one and the same thing, ontologically and cosmologically unified as values for the person to realize in the mind-heart as the true or fundamental nature of the mind-heart as human nature. As Wang put it, "Knowledge is the direction for action and action is the effort for knowledge" and "knowledge is the beginning of action and action is the completion of knowledge" (Ching 1976:68). As Julia Ching has pointed out, Wang never tired of stressing the unity of knowledge and action in any of his teachings: "Knowledge and action are really two words describing the same one effort. This one effort requires these two words in order to be explained completely. If one sees clearly the essential point of departure, he would know this is only one, and that though (knowledge) and (action) may be described as two activities, they really remain one effort" (Ching 1976:69).

Wang's understanding of the unity of the mind-heart as principle meant that he had to deal directly with Chu Hsi's teaching about the examination of things. Wang was cautious in his criticism, always preferring to argue that what he taught about the examination of things was what Chu really meant, even if Chu's language and the interpretations of Chu's students erred in seeming to imply some kind of cosmological division between principle and the mind-heart. One suspects that Wang was too good a general (and we need to remember that he was actually one of the greatest Confucian military leaders of all times) to give up entirely on some notion of authority beyond mere personal inclination.

Wang Yang-ming, even when arguing for the priority of the realization of principle in the mind-heart, did not dispense with the reading of the classics. But Wang urged his students to return to the classics themselves and not to rely on the later Han, T'ang, and especially Sung commentaries to understand principle. True understanding could only come when the mind-heart was judged to be in conformity with the classics themselves. Each one of the classics seeks to impart some kind of truth if we can but attune ourselves to it: "In using the Six Classics, the gentleman seeks the movements of the *yin* and *yang* of the mind (*hsin*), in order to act according to them by his respect for the Book of Changes" (Ching 1976:95). Similar forms of wisdom and special arts can be found in each of the other classics when viewed with an unobscured mind.

On the whole, Wang's theory of learning revolved around his idea of extending the basic goodness of the person, the famous dictum of *liang-chih*/extending the good. "A scholar who has already determined to become a sage, need merely to extend his *liang-chih*, in its intelligent and conscious aspects, to the uttermost, proceeding gradually day by day. He does not need to worry about externals or details" (Ching 1976:101). In fact, along with the recognition of the pivotal role of the mind-heart—the doctrine of the unity of knowledge and action—the whole teaching of the extending of the good will, or one's knowledge of the good (Ching 1976:105), is another key to Wang's thought. Ching and other Wang scholars have documented that both Wang's political career and philosophy reached a peak from 1519 to early 1521, and it was in this period that he elaborated on the extension of the knowledge of the good.

According to Wang, the mind-heart, when it has extended its moral goodness to the uttermost, becomes what the *Doctrine of the Mean* calls the states of equilibrium and harmony, a balance of the forces that control the human person so that the person is able to realize the good nature. This perfected knowing is the fundamental bedrock of the mind-heart. For Wang, this state of harmony was achieved by tireless action *and* the tranquil awareness that this moral goodness was actually and fundamentally the core of the being. We are able to extend this moral sense because we are simply born with it. The only difference between ordinary people and the sages is that the sages were people who could extend the good in an effortless way; extending the good is more difficult for the rest of us. What we need to do is "extend" this fundamental good nature rather than examine things outside ourselves. Hence, Wang argued that the real examination of things was to be found in this extension of the good rather than in external ruminations. The examination of things was the task of overcoming all selfish desire in order to realize the truth of fundamental goodness.

Wang had a holistic if not monistic view of reality in that he recognized the reality of different events and things in the world. The font of the interpretive problem is Wang's famous Four Sentence teaching that he linked to his maxims about *liang-chih* more and more after 1527. It was the first sentence that caused all the trouble. "The absence of good and evil characterizes the mind-in-itself (*hsin-chih-t'i*)" (Ching 1976:149). The debate was on. Did Wang really mean to teach that the mind-heart was somehow beyond good and evil even in the practical level of mundane affairs? Did this teaching come dangerously close to some kinds of Ch'an Buddhist teachings about nothingness? Or was Wang simply following hallowed Confucian forms of pedagogy in using a complicated teaching for different students? Did the studied ambiguity of the Four Sentence teaching allow Wang to work with different human material in the same way that different classics embodied different icons of virtue? The debate has continued wherever Confucian discourse is considered worthy of attention. Julia Ching concluded her study of this aspect of Wang's thought by suggesting that Wang was a mystic and a philosopher, ultimately a wise man or even a sage. Wang was a thinking mystic who tried to explain what he found in the mind-heart because this mind-heart was expressive of the concern-consciousness of the Tao and hence part of all of us.

Debates with Wang Yang-ming

Of course, just as had been the case with Chu Hsi, not all of Wang's colleagues were convinced by Wang's new and potentially subjectivist theories about the mind-heart. For instance, Chan Jo-shui (1466–1560) sought a middle ground between Chu and Wang. Chan began his own teachings on *hsin* by reminding the reader of the difference between the mind of the Way and the obscure human mind-heart. Nonetheless, Chan, like Wang, did not want to emphasize the distance between the two states of mind too greatly. But Chan showed that he did not mean just what Wang did either.

> The Sage Learning is the learning of the mind-and-heart. What we refer to as "heart" does not one-sidedly point to the square inch within the breast in contradistinction to (objective) things and affairs. Without things and affairs there is no mind-and-heart . . . Wang Yang-ming's and my way of viewing the mind-and-heart differ. What I refer to as the mind-and-heart embodies the myriad things and affairs and leaves nothing out. When Yang-ming refers to the mind-and-heart it indicates what is within the human breast. (de Bary 1989:93)

Chan worried that in his theory, Wang had reduced all dimensions of life to the one point of the mind-heart and that this would end in a kind of truncated monism of *hsin* and a lack of attention to objective scholarly work. Chan was also interested in the role of *ch'i* because he held that the world is *ch'i*: "The world of time and space as a whole is constituted by *ch'i*. The function of mind is to contemplate the order of things in the universe without omitting any item . . . Human nature or human essence is the *form* of thought. Human nature and mind cannot be considered as separate from one another" (Chang 1957–1962:2, 88).

In Chan's "Diagram of Nature and Mind," there are a number of smaller and larger circles that illustrate what Chan takes to be the proper relationship of the mind-heart to human nature and to the wider world. Whereas Chan holds that the mind-heart can penetrate anywhere and everywhere and that diversity exists, he still encloses the diagram with one large, inclusive circle for the mind-heart that shows that there is nothing outside of it. Furthermore, in order for the mind-heart to truly penetrate everywhere, strenuous effort is needed. An excess of tranquillity, Chan argued, would be too much like the Buddhists.

Perhaps the most cogent early critic of Wang yang-ming was Lo Ch'in-shun (1465–1547). Nonetheless, as Irene Bloom (1987) has noted in her study and translation of Lo's *Knowledge Painfully Acquired*, Lo himself believed his paramount task was not really to conduct a dialogue with Wang Yang-ming but to try to undo the problems caused by Confucians incorporating too much Buddhist thought and practice into their own philosophies. As with many other thoughtful Confucian critics of Buddhism, Lo did not focus on surface issues such as the charge that Buddhism was too otherworldly or selfish about individual salvation. Rather, Lo believed that Buddhists were overcommitted to a view of reality as mental and hence developed an epistemological stance that was too subjectivist for Confucian understanding. Lo also included Lu Hsiang-shan and Wang in this, in "that their conception of ethical cultivation, while apparently deep, is yet confined and limited" (Bloom 1987:15).

Where Lo diverges from Wang is in maintaining a place for the study of the classics and nature as part of Confucian self-cultivation. The reason for this is that Lo encouraged a real place for sense experience in his form of study, and this reminds Bloom of Francis Bacon in the early modern West, save for the fact that Lo, like the good Confucian he was, held that he was merely reconfirming the basal Confucian position in attending to the world of sense experience. Lo noted that whereas Chu's method of study might lead to a fragmentation because of its diversity, Wang simply did not spread his net wide enough and had too limited a view of reality: "The oneness of principle (*li*) must always be understood from the standpoint of the diversity of its particularizations before it can be truly and thoroughly perceived" (Bloom 1987:157). Slightly later, Lo takes the Buddhists, and by extension probably Wang, too, to task because Buddhists "regard both phenomena (*shih*) and principle as obstructions and merely wish to eliminate these two obstructions so as to arrive at the ultimate Way. How is it that they do not consider this to be overly general and vague?" (Bloom 1987:157).

Lo kept coming back to a very characteristic theme when he said that "the Way is constituted of principles shared in common by heaven and earth and all things and is not something that I alone possess" (Bloom 1987:160). Although Lo is as concerned as Wang with getting the Way right, one cannot but be struck by how different his approach is. Later Marxist historians of Chinese thought spend a great deal of time worrying about whether Lo can be considered a materialist. Bloom has said that this is a mistaken way to try to categorize Lo and forces Lo's Ming Confucian concerns into a modern pattern that does not do justice to what Lo is about. Lo's interests are empirical and based on sense experience; but what Lo considers empirical and the solid evidence of the senses is far beyond what modern Western philosophy calls material reality. Lo is a good philosopher of *ch'i,* and it should be clear by now that *ch'i* is a more inclusive idea than the modern Western commonsense notion of matter per se. Lo wanted to find a place for all experience and believed that to do less would be to default on the genius of the Confucian Way.

Another way the Confucian scholars of the Ming-Ch'ing period sought to understand the diverse strands of their tradition beyond the comments and dialogues between and among individual scholars was to frame the question in terms of genealogies. As Thomas A. Wilson (1995) has explained in his study of the various theories of tradition in later imperial China, the idea of genealogy has a long history in Chinese thought. Because of the centrality of family and family relations as models for social organization within the Confucian Way, it is not hard to see why this kind of intellectual construction would be appealing to Confucian scholars.

The model suggests that just as with a family genealogy that traces the linkages within a family over time, scholars could also develop intellectual genealogies that would assist students to understand the twists and turns of the development of the Way. However, as Wilson has shown, no such listing of the links along the way is innocent of interpretation. Someone has to decide who is in and who is out. For instance, does Chu Hsi's inclusion of his favorite Northern Sung masters really do justice to the Sung revival as a whole? The formation of this genre of intellectual history allowed Confucian scholars to try to define and then redefine the transmission of the Way.

Turning Toward the Confucian Person

Wang Yang-ming's teachings began a process in the middle and late Ming period that gave rise to a turn to the individual, a turn that is unique in Confucian history. As with all such turns in philosophy, its legacy was controversial both in its own day and in the judgment of historians of philosophy ever since. This turn to the individual was a hotly contested issue even within Wang's own school. There were some who believed that it was pushed to an excess and perverted the master's true intent. But once the genie of the individual was out of the bottle, it was hard to get it back in without a great deal of struggle and examination of what the cultivation of the person meant in such a sophisticated society as that of the late Ming. In fact, it took the fall of a dynasty to dislocate the late Ming experiment with protoindividualism. The chastened Confucians of the early Ch'ing dynasty looked back at the extreme form of this movement, represented by the famous T'ai-chou school, as contributing to the fall of the Ming.

The examination culture, the only formal way to enter official life, spawned and expanded a number of other social institutions. Along with the schools and specialized academies, there was an explosion of growth in the publishing industry. There was a need for all kinds of materials to help the students prepare for examinations. These materials ranged from textbooks on how to prepare and write the examinations to collections of model answers to the formulaic kinds of questions that would be posed at all three levels. And at the other end of the spectrum, there were all the serious scholarly works that provided scholars with the even more detailed information about the various schools and teachings of the ancient and modern masters.

The school most identified with the radical or left-wing tendencies of Wang Yang-ming's thought is known as the T'ai-chou school. It is hard not to be impressed with the thinkers of this school if you share any inclination toward recognizing the fundamental value of the person. In his famous account of Ming thought, Huang Tsung-hsi, himself one of the most famous of late Ming Wang Yang-ming scholars, states the case with classic sharpness in his account of the two founding fathers of the T'ai-chou, Wang Ken and Wang Chi.

> Wang Ken and Wang Chi were frequently dissatisfied with their master's teachings, seeking all the while to unveil more of the Buddha's mysteries and attribute them to the master . . . In Wang Ken's case, many of his disciples could fight the dragon and snake with their bare hands. By the time his teaching passed down to men like Yen Chün and Ho Hsin-yin, it was no longer within the boundaries of Confucian moral philosophy. (Huang 1987:165)

These are harsh but not untypical words of condemnation of the whole T'ai-chou school. What disturbed other Confucians, even other followers of Wang Yang-ming, so much about this school? Dragon fighters who took the message that there are "sages in the streets" to the people in the streets often tended to unsettle the less active of their brethren working in the civil service and private academies.

The most interesting and unconventional of the early T'ai-chou teachers was Wang Ken (1483–1540). He began life as the son of a salt merchant and ended as a Confucian teacher. It was Wang Ken who most vigorously championed the idea that common men could also be sages. Although theoretically this had always been an open possibility within the Confucian tradition, going back as it did to Confucius' own enigmatic statement that he would teach without concern for class distinctions, the actual situation had always been different because Confucians assumed that one needed to master a considerable body of classical literature and that such an education necessitated a great deal of leisure and wealth—at least enough leisure and wealth to put the Confucian ideal beyond the reach of most commoners. Wang Ken challenged all of this in the name of the idealism of the tradition.

Wang Ken was a powerful individual. Based on his early and self-taught readings of the classics, he designed teaching robes based on what he thought he had learned from the *Book of Rites*. Like Confucius before him, Wang Yang-ming should be given credit for recognizing the talent and sincerity of this rather amazing young scholar. Yang-ming acknowledged that Wang Ken was searching for a way to obtain and then teach the Confucian Way. In fact, Wang Ken was already a teacher on his own when he meet Wang Yang-ming. The story of how Wang Ken, in his strange robes, demanded an audience with Yang-ming, already a famous governor and general, is the stuff of legends. Rather than beg to become Yang-ming's student, Wang Ken first debated the master and then and only then accepted that Yang-ming was his teacher. Wang Ken even changed his mind overnight and went back for a second round of debates before the issue was finally resolved in Yang-ming's favor.

Wang Ken, although accepting Yang-ming's teaching about the innate goodness of the fundamental mind-heart, gave a distinctively individualist interpretation to Yang-ming's doctrine. Yang-ming, according to de Bary, stressed the cultivation of a person's moral awareness of *liang-chih*, whereas Wang Ken saw the fundamental mind-heart as "the active center of things" (de Bary 1970:163).

> To make the self secure, one must love and respect the self, and one who does this cannot but love and respect others. If I can love and respect others, others will love and respect me . . . Therefore, if others do not love me, I should realize that it is not particularly because of others' inhumanity but because of my own, and if others do not respect me, it is not particularly that others are disrespectful but that I am. (de Bary 1970:163)

Rarely in the Confucian tradition has so much emphasis been placed on the actions and dispositions of the individual person. Wang Ken drew the conclusion that this kind of great love must move out into the realm of social action and teach its message to all people, not just the elite. Wang Ken found this a remarkably joyful process, and the wonder of it all shines through his simply written sermons and poems. In this regard, Wang Ken, after his work with Yang-ming, stressed that all of this joyful teaching of the sages must be put to the test of the everyday needs of the common people. Nonetheless, Wang Ken's teachings remained quite Confucian in that they focused on the need to renovate the individual and never depended on a complicated system of social reforms as a means of social revolution, even though Wang Ken expressed an egalitarian passion for all human beings.

Among Wang Ken's most famous students of the heroic way was Ho Hsin-yin (1517–1579). Ho had the conviction of his beliefs and was jailed for his views; he died in jail as a martyr to the T'ai-chou dream at the age of sixty-two. In essence, Ho took the message of the person to mean that we must embrace our desires and reject the notion that desirelessness is the best state for the cultivated Confucian. Although many Confucians did not go as far as the Taoists and Buddhists in rejecting human emotions, few would go as far as Ho in celebrating them as the distinctive feature of humanity. One gets the distinct impression that almost alone among Confucians Ho would have appreciated Walt Whitman's poetry.

Ho Hsin-yin put his argument like this: "To love life and love righteousness is to restrict one's desires. But can one reduce and reduce to the point of nothingness and still preserve one's mind-and-heart?" (de Bary 1970:182). The rhetorical flourish is that, of course, one cannot reduce desire and still carry out the Confucian Way because the Confucian Way is a teaching situated in the midst of the common world, the world of desire it-self. In this regard, Ho is broadening the view of the human person even further, deepening it to include not only the active mind-heart as reason but also the passions as well as part of the active nature of true humanity.

One of the ways Ho Hsin-yin sought to carry out his vision for self and society was to focus special attention on the virtue of friendship. The later archindividualist Li Chih (1527–1602) even went as far as to say that Ho had abandoned the first four of the five virtues in order to focus exclusively on friendship. Although this is going too far, Ho was indeed the teacher of friendship as a model for proper Confucian social relationships. This makes a great deal of sense because alone among the five relationships, friendship points to a connection that was not innately hierarchical but was rather based on personal choice and respect. Ho was also one of those rare talents who tried to live his vision to the extent that after having passed some of the preliminary examinations and having then discovered the teachings of Wang Ken, he abandoned any future pursuit of higher examinations and entrance into the civil service.

In Ho Hsin-yin's mind, friendship and teaching go hand in hand. Thus, although Ho may seem extreme in some regards, he is resolutely Confucian in his demand that we must discipline ourselves to learn the Way in the company of good friends and teachers. He taught that "friendship is main-tained by interaction, and the Way and its study is found fully in the inter-action between friends" (Dimberg 1974:86). And slightly later, Ho adds that "the student learns the Way from his teacher and thus is able to com-municate with Heaven and Earth" (Dimberg 1974:87). In Ho's estimation, teaching and studying represent the epitome of humanity's physical nature such that the physical and moral are fused in the comprehension of the Confucian Way: "Sagehood brings the physical being to fulfillment as it brings study to fulfillment. Doesn't the physical being give rise to sagehood as it gives rise to study? (Dimberg 1974:89).

At the Boundaries of the Confucian Way

It is fascinating to see just how far thinkers stimulated by the teachings of the T'ai-chou school went in their search for the individual. As we have seen, and will see in the next chapter on Ch'ing thought, most Confucians believed that they went too far. Two prime examples are found in Li Chih (1527–1602) and Chiao Hung (1540?–1620), albeit in very different modes of thought and action. If there ever was a Confucian who deserved the title of individualist, it was Li Chih, although it is unlikely that Li would have accepted the title of Confucian. As de Bary (1970) has pointed out, Li was repulsed by the thought of having any kind of doctrinal label. The world was too idiosyncratic for Li. Although Li had a classical Confucian education, he rebelled against it and at the end of his life was a very odd kind of Buddhist monk.

The first part of Li's life was conventional. After passing the civil service examinations, he spent over thirty years as an official. But for all these years of service, Li reported that he longed to "hear the Way." It was only when he was about forty that he made his decisive turn to the individual, much influenced by Wang Yang-ming and the T'ai-chou school. It was after this period that he became a "monk," although he was not officially recognized and was much given to scandalous and passionate behavior. It was in this period that he wrote his two most famous works, *A Book to Burn* and *A Book to Hide*. The titles were prophetic because as his views became known, he was criticized for going beyond any possible Confucian, Buddhist, or even Taoist bounds of proper conduct. Li did not seem to care because he was finally trying to hear the Way for himself.

As Li Chih wrote about himself: "His nature was narrow, his manner arrogant, his speech coarse, his mind mad, his conduct rash and imprudent. He did not mix much with others, but in personal contacts could be warm and friendly" (de Bary 1970:193). These are not the typical kinds of claims for the enlightened sage. Li defended his passionate nature, rode it, appreciated it, and lived with it like no one before him. The root of Li's theory was the recurrent Confucian theme that a person's fundamental nature was pure and that one should cultivate it and follow it where it willed. This is what Li would call the "childlike mind-heart." As scholars such as de Bary and others have pointed out, there is a certain convergence in Li's thought with radical Buddhist, Taoist, and Confucian egalitarian sentiments.

True to his Confucian education, Li Chih attempted a complete transvaluation of human relations. Li went even further than Ho Hsin-yin in this, who at least held on passionately to the concept of friendship and sincerity. Li wanted to doubt everything, to question all human relationships. For instance, Li argues that the truly primal human relationship is that of husband and wife as a procreative unit. All other units of society ultimately exist because of the male-female relationship. Another favorite Confucian virtue, that of being concerned for others, was challenged by Li because he believed that a person must be selfish in order to be true to human nature. "What people consider right and wrong can never serve as a standard for me. Never from the start have I taken as right and wrong for myself what the world thinks right and wrong" (de Bary 1970:199). For Li, the very substance and passions of daily life are the Way, and they must be served and satisfied.

But a good Confucian education dies hard. Li Chih devoted a great deal of his time in the massive *A Book to Hide* to a study of history, in order to prove his point about the pivotal role of human passions and selfishness. Although Li takes great pleasure in pointing out how many failures there are in history when Confucians try to live in their moralistic way, Li is still the archmoralist. He believed that he had found a better form, though unorthodox, of morality, one truer to human nature by embracing the passions for all they are worth. If Li is self-centered, he is still pragmatic in arguing that his way will lead to a more fulfilled life. In the end, de Bary surmised that Li Chih is ultimately more a Confucian than anything else, even if he pushes against the boundaries of the tradition. As Li himself put it, the three teachings still converge on Confucianism, for good or ill. In the end, Li was a martyr to his vision of the liberated self.

The second of our boundary pushers, Chiao Hung, took up the idea of the unity of the three teachings, or the doctrine of three teachings and one end, as Chiao put the issue. Like many other Chinese intellectuals before him, Chiao Hung sought a way to study all three of China's great teachings together as a common illumination of the Way. In this he was not alone, joined by other late Ming thinkers such as Lin Chao-en (1517–1598) in arguing that the three teachings can be seen as one, though each philosopher had a different take on what this syncretism signified. Edward Ch'ien (1986) argued the case that Chiao's teaching was a special kind of late Ming syncretism. According to Ch'ien, Chiao did not abandon his Confucianism but rather turned to Taoism and Buddhism in order to shed more light on distinctive Confucian problems, especially the ongoing debate between partisans of Chu Hsi and Wang Yang-ming. Chiao, like so many late Ming Confucians, was seeking to restructure the Confucian tradition and was willing to use whatever useful material he could find to do so.

Chiao Hung argued that Chu Hsi has gone wrong in condemning Ch'an Buddhism because of its extremely rigid view of scholarship and narrow understanding of orthodoxy. Chiao appealed to the *Book of Changes'* notion of broad comprehension as a way to expand the range of the tradition. To paraphrase Whitehead, Chiao wanted to explain the world and not try to explain away anything in it, including the doctrines and practices of Buddhism and Taoism if they could be of use in the search for the Way. In this regard, Chiao Hung believed that the Grand Historian Ssu-ma Ch'ien (d. 110 B.C.E.) was a better model in that Ssu-ma was willing to look at all the classical schools and pick their best points, hence embracing the proper Confucian attitude of broad comprehension.

Chiao Hung is particularly interesting because he holds a pluralistic view of the three traditions. Chiao values each tradition because of their views of the Way but realizes that no one tradition can give us a perfect interpretation of the Way. In this regard, Chiao is a mystic, believing that the Tao is greater than any of our abilities to give it a name. Nonetheless, Ch'ien (1986) argued that Chao still believed that there is an essential unity to the world even if the various teachings represent it in diverse ways. Chiao can be lodged within the Confucian framework because his articulation of the

Way depends on Confucian motifs to bring order to the other teachings, without ever claiming that Confucianism is the only way to explain the world. Armed with his new understanding of intellectual pluralism and the diversity of the three teachings, Chiao Hung undertook a restructuring of the entire tradition. This was shocking to those who held that only the Confucian texts contained the records of the sages.

The Active World of Late Ming Thought

Not all the radical thought of the late Ming was done by the radical wing of Wang's followers. One of the other radical currents, which became more prominent in the Ch'ing period, was statecraft studies. Whereas most Confucian Tao school philosophers worried a great deal about social ethics, personal self-cultivation, and, within T'ai-chou circles, even about the perfection of the individual, other Confucians tried to take a serious look at what might be done at the local, regional, and national levels of government.

Lü K'un (1536–1618) is particularly interesting because he sought not only to work with other scholar-officials but with local people, including women and children. We must never forget that even the most refined Sung moral philosophers, with Chu Hsi as the perfect example, wrote extensively for the less-educated elements of society as well as for their fellow philosophers. They maintained that if the scholar could not be a model for the entire community, then scholarship was in vain. Lü agreed and tried to find ways to make Confucian teachings even more accessible to the common people. Lü sought to do this by crafting local reform. His memorials to the throne included programs for military affairs, studies of plants and fertilizers, and local handicrafts.

Lü argued that "by and large eight or nine out of every ten people are average" (Handlin 1983:114). This meant that one had to devise ways to reach these average people effectively. Along with realizing that this averageness is also the mark of Confucian officials, Lü tried to find ways to reform the bureaucracy. But what is fascinating is that Lü composed various essays for wide dissemination. As Joanna Handlin has noted, "Lü often forsook the classical style for the language of the market place" (1983:143). For instance, he wrote works for women because he believed that education obviously begins at home. This was an argument that the women teachers we will meet next embraced with great passion and logic. If Confucians want more good Confucians, it would not hurt if their mothers, daughters, sisters, and wives were educated Confucian ladies who could share their respect for moral philosophy and culture. There were not only sages in the streets but in the inner quarters, though Lü would probably not have put it this way.

Lü was motivated by a fundamental Confucian conviction about the necessity of reciprocal relationships within society. By expanding this to include the poor and women, he was following the logic of later Ming thought. Lü also illustrates the answer to the question as to why Confucianism had had such a broad appeal in East Asian life for so long. There is a moving story in Lü's biography about how all the local people, men and women alike, followed after him for miles when he was leaving their service as their magistrate. In Confucian terms, Lü was indeed a mother-father official who really cared for the people under his charge; he actually saw them as people who could be educated and who had a role to play in Confucian civil order. Why would some bright young peasant not find inspiration and encouragement from this kind of scholar-official? Lü was just the kind of man who made the Confucian claim that careers ought to be open to talent a reality and not just a platitude.

Women of the Tao

As Dorothy Ko, in her remarkable 1994 study of women teachers in the late Ming titled *Teachers of the Inner Chambers*, has noted, it was only in this period that women were able to break the bonds of silence and print works of their own for general circulation. Although there had always been educated women in China, in the late Ming period women were allowed and sometimes even encouraged to teach and become educated in their own right. Of course, this was not done for purely humane reasons; the educated elite noticed that education improved the marriage chances of their daughters along with the traditional female arts of household management.

It is memorable that we now have some of the women's own voices telling us what they thought about their education. Of course, we can find echoes of similar voices in the past. For instance, Chu Hsi, in writing to a good friend about the death of his friend's wife, told his friend that it was entirely human and proper for him to mourn his wife. Apparently this lady had a fine education and shared many cultural interests with her husband; Chu reminded his friend about how the wife and his friend had enjoyed writing poetry together with friends. Chu gave his friend the assurance that it was normal to grieve such a wonderful spouse, a woman of wit and taste, whom any man would have been lucky to have as a wife. Then Chu returned to talking philosophy; normally, speaking about one's personal life was not a Neo-Confucian convention.

Ko (1994) has provided a definition of these educated Ming women by using a tripartite model that takes into account their own ideals, practice, and self-perception. This is a unique moment in history. Most of what we know about women in Chinese history was written by men; although it is true that some of these men thought well of their brilliant daughters, wives, mothers, and mistresses, it is still not the same as having the women speak for themselves. It was only in the rich urban and commercial culture of the late Ming that women were able to express themselves. And even here, that we have these records is not due to pure virtue; it had more to do with the fact that publishers recognized a market for material written for women by women.

If late Ming men such as the T'ai-chou scholars and the iconoclastic Li Chih were discovering themselves, then so too were Ming women. The interest in individuals and their passions was legitimated in philosophical discourse by a passion for passion. And of course, as in many other cultures, women were viewed as being more interested in the emotions than were men. But when it was possible to write honestly about emotion, women sought to do so in prose and poetry. There were even whole collections of famous women poets published by male editors who extolled the power of these women to express more deeply the emotions of love and devotion than their more constrained and less spontaneous male counterparts. It became clear as women wrote that they could reason as well as express deep emotions.

Women wrote commentaries about material that would not have been considered proper for men. The following story, although it took place in the Ch'ing, illustrates the new role of women as intellectuals. Ko tells the wonderful tale of the famous *Three Wives Commentary* on the famous Ming drama *The Peony Pavilion*, first published in 1589. The story begins with the life of the first wife, Chen Tong (ca. 1650–1665). She was engaged to be married to a noteworthy young scholar, Wu Ren. Chen died before she was actually married to Wu, but through the intervention of Chen's old nurse, Wu was given Chen's commentary on the play. Soon after, Wu remarried another talented young woman, Tan Ze (ca. 1655–1675). Tan also read Chen's commentary and added to it herself. Then Tan, after just three years of marriage, also died.

In 1675, Wu Ren married a third time, and his new wife, Qian Yi, was also devoted to the play and collected and continued the commentaries of her two "older sisters." Qian convinced her husband to publish the material under the name of the three women and even sold her own jewelry to pay for the publication of the commentary. The book was published in 1694 and was "graced by prefaces and afterwords from Hong Sheng's daughter and members of the Banana Garden Club, the most famous women's poetry club in Hangzhou" (Ko 1994:71). Although some men refused to believe that the work was actually written by the three women, Wu Ren always acknowledged their authorship and defended their genius. If people doubted that the women had written the commentaries, so much the worse for men who could not recognize intelligent women.

Chen, Tan, and Qian defended a notion that was also held by the T'ai-chou school, namely, that romantic love and its emotions could become "a noble sentiment that gives meaning to human life" (Ko 1994:84). These young women made use of an avant-garde current in Ming Confucian thinking in order to propose something radical indeed, the notion of a loving, emotional, and even romantic companionate marriage. In one of those odd twists of fate, at the other end of the world the much maligned Puritans in England and America were proposing companionate marriage on the basis of Christian love and charity as well. These Confucian ladies made the point that the fundamental Confucian virtue of reciprocity should obtain in the world of emotion as well as in the realm of reason and civil society. The relationships of the inner chambers, the relationships between men and women, could also embody these high goals and ideals. These women argued, on Confucian grounds, that the search for love, moral and carnal, was an acceptable part of the Confucian Way.

In many cases, the lives of these talented women defied the normal conventions of Confucian society, but that did not seem to bother them very much at all. For instance, Ko tells the story of Huang Yuanjie (ca. 1620–ca. 1669), who managed to destroy every image of convention she could find. For instance, because of her literary genius, she actually supported her family as an artist and author for her whole life. And moreover, she often traveled around the country without her husband, visiting other educated women, including the wives of officials as well as courtesans and even male scholars. In all of this, Huang had the support of her bemused husband, Yang Shigong, who realized that she was more talented and ambitious than he would ever be. It is fascinating to note that other men, including her biographer, came to the defense of her virtue against attacks that she violated all the norms of a respectable woman.

These women were aware of the gender problems inherent in the Confucian tradition from a woman's point of view and attempted ways to reform its shortcomings. For instance, the renowned matriarch Gu Ruopu (1592–ca. 1681) established a poetry club to work with other women in their literary pursuits. Moreover, Gu also sought to create the ideal of the mother-teacher, arguing that girls should be educated to understand the difference between right and wrong so that the ancient Confucian moral standards could be inculcated in the home itself. Gu was a founder of the previously mentioned women's poetry club, the Banana Garden Club. But Gu was no social rebel; she sought to support her lineage as a respected elder and educator. After she was widowed at a young age, she dedicated herself to the education of her sons. In doing so, Gu fell in love with Confucian learning. She read the Four Books and confessed that she often read them far into the night: "I was so delighted that I did not think of getting tired" (Ko 1994:238). Perhaps in Madame Gu, Confucius would finally have found someone who loved learning as much as he did.

Even more beguiling about women's intellectual connections is that educated courtesans were included in the poetry clubs sponsored by the wives of officials. The wives of the senior officials believed that there was nothing wrong with enjoying the company of this other class of educated women. In one case, when questioned about the matter, a senior wife pointed out to her husband, who happened to notice that there were courtesans present at his wife's club, that she and her "respectable" sisters and the courtesans all had the same male clientele. Furthermore, some of these courtesans, such as the famous Liu Rushi (1618–1664), became involved in the loyal yet doomed Ming resistance to the Ch'ing conquest. Liu demanded that her patrons show the Confucian virtue of loyalty to the fallen dynasty. Unfortunately, these experiments in revising gender roles did not continue to gather strength under the new Ch'ing dynasty. But the point that all these educated women made is still valid: Confucian education and virtues, if expanded beyond the social confines of socially constructed gender roles, can become even more universal in application.

Liu Tsung-chou and the End of the Ming

At the end of the Ming, the country was beset by all kinds of internal quarrels between court factions and the emperor. As if these were not problems enough, the country had to spend even more of its precious resources in assisting Korea, a vassal kingdom, in fending off a series of Japanese invasions in the 1590s. And last but not least, there were even a number of major internal insurrections that threatened the empire. In fact, it was one of these internal rebel groups that actually captured Beijing, effectively ending Ming rule and opening a way for the Manchus and their Ch'ing dynasty to march south on the pretext of restoring law and order; the Manchus restored order and then showed no inclination to turn the empire back over to the Chinese. But this is a story for the next chapter.

Huang Tsung-hsi, in his great history of Ming thought, introduced the Tung-lin school, named after its original home academy, with the following words: "Today, when people talk about Tung-lin, they associate the Tung-lin party's political disaster with the fate of the Ming house . . . (After recounting the real teaching and impact of the school, Huang concludes) that a group of teachers and disciples belonging to one academy should give their blood to purify Heaven and Earth and that fools should criticize them in secret is cause for lament!" (Huang 1987:223–224). Not only were the Tung-lin scholars heroes to later Ch'ing thinkers, but even the great modern Confucian scholar Mou Tsung-san argued that the Chi-shan scholar Liu Tsung-chou was really the last and greatest of Ming thinkers in that he preserved the greatness of Confucian moral philosophy in a direct line from Mencius to Ch'eng Hao. Other scholars can be orthodox Confucians according to Mou, but Liu deserved to be placed not only in the mainstream of the transmission of the Tao but as part of the mainline of the mainstream.

Liu Tsung-chou was a harsh and relentless critic of the eunuch-dominated government of his time. Even in the difficult last days of the empire, Liu demanded that the government pay attention to the cultivation of the virtues of its ministers, advice that the emperor regarded as out of touch with the dynamics of rapid dynastic decline. Nonetheless, Liu maintained that only good men could return the Ming to better times. The emperor might want practical advice, but Liu countered that truly practical advice was based on the employment of good men in positions of real power.

Tu Wei-ming's 1993 essay on Liu Tsung-chou identifies Liu's moral anthropology as his signal contribution to late Ming philosophy. Liu is often portrayed as a follower of Wang Yang-ming, but modern scholars all argue that this is much too simplistic. Like all the late Ming thinkers, Liu analyzed the nature of human subjectivity and intersubjectivity as the basis of moral anthropology. Tu has submitted that to understand Liu we must look at his thought in two ways. On the one hand, it is true that Liu was passionately concerned about the individual, and in fact he is known for his dictum of "vigilance in solitude." This vision of the self is predicated on the Mencian belief that a person can indeed become a responsible social agent. But on the other hand, Liu is equally committed to the desire to overcome the selfish tendencies of the mundane individual in order to be in communication with others and to give real service to self and others in society.

The key question for Liu was whether we begin with the will or with knowledge when we seek to cultivate the mind-heart. Liu leaned in the direction of the will, and for this reason, later scholars see Liu as refining and correcting Wang Yang-ming's approach to moral anthropology. But Liu was aware that this is a truly difficult task, namely, the primal cultivation of a good will without any kind of knowledge about what goodness means as we check our subjective feelings against the reality of the world around us. Although Liu agreed that the person is fundamentally good, the process of uncovering and cultivating this fundamental goodness is an endless and difficult task. Liu refused to indulge in any kind of moral relativism. We are human because we must choose between good and evil.

If Wang Yang-ming focused on the perfection of our innate goodness, Liu refined this insight even more as a student of the cultivation of the will as the crucial factor in the perfection of the human mind-heart. Liu suggested that there are really two kinds of willing that we must attend to in moral cultivation. Tu Wei-ming (1993) calls the first form of will "volition" and the second "intention." If we do not make the proper distinction between the two then we will confuse the use of knowledge and willing in seeking the good. For Tu, Liu's insight into the role of the will took the form that "the will, on the other hand, assumes an active role in moral self-cultivation. Primordial knowing, accordingly, functions not as a posterior reflection on the good and evil engendered by the motions of the will; it knows as the will transforms" (Tu 1993:108). This is a kind of intellectual insight into the reality of the world that includes volition, knowledge, and action in a very delicate balance. The will is then what gives life to the whole process and includes the seeds of its own perfection in knowing good from evil.

Liu Tsung-chou provided a reinterpretation of Wang Yang-ming's famous Four Sentence Teaching that illustrates his revision of Wang's thought. This was why Liu was so concerned about solitariness. It is only in the solitary reflection on the movements of the will that we can begin to divine the root of human goodness. We must learn to be watchful of the will in solitude in order to be aware of the moral creativity of the self as an agent of Heaven and Earth. As Tu Wei-ming has noted, solitariness is truly an ontological state of moral being for Liu. In Liu's terminology, solitariness is a dual process: "To transform volitional ideas into the mind (*huanien kuei-hsin*) . . . (and) manifest nature through the mind (*i-shin tso-hsing*)" (Tu 1993:111–112). Hence, Tu argued that for Liu the very root of intention defines the substance of the mind (Tu 1993:112).

Therefore, Liu Tsung-chou suggested that the proper way to read Wang Yang-ming's Four Sentence Teaching was:

> In the movements of the mind, there is good and evil.
> In the tranquillity of the will, there is liking the good and disliking the evil.
> Knowing good and evil is primordial knowing.
> Doing good and eliminating evil is the principle of things. (Tu 1993:108)

Liu rethought the whole question of the nature of the mind-heart, the nature of the will, how we know the will, and what the moral nature of a human being is like. He suggested a method by which the mind-heart can be brought back to the fundamental knowledge of good and evil in terms of its solitary awareness of fundamental goodness. It is impressive that even within the empirical movements of the human mind-heart, Liu isolated the process by which this will itself can become the guide to moral philosophy and life. If this was all Liu did for the tradition, it would have been a signal contribution. But we must remember that someone like Liu believed that he had to live this vision as well as teach it. Liu did just that and gave his life as a token of loyalty to the empire he served, but which did not serve him or others nearly so well.

At the end of the Ming, Liu sought to support the dynasty and moved with it when it fled Beijing and transferred the capital to Nanking. To the bitter end Liu tried to give advice to the falling Ming house, but to no avail. The court refused his advice, and it is even reported that evil ministers sent assassins to try to kill him. The assassins found Liu sitting erect and without fear and "left him in admiration" (Huang 1987:260). But with the fall of the southern capital, Liu wept for the Ming and realized that the dynasty had lost the Mandate of Heaven. At the end, Liu decided that he would flee no more: "I can now say that I am dying without having to die, that I am dying with a proper expectation, and that dying is a closer duty than not dying. Should I now run away, I would only be a fellow who is attached to his own life and fearful of death" (Huang 1987:261). It is reported that this last great Ming philosopher fasted for twenty days and died on July 30, 1645, surrounded by his students, at the age of sixty-eight. Liu's exploration of human morality meant that there were things more important to him than life itself. Along with Socrates in the West, there were philosophers in China who would face death itself because they had heard the true teachings of the Tao and would not abandon it for personal gratification.

6

Korean and Japanese Confucianism and the Ch'ing School of Evidential Research

𝓟RIOR TO THE SIXTEENTH CENTURY any educated Korean, Vietnamese, or Japanese knew about Confucianism as an aspect of Chinese high culture. In an ironic twist of fate, it was the educated Buddhist clergy of Korea and Japan who were the guardians of Confucian lore in their respective countries because they were the transmitters of Chinese culture throughout East Asia. For instance, the Ashikaga Zen school in Japan functioned as a school as well as a monastery, and part of the curriculum for the young nobles was Confucian and Neo-Confucian texts.

In fact, the Koreans were later to claim, with a great measure of justification, that Korea had become the most Confucian country in East Asia. On the other side of the narrow sea, Japan likewise received Confucianism with fervor and creativity, along with a willingness, typical of Japanese intellectuals, to embrace Neo-Confucianism without abandoning the older Shinto and Buddhist affiliations. Although Japan did not become as "Confucianized" as Korea, during the long and successful Tokugawa period Confucianism became the dominant intellectual and philosophical movement and enjoyed official support from the Tokugawa and other regional rulers.

The Rise of Korean Confucianism

James Grayson (1989) and Martina Deuchler have pointed out that the initial transmission of Confucianism to Korea probably took place as early as the first three centuries of the Common Era. As early as 372 C.E., it was reported that there was a Confucian academy in the post-Han dynasty state of Koguryo (Deuchler 1992:14). During the United Silla period, the Koreans established an examination system based on the Confucian classics, even though the major intellectual trends were dominated, as was the case for most of East Asia, by Buddhist philosophical concerns. Korean travelers continued to bring back information about the development of Confucianism to their home country, even if the Confucian Tao did not flourish to the same degree as Buddhism.

Nonetheless, Koreans remained interested in Confucian developments in China before the rise of the Yi dynasty. For instance, An Hyang (1243–1306) accompanied his prince on the visit to the Mongol court in Peking and returned to promote Chu Hsi's Neo-Confucianism in a number of offices back in Korea. Later in the Yüan dynasty, it is reported that Koreans passed the Chinese civil service examinations, indicating that they had not only mastered classical Chinese but also Chu Hsi's commentarial tradition as well. Such occasional contacts between Korean scholars visiting the Chinese court continued during the Ming dynasty, and these visits helped to cultivate the Korean taste for Chu Hsi's philosophy. As Deuchler (1992) has noted, these various Korean Confucian scholars worked to reform the educational system, and this allowed them to pave the way for further scholarly endeavors.

Although it is difficult to ascertain the precise nature of early Korean Confucian studies, the Chu Hsi school was dominant from the beginning of the Korean reception of Neo-Confucianism. Choi Min-hung wrote that the "Yi dynasty Neo-Confucianism was directed towards two objects: the reverence for and cultivation of man's nature . . . and the investigation of truth"(Choi 1980:15). These are certainly themes central to the Chu Hsi tradition. The focus on the cultivation of human nature, of course, is common and even central to Wang Yang-ming's tradition as well, even if the Koreans choose to follow Chu Hsi in these matters.

In 1392, General Yi Songgye (1335–1408, r. 1392–1398) decided, after having seen the establishment of the new Ming dynasty, to found a new dynasty. Although General Yi was no scholar himself, he made use of a coterie of young Confucian scholars to assist in the founding of his new dynastic house. Principal among these men was Chong Tojon (1342–1398). Joining in the task of helping Chong to advise General Yi on the formation of a Confucian state ideology were Cho Chun (1346–1405), Ha Yung (1347–1416) and Kwon Kun (1352–1409).

Chung Chai-Sik (de Bary and Haboush 1985:75–80) identifies a characteristic feature of the early Yi Confucian reformers: They installed a version of Chu Hsi's synthesis as orthodoxy by means of reorganizing the state and education, by providing a new set of social rituals modeled on Chu Hsi's ritual reforms of the family, and through an apologetic attack on Taoism and Buddhism. Chong Tojon believed that such a refutation of Buddhism was a precondition for the successful imposition of Confucian norms on Korean society. The young Confucian reformers were living and working in a society that was still dominated by a strong network of Buddhist institutions. The Confucian apologetic was delegated the double duty of reducing Buddhist influence on the older aristocracy and providing both a Confucian basis for the new state and an educational system to cultivate proper Confucian scholarship and practice.

Chong Tojon was the political leader of the group, but the main philosophical adviser to the new king was Kwon Kun (1352–1409), a slightly younger and more aristocratic Confucian scholar. As was typical of the early Korean Neo-Confucians, he mixed together a combination of anti-Buddhist apologetics with the propagation of Chu Hsi's thought as well as studies of ritual texts. In fact, Kwon's work on the *Book of Rites* and his revised edition of Chu Hsi's famous *Chu-tzu Chia-li,* or *Master Chu's Family Rituals,* were the first of their kind and set the standard for the rest of the dynastic period. Kwon took the general position that although there was something of worth in Buddhism and Taoism as well, the best manifestation of the true way was found in Confucian teaching.

Stimulated by reading Chou Tun-i's *Diagram of the Supreme Ultimate Explained* as well as Chu Hsi's commentary on it, Kwon Kun, as early as 1390, developed his own cosmological diagram and commentary to help his students comprehend the Sung vision of reality. According to Michael Kalton's interpretation of the text, it is a clever melding of Chou's cosmological concerns with the vocabulary and style of the *Doctrine of the Mean*'s moral psychology. The genius of the work is not in a novel interpretation of Chu's thought but in its faithful representation of this new form of Confucian discourse for an expanding Korean audience. From a philosophical point of view based on the *Mencius* and the *Doctrine of the Mean,* Kwon separated the Four Beginnings of the emotions from the Seven Emotions themselves, implying a rather strict form of dualism for moral anthropology. In this model, the Four Beginnings are interpreted as principle, whereas the Seven Emotions are simply identified with *ch'i*/matter-energy. The question of the relationship of the emotions to the life of principle became immortalized in the Four-Seven Debate in the sixteenth century between Yi T'oegye and Yi Yulgok.

However, the true glory of the Korean Confucian traditions fully flowered in the sixteenth century. As many scholars of Korean Confucianism have noted, the fifteenth century was a period of consolidation of the new Yi dynasty and its Confucian ideology. As Kalton (1988:10) has written, "Neo-Confucian energies in Korea were devoted mainly to the transformation of government and social institutions." In a remarkable transformation, Korea became a model Confucian society. It is no exaggeration to say that in the sixteenth century the most innovative Confucian philosophy in the Chu Hsi tradition was being written in Korea. Leading the way, of course, was the great Yi T'oegye.

Yi T'oegye (1501–1570)

Yi T'oegye (1501–1570) has long been considered Korea's preeminent Confucian philosopher. T'oegye was deemed one of those rare thinkers who had the ability to expand on the work of his Chinese master Chu Hsi. In this case the kudos awarded T'oegye are not an exaggeration, given his contribution of the global Confucian Way and its particular flowering in Korea. From a philosophical point of view, T'oegye is important because of his refinement of Chu's synthesis and because of his celebrated discussion of what is called the Four-Seven Debate on the nature of the emotions and principle. The Four-Seven Debate is the most extended, systematic, coherent, and famous debate in the entire history of the Confucian tradition. We shall return to it after we have first reviewed T'oegye's philosophical deposition.

The presenting problem for T'oegye was this: If we take Chu Hsi's statements about the analytic or rational nature of principle with utter seriousness, then it is not very far logically from a kind of metasystemic dualism. At least in theory the dual origins were principle and matter-energy. Of course, many scholars argued that Chu Hsi went even further toward an ontological dualism by suggesting that principle is really the primordial source and is prior to matter-energy. Notwithstanding the fact that Chu Hsi himself never tired of showing how principle and matter-energy are everywhere and always one, there was a suspicion that even if this is what Chu Hsi thought, the very logic of his own system inexorably pointed to the priority of principle as the font of reality.

The question of dualism or monism was the philosophical background of the Four-Seven Debate. As we shall see, this debate was actually a series of philosophical conversations beginning in 1559 and ending in 1566 between T'oegye and the younger scholar Ki Kobong (1529–1592). There was a second stage to the discussion, initiated between Yi Yulgok (1536–1584) in 1572 with Song Ugye (1535–1598), which generated another ten letters concerning the nature of the emotions and their principles. The whole quality of intellectual civility that pervades the letters is remarkable. Although each man defended his position with passion and wit, all the participants recognized that they were engaging in a corporate Confucian search for the truth and treated each other with genuine respect. If ever there was a case of the manifestation of Confucian theory and praxis in debate, this is it.

The source of the argument resided in the interpretation of a passage from Mencius about the Four Beginnings, or seeds of morality. Mencius held that these four seeds are the foundations of our basic morality. Later, the *Doctrine of the Mean* raises the same issue in terms of what are called the Seven Emotions, not a term used in the *Mencius*. The *Doctrine of the Mean* states that we have a state of moral incipience called the state of equilibrium. But once our emotions have been stirred by contact with the world, we develop, rather spontaneously, the Seven Emotions. These Seven Emotions are in need of careful tending in order to achieve the state of harmony proper for the aroused emotions. Hence, the argument is that there is a state of prior equilibrium and then a state of emotional harmony, if and only if the emotions are correctly cultivated. The relationship between the two sets of "emotions" was the problem that perplexed the Korean Confucians.

Yet another way Chu Hsi approached the question of the emotions needs to be added to the puzzle. In talking about the mind-heart, Chu taught that the mind-heart was to be found either in the *wei-fa,* or unmanifested mind-heart, prior to contact with things or in the *i-fa,* or the manifested state after contact with the object-events of the world. Chu pointed out that the unmanifested mind-heart represents pristine human nature, whereas the manifested mind-heart is the *yung*/stimulated function of the mind-heart. With all these varying traits to work with, the Korean Four-Seven Debate tried to discover the philosophical issues behind the problem as it had been bequeathed to them by Chu Hsi.

The crux of the puzzle for the Korean scholars was this: "If both the Four Beginnings and the Seven Emotions are basic human feelings, why make *any distinction* between them, using two different names?" (Edward Chung 1995:49). Is there some kind of meaningful, perhaps even ontological, distinction to be made between these two ways of looking at emotions? Or, if human nature is one, as Chu seemed to teach, then how are these two different manifestations to be understood as one and yet separate? Or does this difference imply, however unintended, that the fundamental Mencian claim that human nature is good is a flawed or inaccurate theory of human nature? According to Edward Chung, "The question was, If the mind is ontologically one, how can it be discussed in term (sic) of what Chu Hsi calls the *moral mind* . . . and the *human mind*? (Edward Chung 1995:52).

The debate began with Kobong denying any dualistic rationale to be found in the distinction between the Four and Seven. T'oegye agreed with Kobong's thesis that Chu never intended any kind of radical or even mild dualism to arise from his theory of the linkage of principle and matter-energy in the unmanifested/manifested nature of the emotions. It is absolutely fascinating to watch the debate unfold with precision and candor. However, we need to attend to the underlying philosophical issue about the true nature of principle because this is the place wherein T'oegye provides us with a vision of a living, active principle and hence a defense of Chu Hsi's thought as something more than a rationalistic quasidualism.

Chung has summarized the living quality of principle for T'oegye with the following astute observation:

> For him, human nature, as principle, has to be an *active,* not passive, thing capable of manifesting itself in self-cultivation. Unlike Chu Hsi who emphasized

the rationalistic "investigation of principles," he has a stronger tendency for the *self-realization* of principle. And his conviction was to take principle as the ultimate foundation of the Neo-Confucian learning for sagehood. (Edward Chung 1995:124)

As with his Ming Chinese compatriots, T'oegye also made a turn from a rationalistic reading of Chu Hsi toward a reading focused on cultivation that embraced Chu's basic insights but inscribed them in terms of the cultivation of the mind-heart. But what makes T'oegye so interesting is that he does so without abandoning Chu Hsi's basic philosophical stance on the centrality of principle for something like Wang Yang-ming's position. In this sense, T'oegye developed his own school of the mind-heart without giving up on the notion of principle as essential to understanding the complex human emotional manifestation within the matrix of matter-energy.

Yi Yulgok (1536–1584)

The younger of the two great pillars of Korean Confucianism was born into an elite family and enjoyed not only a life crowned with academic success but is also remembered as an influential reformer of governmental institutions. He had a chance, when he was twenty-two, to meet T'oegye, by then the most respected of scholars. Although he had deep respect for the older man, Yulgok was uneasy about T'oegye's reformulation of Chu Hsi's thought and sought in his own work to provide an alternative interpretation. It was in 1572 that Yulgok, then thirty-six, recommenced the Four-Seven Debate with his friend Song Ugye (1535–1589). In the second round of the debate, ten long letters were generated. T'oegye focused his attention on devising a new interpretation of a living principle, but Yulgok is remembered for being more concerned with a renewed theory of the role of matter-energy.

According to Young-Chan Ro, what bothered Yulgok about T'oegye's work was that it appeared to embrace the dualistic tendencies that have always lurked around Chu Hsi's theory of principle and matter-energy. Yulgok sought "to overcome a dualistic system of thought without falling into an absolute monism" (Ro 1989:xiii). Yulgok tried to keep this balance by reanalyzing the cosmological aspects of the Sung philosophers and Chu Hsi's fundamental ontology, and through a revalorization of the notion of *ch'eng*/sincerity as the linchpin, he tried to hold all of these contending forces together without their becoming either monistic or dualistic in orientation.

The first move Yulgok made was to refocus on the cosmological aspects of the *t'ai-chi*/Supreme Ultimate that Chu Hsi used to designate the ontological and axiological status of the world. Yulgok indicated that the true nature of the Supreme Ultimate was to act as the "spirit" of the world, in the sense that it was the function of creativity in the ceaseless production of the myriad things. It is spiritual in the sense that its functions as creativity are beyond the ability of human cognition to fully comprehend. Of course, the Supreme Ultimate acts through the agencies of yin-yang and the Five Phases.

> The myriad things are one; (this one is) the Five Forces and the Five Forces are one; (this one is) *yin* and *yang*, and *yin* and *yang* are one; (this one is) *T'ai-chi*. *T'ai-chi* is nothing but a name that we are forced to name it. Its substance (*t'i*) is change (*I*), its principle (*li*) is called the way (*tao*), its function (*yung*) is called spirit (*shen*). (Ro 1989:30)

Yulgok argued that principle as the Supreme Ultimate was one but that it was manifested in diversity because of the nature of matter-energy as dynamic generativity: "The original essence of *i* (Chinese *li*) is one; however, when it flows and circulates, its particularizations are diverse. It is wrong to seek for the original *I* only while neglecting the *i* that flows and circulates" (Edward Chung 1995:110). Actually, Yulgok formulated his own teaching about the relationship of principle and matter-energy in a formula in which "*i* is penetrating and *ki* (Chinese *ch'i*) is limited" (Edward Chung 1995:114). Yulgok went on to explain that principle is penetrating because it is without limit, without a beginning or an end because of its ideal nature as expressed as the Supreme Ultimate. Matter-energy is limited because it is always involved in physical form. "*Ki* (Chinese *ch'i*) already involved its physical form and traces; therefore, it has beginning and end, priority and posteriority" (Edward Chung 1995:114). For Yulgok, principle represents the transcendent element of ceaseless creativity, whereas matter-energy implies the constant particularization of this creativity.

In order to show how this unity can be understood as a moral epistemology, Yulgok turned to the concept of *ch'eng* or sincerity. He began by noting that Confucian epistemology begins with the examination of things in order to arrive at a true knowledge of the various object-events: "If we talk about the principle of things, its means *wu-ko* (ed., to examine things); if we talk about our minds, it means *chih-chih* (ed., extension of knowledge)" (Ro 1989:85). Only when a person has made a thorough (*ch'iung*) effort to understand the principles does the person come to a true knowledge of the things themselves, and this, Ro noted, indicates that Yulgok believed in the "unity of subject and object" (Ro 1989:85). Hence, sincerity in Yulgok's view is not only an epistemological stance but also the very nature of the human condition qua moral effort. And because human life is relational, only a relational icon like sincerity can be employed to show all the interconnections of heaven, earth, and humanity that are crucial to Confucian discourse. Ro has summarized Yulgok's thesis in this fashion:

But the concept of *ch'eng* also contains an imperative, for it states that only one particular relationship between humanity and the cosmos is in fact fully good and harmonious, and it pictures humanity and the cosmos as involved in a process of mutual self-perfection leading towards the establishment of this ideal relationship, its *ch'eng*, as the agency of the realization. (Ro 1989:94)

Before closing, it is important to note just how effective these Confucian scholars were in transforming Korean society. For instance, the Koreans were more scrupulous in using Chu Hsi's *Family Ritual* as the basis for marriage and other ceremonies than were the Chinese. Although intellectual fashions change from generation to generation, it is a rare philosophy that can convince a whole society to change its patterns of birth, life, marriage, and death.

Japanese Confucianism: The Tokugawa Achievement

As one would expect, the Japanese appropriated the Confucian Way in ways unique to their distinctive history. Although Confucianism had a long history in Japan prior to the rise of Tokugawa rule in 1600, it is incontestable that the golden age of Japanese Confucianism coincides with the rise of the Tokugawa Bakufu in the seventeenth century. The Tokugawa shoguns made explicit use of Confucianism in order to craft their official ideology. But unlike in Korea where the Yi dynasty scholars set out to make Korea a Confucian state, the Japanese were selective in what they appropriated from the Confucian tradition in East Asia.

Along with the military victory, the Tokugawa founders also needed a way to establish a new moral order for the shogunate. The shoguns realized that even if they conquered by the sword, they would need to rule by the writing brush and the arts of civilization. Ieyasu, though famous for being clumsy in the traditional cultural skills of Japan, understood the need for a cultural as well as military revolution. The new Tokugawa leaders needed a composite ideology that built on all the cultural capital of the country.

Oddly enough, because of the lack of a formal examination system in Japan, the decoupling of formal careers from education allowed for a freer kind of Confucian study in Japan than in Korea or Ming-Ch'ing China. Japanese Confucians were free to follow their studies wherever their interests took them. Another major difference between China and Japan was the fact that many great Confucian scholars were also interested in preserving their own Shinto traditions as well. It might have been suspect, after Chu Hsi, for a Chinese Confucian to be a Buddhist, but there was nothing strange at all for a great Japanese Confucian like Yamazaki Ansai (1618–1682) to try to combine a strict Chu Hsian Confucian worldview with Shinto spirituality. And last but not least, unlike in Korea, many

Japanese scholars, lead by Nakae Toju (1608–1648), were interested in Wang Yang-ming's thought. All in all, Japanese Confucianism was a variegated and fascinating mix.

In order to bring out the unique character of the Japanese Confucian experience, I will stress three aspects of these traditions: (1) the formation of the Tokugawa state ideology, (2) the orthodox and unorthodox scholarly work on received Chinese and Korean models, and (3) nonelite forms of Confucian discourse.

The Formation of the Tokugawa State Ideology

Yamazaki Ansai. If Hayashi Razan (1583–1657) was the founding father of the new Tokugawa Confucian world, Yamazaki Ansai (1618–1682) was the greatest Chu Hsi scholar of his generation. As Masao Maruyama wrote, "Ansai has religious reverence for Chu Hsi philosophy. 'If a person errs by studying Chu Hsi . . . he errs with Chu Hsi. He has nothing to regret'" (Maruyama 1974:37). Yet, as we shall see, Ansai continued an interest in fusing Chu Hsi's thought with a reconstructed Shinto—hardly something that Chu Hsi would have approved of. Nonetheless, it was Ansai who, in Herman Ooms's words, "was transforming Shinto into a powerful and lasting political doctrine" (1985:195). But Ansai's willingness to conjoin a Chu Hsi style Confucianism with his version of Shinto did not extend to an equal recognition of the virtues of Buddhism. Ansai's first major work was entitled *Heresies Refuted* and marked his strong distaste for what he claimed were all the social and theoretical ills of Buddhism. Along with a denunciation of Buddhism, *Heresies Refuted* revealed an excellent working knowledge of Chu Hsi's thought.

Ansai's task centered on a Neo-Confucian interpretation of Japanese history. If the Sung Confucians could find something of the Way in the study of Chinese history, Ansai reckoned that he could do the same with Japanese history by writing the monumental though unfinished *A Mirror of Japan.* Nonetheless, this veneration of history as a Confucian truth did make Ansai come to terms with the impact of Shinto on Japanese history. In short, Ansai came to believe that the way of Confucius and the way of the founding Shinto deities were one and the same teaching.

Ansai drew from his Shinto studies the elevation of the notion of loyalty as a key theme for Japanese Confucianism. Although his Neo-Confucian studies dealt with the standard Confucian themes of the Way and humaneness, Ansai shaped a Japanese ethos wherein loyalty was considered a dominant virtue. And why should this surprise us, given the nature of Japanese political institutions based on the loyalty of the retainer to his feudal lord? For Ansai, the true Confucian Way was "unswerving loyalty and selflessness, guarded by an ever-vigilant mind" (Ooms 1985:233). In order to prove his points, Ansai wrote a *Japanese Elementary Learning* to show how the true Way was embodied in the Japanese Shinto founding myths, including unreserved loyalty to the imperial system and feudal order. It would never have occurred to the Japanese Confucians that loyalty and *jen* were not intimately related.

Nakae Toju.   Although followers of Chu Hsi persistently claimed to be the guardians of orthodox Confucianism, this claim was no more universally accepted in Japan than it was in China. Even if Razan and Ansai said it was true, scholars such as Nakae Toju (1608–1648) defended Wang Yang-ming's claim to respectability within the unfolding of the Confucian Way. Quite typically, Toju began his career as a Chu Hsi scholar who received his introduction to Neo-Confucian thought from a Zen monk. As Toju himself confessed, even fairly early he harbored some doubts about Chu's thought but had no way to find a purchase for his hesitations from within the Chu Hsi school itself. It was only after he gained access to the *Hsing-li hui-t'ung* of Chung Jen-chieh, published in 1634 in China, that Toju was introduced to alternative thinkers such as Wang Yang-ming. Toju was intrigued by the Wang school as a form of Confucian discourse that clearly had a more re- ligious tone than he was accustomed to finding in Chu Hsi's thought. Furthermore, as Yamashita Ryuji noted, "This kind of religious philosophy existed on a fairly broad front in the late Ming as a theistic mysticism or anti-rationalism which stood in opposition to the rationalism of the Chu Hsi school" (Yamashita 1979:314).

This religious dimension of Wang Yang-ming's thought, as Toju inter- preted it, not only allowed the rulers to worship Heaven but allowed the literati and even the common people to reverence High Heaven. It was ac- tually through Wang's disciple Wang Chi that Toju became aware of a pro- foundly religious way to understand matter-energy as the way of Heaven. In short, Toju came to believe that "the August High Lord of the Supreme Vacuity is the great ancestor of the human race" (Yamashita 1979:320). And like his later Ming colleagues in China, Toju thought well of Buddhists, Taoists, and Shintoists because they were all subjects of the August High Lord—this was Toju's version of the unity of all religious teaching.

Toju's thought found a special place for filial piety as a cosmic virtue with a sweeping religious dimension. Robert Bellah has gone as far as to say that Toju develops a theology of filial piety based on his understanding of the unity of knowledge and action:

If we seek for the origin of things we find that, as our bodies are divided from our parents, but still are one with them, so are their bodies divided from the spirit of heaven and earth, and the spirit of heaven and earth is the offspring of the universe; thus my body is one with the universe and the gods. Clearly perceiving this truth and acting in accordance with it is obedience to the way. (Bellah 1957:79–80)

Kaibara Ekken. In the next generation of Tokugawa thinkers, the brilliant Kaibara Ekken (1630–1714) continued this Japanese fascination with the religious and empirical side of Confucian thought. Like so many other Japanese Confucians, Ekken was a true Renaissance man, a scholar interested in the whole range of topics and not just traditional Confucian studies. For instance, his commitment to the practical side of Confucianism allowed him to write important studies on farming and botany as well as to frame a new cosmological vision based on both Chu Hsi and Wang Yang-ming. Mary Evelyn Tucker's 1989 study of Ekken includes reproductions of illustrations of Ekken's studies of plants, fish, and shellfish.

Rather like Chang Tsai in the Northern Sung, Ekken moved from filial piety for his own family outward to the whole world. Tucker has suggested that "Ekken's thought may best be summarized as a religious humanism based on a vitalistic naturalism that found expression in practical empiricism" (1989:123). In order to deal with all of his varied interests, Ekken focused his work on three main areas: traditional Neo-Confucian metaphysics; ethics and spirituality; and practical, empirical learning. Or as Ekken put it, "If we constantly appreciate this varied beauty of creation, our spirit of harmony will be ceaseless by expanding our mind-and-heart, purifying our emotions, cultivating a moral sense, enkindling joy, and washing away all regrets from our heart" (Tucker 1989:125).

Another fascinating feature of Ekken's thought is that he often wrote in colloquial Japanese and not classical Chinese. The reason for this was simple, and very much in tune with Chu Hsi's original intent, namely, to teach as many people as possible. Ekken knew that most Japanese could not read the difficult classical Chinese, so he wrote his famous *Precepts for Daily Life in Japan* "in contemporary language about the principles that have been received from ages past" (Tucker 1989:135). In this summary of Confucian principles, Ekken sought to present a straightforward account of the tradition as he understood it. He began by teaching that "the sages taught in the *Book of History* that heaven and earth are the parents of all things and that human beings are the spirit of the universe" (Tucker 1989:136).

Ekken immediately drew a number of conclusions from his first premise: "The principle of humaneness makes it a virtue to show kindness toward human beings and compassion for all things" (Tucker 1989:138). For Ekken, there is a kindness that comes from the parenting activity of human beings. In fact, there is a limitless quality to the kindness of heaven and earth that obligates all people to do the best they can as ethical agents: "Since humans have heaven and earth as their great parents, just as they receive the kindness of their own parents, so they receive the limitless kindness of heaven and earth" (Tucker 1989:139). The sense of obligation and duty is palpable in Ekken's thought, but this is not the cause of grief or guilt because human beings have the means to repay this cosmic debt of gratitude.

The reason that people can repay their filial debt is that human beings are fundamentally good, even if they fall away from this goodness because of confused desire, emotion, and misguided self-interest "The nature of all people is good and, based on this fact, they can be induced to activate their innate goodness" (Tucker 1989:146). Ekken is under no illusion, however, that this is an easy task. We are clearly not all born sages, and we must make a great effort to find good teachers, practices, and doctrines that will assist us in returning to our originally good nature. In fact, this is why Ekken wrote a book like the *Precepts*—in order to provide just the proper kind of repetitive and organized Confucian instruction for the good. According to Ekken, there are many ways to learn. Of course, there is the study of texts, and good Chu Hsi scholar that he was, Ekken did not disparage textual work. But for Ekken the whole of creation was a text waiting to be read correctly in an empirical fashion: "The Way of heaven and earth is the root and source of the Human Way, and unless we know the Way of heaven and earth we will not understand the root from which truth emerges" (Tucker 1989:147).

According to Ekken, "There are two essentials for learning. When we still do not know, we should seek to know, and if we already know we should practice it. If we do not know it is difficult to act. If we know but do not practice, it is the same as not understanding, which makes it useless" (Tucker 1989:164). As with all Confucians, Ekken believed that teaching should end in practice, and in his case, a socially useful kind of practice includes good farming as well as comprehension of the key Confucian ethical duties. One of the keys to Ekken's theories about education is his contrast between what we know and what we do not know and the doubt that we must always have, in humility, when confronted with our lack of true knowledge.

Ekken was, like Descartes, famous for his principle of using doubt as a method to increase our actual knowledge of the world: "After one studies one has doubts, after one doubts one has questions, after one questions one can think, after one thinks one can understand" (Tucker 1989:76). Many of Ekken's own doubts arose as he pondered Chu Hsi's teachings about the relationship of principle and matter-energy. Ekken understood that Chu Hsi was not a simplistic dualist; however, it did seem to Ekken that Chu Hsi often spoke as if there was a priority to principle over matter-energy. In fact, after having read Lo Ch'in-shun's *Knowledge Painfully Acquired,* Ekken basically agreed with Lo's revision of Chu's thought in the direction of what had come to be called a monism of *ch'i.*

The way Ekken defended his rereading of Chu Hsi was to argue that the Supreme Ultimate was merely the name of primordial matter-energy before it was divided into yin and yang. Rather like God's presence brooding over the waters of creation, the Supreme Ultimate was not some kind of abstract principle but a living energy bent on the ceaseless creativity of the Way: "It flows through the seasons and never stops. It is the root of all transformations and it is the place from which all things emerge; it is the origin of all that is received from heaven" (Tucker 1989:78). The reason that Ekken reversed Chu's reading of the Supreme Ultimate as principle is that he wanted to sustain the unity of a creative cosmos in which the dynamic nature of reality is really the hermeneutic key needed to read things correctly: "The 'Way of the sage' is the principle of life and growth of heaven and earth; the original ch'i harmonizing the yin and yang is ceaseless fecundity" (Tucker 1989:81).

Ekken's theory of the primacy of matter-energy has implications for other parts of his system. For instance, Ekken taught that "there is no distinction between an ideal nature and a physical nature" (Tucker 1989:82). In this regard, Ekken was willing to argue with Chang Tsai, Ch'eng I, and Chu Hsi about the nature of human nature. Because of the unity of matter-energy, there was no ultimate separation to be found between the original nature of something and its manifested characteristics as an object-event. Ekken therefore argued that sincerity was the necessary tool for correcting our potential and actual faults. We cannot merely be serious about our nature, but we must try to carry out the practice of sincerity as outlined in the *Doctrine of the Mean*. What we need as human beings is the ability to sincerely identify with other people and the whole creation as our companions on the Way. Ekken was moving toward a truly ecological vision of the Confucian cosmos.

Teaching the Secular World

In many ways the Japanese Confucians were highly successful in finding ways to teach the Confucian Way to the common people, even the much-despised merchant classes. In fact, if we consider the Japanese case for a moment, there was a pressing need to find new pedagogies for people beyond the feudal lords and their samurai retainers. The paradoxical reason for the spread of Confucianism in Japanese society was the very strength of its class structure.

Even in spite of the official theory that denied elevated social standing to anyone but the samurai, there were merchant Confucians, and their story is unique in the annals of Confucian history. Just as the great feudal lords established their own Confucian academies to instruct their retainers and civil servants in Chinese administrative and philosophical lore, so too did some great merchant houses found their own version of Confucian academies. Tetsuo Najita (1987) has chronicled the rise of just such a house in *Visions of Virtue in Tokugawa Japan: The Kaitokudo Merchant Academy of Osaka.* In this rich study of Tokugawa society, Najita tells the history of a great merchant academy in Osaka, the commercial center of Tokugawa Japan. The Kaitokudo's greatest success came during the eighteenth century. With the end of the Tokugawa, which had chartered the academy, the school ended formal instruction. However, in the nineteenth century, after the beginning of Japan's successful modernization, many great merchant houses, such as Sumitomo, raised funds to rebuild the academy in order to honor the memory of the Japanese Confucian commercial past. This Meiji building was destroyed during World War II, although there is still a plaque on the side of a giant modern office building today in Osaka memorializing the Kaitokudo.

The scholars at the Kaitokudo framed their position in terms of a major debate in Japanese Confucian circles. It is known as the controversy between a philosophy of nature and norms of history. As with all such culturally coded jargon, this debate needs some unpacking. From the viewpoint of the Kaitokudo scholars, the person they were responding to was the famous classical scholar Ogyu Sorai (1666–1728). Sorai was famous for developing a full-blown historical reading of the Confucian tradition. This historicist understanding of the tradition was not just a way to chronicle the past, something important to all Confucians, but a radical new epistemological stance aimed at the heart of Sung moral metaphysics. As we shall see, the Kaitokudo scholars rejected Sorai's stance and framed their own way of dealing with epistemological issues.

Sorai began by arguing that we need to get back behind the writings of the Sung and Ming thinkers in order to uncover the real, foundational Confucian thought. Sorai saw this as a shift from reading the Four Books via the medium of Chu Hsi's commentaries to a direct reading of the Thirteen Classics. Like other reformers, Sorai's cry was an appeal of "back to the classics."

> Sorai was also of the opinion, and here he could quote Confucius, that too much talk about human nature would lead scholars away from social ethics into the realms of metaphysical speculation wherein nothing was sure and everything was without a firm foundation. Speaking of the problem of understanding the cosmos, Sorai wrote, "The riddle cannot be solved. The causes of the birth and rebirth of all things, good luck and bad, fortune and misfortune, cannot be known, but they exist. (Maruyama 1974:79)

Sorai did not deny that there were patterns to the cosmos but only reasoned that they were so vast because of the immense dimensions of the natural world, putting them beyond the scope of careful human reflection.

However, this inability to grasp all the details of the natural order did not keep Sorai from finding a pattern to follow for human conduct. Sorai recommended studying the way of the sages because this was the only thing that human begins could really know for certain. Sorai called this the Way of Man, or the Way of the Sages. For Sorai, this was the concrete world of human facts and institutions. He accused the Chi Hsi scholars of his day of ignoring the facts of human history in order to deal with their abstract metaphysical theories:

> It is necessary above all to look at history. It is of the utmost importance to understand each age. Unless the studies of literature, government, and classical texts are all undertaken by first understanding *the changes that occurred in each age*, there will be difficulties. *Changes in a particular age produce changes in languages and institutions.* In order to study history without difficulties, it is necessary to bear this in mind. (italics in original) (Maruyama 1974:100)

The Kaitokudo scholars disagreed with Sorai's reading of the cosmos and history. As Najita has noted, from the Kaitokudo point of view, "Regardless of how limited human intelligence was, men must proceed from the elemental proposition that the universe was not organized in a random way and things did not move about in a state of meaningless flux" (Najita 1987:125). In this regard, the Kaitokudo scholars shared a great affinity with Kaibara Ekken: They were heirs of Chu Hsi's grand view of the cosmos and held a great deal of respect for the empirical conditions of the world as it was. Although the study of the management of fiscal policy was not something found in the classical Confucian texts, there was a certain order to fiscal policy that argued for a kind of orderly world—at least in theory.

The Kaitokudo thinkers did not believe that ancient philology could provide us with a perfect vision of the Confucian Way. As Najita wrote, "The usefulness of 'philology' was not that it could make that origin factual, because it could not, but that it helped to clarify the long historical unfolding of the human intellectual effort to understand nature and man's place within it" (Najita 1987:135). The scholar best remembered for giving voice to the educated merchant's point of view was Yamagata Banto (1748–1821). Yamagata, along with being a brilliant thinker, was also a highly successful merchant banker. His most famous book, composed just at the beginning of the nineteenth century, was called *In Place of Dreams*. Najita has argued that it summarized the work of the academy and blazed the way for an entirely new way of looking at epistemological issues.

Yamagata provided what Najita calls a natural ontology, wherein both human nature as a norm for moral philosophy and the careful study of history find a place:

To Yamagata . . . phenomena close at hand, inclusive of natural and social objects, must first be located in relation to a prior universal "center" that could
not be grasped through commonsense "observation." Plants, animals, creatures, the physical landscape, history, social classes, all must be reinterpreted
or recentered in accordance with an ultimate first principle of the universe.
(Najita 1987:253)

Yamagata was stimulated to think about how to decenter all things traditionally Japanese by his study of Western astronomy. The reason for this
was that modern Western astronomy teaches that the cosmos is gigantic in
size. It is only after the cosmos that we come to the earth, much less to the
more minor creatures such as human beings. And last but not least, this
Western astronomy is carried out with a precision of rational calculation
that is more refined than even the best philology.

It was in the working of the market that Yamagata, almost like Adam
Smith, found an invisible, rational hand at work: "When addressing the
matter of price, cheap level should not be thoughtlessly set. When items are
too expensive men choose not to buy them. The matter of price simply put
should be left in the hands of merchants. When prices are too high and buy-
ers decline, they will be lowered . . . All this is based on general principle"
(Najita 1987:270).

Here Yamagata brings us back to the Confucian ideal of a norm or measure for all things. Najita has argued that for Yamagata this norm is to be
found in the Mencian idea of the mind-heart that cannot bear the suffering
of others, in other words, the human sense of universal compassion.
Yamagata went on to conjoin this Mencian sense of sympathy with the
recognition that we have "the mental power to cognize things and to organize this knowledge in ways that were truthful and to the mark" (Najita
1987:271). Hence, Yamagata unified the notion of rightness found in
Mencius with the idea of center, or mean, found in the *Doctrine of the
Mean* in order to give full expression to the original human nature.

Popular Confucian Teachers

Just as the Kaitokudo merchant scholars crafted a place for their knowledge within the Confucian circle, the teachers of the Sekimon Shingaku did
the same for an even more popular audience in the eighteenth century. The
two most famous leaders of this popular Confucian educational movement
were Ishia Biagan and his foremost disciple, Teshima Toan (1718–1786).
Along with trying to redescribe Confucian thought in terms that could be
understood by commoners with little formal education, these thinkers were
famous for making use of the large public lecture as a means of propagat-
ing their doctrines. They were renowned as teachers of the cultivation of

the mind-heart, and in fact they developed sophisticated means for less-sophisticated common people to learn about Confucianism. Like other popular teachers, they were also famous for writing in colloquial Japanese rather than in classical Chinese; Toan in fact always said, though it was an exaggeration, that he could hardly read the classical Chinese texts. Toan meant by this that he had not received a formal elite education.

Although many scholars have reviewed the work of Ishia Baigan, his student Toan was the person responsible for spreading his master's message around Japan; Toan was the organizational genius that made Shingaku a mass movement in the eighteenth century. Toan and his commoner followers turned this method into the basis for a large and focused Confucian movement. Along with public lectures, Toan also organized meetinghouses and classes where students could congregate to study Confucian thought. Some of his techniques bring to mind the work of the great Methodist John Wesley on the other side of the globe in the eighteenth-century world. Both Wesley and Toan used public lectures or sermons in order to bring their followers into fellowship and become seekers of the way, one Christian and the other Confucian. Like Wesley, Toan even gave his students a set of formal rules to conduct their meetings and rules to order their lives.

All of Toan's work was focused on helping his students "see" the original good mind-heart.

> Our teaching strips away students' layers of wisdom one by one . . . Either one hears the sound of a bell, or is startled by the noise of a drum or a dog's bark, or one looks at a bird, or views a blossom. At that moment, one suddenly forgets that one last layer of skin, and sees and hears directly—this is the emergence of the original mind. (Sawada 1993:75)

Toan helped the student identify a Mencian view of the moral mind-heart as the font of all true humane values. Nor was this an individual quest. Toan organized group study to assist people in cultivating this insight into the original moral-mind. In his *Principles for the Assembly of Companions,* Toan wondered how anyone can make progress without friends along the way: "All the more reason to ask how our comrades can remove the impurities with which they have long been imbued, if they fail to rely, even for a short time, on the support of the assembly of companions" (Sawada 1993:91).

Toan even went beyond working with adult commoners and developed a whole Confucian curriculum for children. After the 1770s, he wrote a number of works aimed at introducing young people to the Confucian Way. Going even further, Toan taught groups of boys and girls together, something that certainly would have given pause to his more elite colleagues. Although Toan was not a classical scholar, he wrote a book for children in six-character verse called *Teaching of Words of Truth*. Here, too, Toan built on earlier Buddhist foundations but gave them a Confucian substance.

> One does not value people because of their individual knowledge.
> One values them because of they are morally upright.
> Literary learning is not the ultimate treasure;
> Real learning is considered the priceless jewel . . .
> The teaching of filial piety and deference is innate virtue.
> What you should learn is filial piety and deference, loyalty and trust;
> Do not envy broad erudition and great talent. (Sawada 1993:119)

Chu Hsi would have approved of the message and the stress on the education of young people. And as if these small verses were not enough, Toan—a true teacher of children if there ever was one—composed popular songs to help reinforce Confucian virtue. Along with the verses of his songs, Toan added pictures to illustrate the moral points he was trying to make.

One cannot but speculate that perhaps one reason for Japan's remarkable ability to deal with the shock of the Western challenge in the nineteenth century has something to do with the flexibility and openness of the Tokugawa Confucian teachers. Although scholars have long noticed that many of the leaders of the Meiji Restoration were inspired by Confucian thought, this would not explain why the common people also bought into the renovation of their country with such zeal and skill. Of course, a cynic might respond that the common people were simply following common sense in overthrowing the samurai oppression. But one wonders whether the poems and songs of Toan, teaching about the universal nature of the moral mind-heart, might not also have had something to do with the intellectual ferment of the Meiji world. But this is the topic of the next chapter.

New Directions for the Ch'ing Summation of the Tradition

Dynastic transitions posed difficult questions for Confucian scholars. Why, for instance, if the Ming dynasty was such an expansive period for the development of Confucian thought, were the Confucian advisers unable to assist the Ming emperors in reforming the dynasty? One of the key intellectual issues, as we shall see, for Ch'ing Confucian intellectuals, was to determine why Ming Confucianism did not stem the tide of dynastic decline. Was there something about Ming Confucianism that had actually, however inadvertently, precipitated the fall of the Ming?

Richard Smith (1994) has pointed out that even within the diversity of Ch'ing thought, there is a core of ideas that remained normative. Part of the stability can be attributed to the fact that the Ch'ing rulers were staunch patrons of Chu Hsi orthodoxy and the cultural uniformity of the civil service examination system. The more cynical believe that it was simply a way for the Manchu Ch'ing rulers to force their Chinese subjects to adopt an ideology that placed tremendous emphasis on the notion of loyalty to the ruler. The less suspicious point out that some of the great Ch'ing emperors like K'ang-hsi and Ch'ien-lung were intelligent men who genuinely appreciated the nature of Chu Hsi's achievement, especially the fact that it produced a cadre of dedicated civil servants loyal to the throne on Confucian principle.

Richard Smith outlined the fundamental points of agreement for Ch'ing thought, using eight main points:

1. A comparative lack of interest in metaphysics
2. A rationalistic outlook predicated on a belief in the intelligibility of the universe
3. A great reverence for the past
4. A humanistic concern with "man in society"
5. An emphasis on morality in government and a link between personal and political values
6. A belief in the moral perfectibility of all human beings
7. The supreme authority of fundamental Confucian principles
8. A general disesteem of law (Smith 1994:139)

For instance, the notion that law is disesteemed must be grasped within the context of the Confucian understanding of ritual and law. From the Confucian point of view, ritual always leads to a better path for social life because law should be applied only when resorting to ritual proves impossible. Unfortunately, from a Western perspective that values positive law, much Confucian thinking about law was always conditioned by the early and bitter Confucian confrontation with the Legalists in the late Warring States and early Han periods. Nonetheless, Ch'ing thinkers recognized that not everyone would be moved by appeals to moral ritual. Besides, as Smith also noted, the whole drive of Chinese thought was to find a balance, a harmony in life, and ritual seemed a more fitting way to achieve a real balance than the imposition of mechanistic positive law.

Along with the School of Evidential Research, the rise of ritual scholarship is a key element of the new Ch'ing intellectual world. Following the lead of Kai-wing Chow (1994), we will focus on Yen Yüan (1635–1704) and Li Yung (1627–1705) as prime examples of this style of the Ch'ing search for the purity of the Confucian Way. As with almost all Ch'ing scholars, these two ritually oriented thinkers were reacting to their perceptions of Sung and Ming excesses. In the case of Yen, the beginning of his critique of

Chu's thought came with the death of his foster grandmother in 1668. Yen, following Chu Hsi's *Family Ritual* to the letter, began an arduous fast. One day, an old man from the Chu clan told him the truth: "If you die of excessive grief, it will be for nothing. Your grandmother never had any children of her own; your father was adopted from another family" (Yen 1972:9). This event shook Yen's faith in Chu Hsi's approach to learning.

The problem, as Yen Yüan and other Ch'ing scholars saw it, was that Chu's methods of study were incorrect. Chu and his Sung friends had jumped too quickly into quasi-Buddhist discussions of ultimate principles, the arcane learning of the mind-heart and the *wu-chi*/Uncontrived Ultimate, without first doing their proper Confucian homework. Yen observed that Chu Hsi may have "jumped out of Buddhism," but he had not been very careful about where he leapt and when he landed he had not gone far enough to rid his thought of pernicious Buddhist influences:

> Although Chu Tzu jumped out of Buddhism and returned to Confucianism, it is a pity that at that time his pointing out of mistakes was not thorough. He thought that filling in the gaps (in our knowledge of) the ceremonies, music, archery, charioteering, writing and mathematics was difficult, and said he would defer attention to this until he could understand general principle better, until his thought had become sincere, his mind rectified, then he could pay attention to these things. . . . Furthermore, when one ignores the concrete facts, which are what general principles are based on, it is impossible to achieve true incisiveness of thought or rectification of the mind. (Yen 1972:131–132)

Along with a desire to return to a study of the classics themselves, and especially the rituals they embody, Yen Yüan was also an advocate of physical exercise as appropriate for a Confucian scholar. All of this quiet sitting could only injure the body that was given to us by our parents. What was needed, Yen thought, was a form of study that would make for a strong body and a strong mind. In this Yen was, like Chang Tsai, adamant in pointing out that that *ch'i* was at the basis of the entire physical and mental person. If people follow Chu Hsi or Wang Yang-ming, then "they will develop effeminate, fragile bodies. How can they then move their flesh and bones to expend their strength in working on the Six Arts?" (Yen 1972:132). Is it any wonder, Yen concluded, that such a muddleheaded group of idealists, with weak bodies, were unable to save the Ming from its downfall? The late Ming scholars had neither the physical strength nor the will to resist the vigorous Manchus.

It is crucial to hear Yen Yüan's impassioned pleas for the study of ritual as practical action because the modern Western notion of ritual carries much the same connotations of weakness that Yen tried to overcome.

Moderns think that people of ritual are neither strong nor vigorous; in fact, many modern people would agree with the Taoists that only a spontaneous person, someone free of the bonds of ritual, can be a truly active, vigorous person. Of course, this kind of mental, moral, and physical torpor is just the thing that infuriated Yen. The key term for Yen, as Kai-wing Chow (1995) has so ably demonstrated, is practice, or *hsi*. Yen was concerned with the proper practice of ancient Confucian ritual, and we must remember that this was the social and physical conditioning of an aristocratic Chou military elite. Yen himself did not seem too much concerned that his reading of the texts was a perfect one; rather, Yen everywhere and always stressed that one had to practice physical exercise in order to follow the ritual life of Confucius. However, because Ch'ing China was a world of books and examinations, Yen's own students would have to defend their claims about which rituals were to be followed.

Li Yung (1627–1705) is a fascinating example of this search for proper conduct. In fact, Li was so committed to a proper understanding of the Way that he never sought to pass the civil service examinations. Li was motivated by his search for the Way and felt that he could best pursue his vision of the Way by becoming a teacher who would transmit learning to future generations. In fact, Li was recognized in his own time as a great Confucian teacher. Li is a fascinating ritual scholar because, as Anne Birdwhistell wrote, he "acknowledged that words were necessary to communicate moral knowledge, but held that actual understanding constantly changed with the circumstances. Although the sages spoke the truth, their words reflected an understanding appropriate only for their times" (1996:56). Li had the difficult task of trying to find out what these teachings were and how they could be applied to the circumstances of the day.

Li Yung's vision of the Confucian philosopher as a doctor and teacher caused him to disagree with the founder of the School of Evidential Research, Ku Yen-wu (1613–1682), about the use of texts and ideas. Ku, for instance, wanted to drop the use of the terms *t'i* and *yung* because they were not of pristine Confucian provenance. Li, on the other hand, as a good doctor, was not that concerned about where the ideas had come from; he was interested more in whether they would work to achieve the desired results of philosophical health. Li sought to revive personal conduct and social affairs. If non-Confucian ideas would help, then Li, because of his realization that times change and that living things grow, was willing to use them to good effect.

Birdwhistell demonstrated how Li Yung went about defending Confucian thought in a way different from more typical Western forms of argumentation. From "Li Yung's perspective the dominant epistemological imperatives consisted of the ideas of unity, harmony, continuity, constant and patterned change, and an ethical (as opposed to logical) standard for test thought"

(Birdwhistell 1996:27). The ethical imperative is the most important, because it is linked to the metaphor of a living entity such that images of plants, families, and water were used to make philosophical points. The main difference between the logical and ethical ways of stating standards is balanced between a view of logic where "there is an implicit order in which ideas are connected in a linear manner, with each idea based on previous reasoning that ultimately leads back to first assumptions" (Birdwhistell 1996:29). This is a contained system of clear and distinct ideas. However, the ethical standard of Li was based on a view of reality in which the boundaries of action and fact were not set because we are dealing with a living system—and living systems are alive in the sense that they change and grow over time: "Since the entire system depended on adaptation to constantly arising contingencies, the boundaries could be expanded with the contingencies" (Birdwhistell 1996:29). This is the reason that Chinese thought is often compared to American pragmatism, a philosophical movement that was interested in ethics and recognized the living and expansive nature of the philosophic project: "The ethical standard is significant because it enabled notions of social learning to dominate the fundamental premises of thought, rather than such notions as logical argumentation" (Birdwhistell 1996:30).

Another reason that ritual action, broadly conceived, was so important for Li Yung was that he was convinced that all proper Confucian teaching has its origin in the practice of governance. Governance needs rituals, ways to coordinate human action, not just for individuals but also for groups of people. "Li thus held that Confucian teachings stood for a specific content, involving ideas and actions morally and socially useful to a Confucian society. Although the ideals had become obscured, they did not fundamentally change" (Birdwhistell 1996:81). However, the application of the ideals did vary from age to age. Because of this variation, Li was highly irenic in his evaluation of previous scholars. For instance, even though he did not always agree with Chu Hsi, Li saw no reason not to recognize that Chu's teaching method had cogency based on the specific needs of his age.

Li Yung always came back to the point that only good actions could ultimately be counted as the fruits of a Confucian life. Of course, Li's sophisticated pedagogy walked the student through a curriculum that paid careful attention to how actions were informed by a Confucian worldview, but the end was proper action. "The Confucian school (originally) regarded virtuous action as its root and literature as its branches. Later generations, however, have solely regarded literature as their concern, and so one can see the changes in the times" (Birdwhistell 1996:126). Like so many other early Ch'ing thinkers, if the "marks on paper" do not lead to proper action, then all literature is wasted.

Another famous early Ch'ing critic of society and government was Huang Tsung-hsi (1610–1695). Huang is lauded as the founder of the critical study of the history of philosophy. He composed the famous *The Records of Ming Scholars* partially to try to make sense of the fall of the dynasty. But along with being a great intellectual historian, Huang was also a harsh critic of Chinese imperial rule. He wrote *Waiting for the Dawn: A Plan for the Prince* as a protest against autocratic practices. It was so effective that it was not actually published until the nineteenth century. However, it circulated enough to become famous as an argument against tyrannical government.

Wm. Theodore de Bary (1993) has noted that Huang began the preface to his philosophical reflections on political theory with the observation that in humankind's original state there were no rulers. In fact, the image that Huang then develops for the early sage kings was that of servants taking up the increasing load of government on behalf of their people. One reason that the early sage kings did not pass the government to their sons was that they did not want to burden members of their own family with such a heavy responsibility. It was only in the later dynasties that the rulership of the empire became a great prize. Of course, by then, rulers were no longer servants, and problems with the autocratic state began to multiply.

De Bary pointed out that once Huang had established the correct way good government ought to be, he then began "targeting dynastic rule as the prime incarnation of political and economic evil" (de Bary 1993:18). What started as the relationship of a servant to the people now became that of the master to the tenant. Things became hopelessly turned around, and no amount of personal self-cultivation on the part of the ruler could undo all the institutional evils of the system itself. Individuals alone could do almost nothing to rectify the wrongs. Generations of Confucian scholars, such as the Ch'eng brothers and Chu Hsi, in addition to the Wang Yang-ming schoolmen, had sought to convince themselves and the emperor that if only the emperor would mend his ways, things would be better. Huang unmasked this vision of political reform as muddleheaded. Some medicine of a more drastic nature was needed to cure the whole system and not just individual emperors and princes.

In order to move around the problem of mere personal self-cultivation as sufficient to reform society, Huang returned to the idea of law, an area of Chinese thought tainted in Confucian memory by the Legalist experiment in the founding of the Ch'in empire. Nonetheless, Huang came to believe that only a system of laws could deal effectively with the Chinese autocratic institutions. Huang even made the remarkable suggestion of placing law above ritual and envisioning ritual as a subset of law. By "law," Huang most definitely did not mean the dynastic law of late imperial China. This was a law designed only to support the despotic forms of government that Huang wanted to replace. These were "unlawful laws": "Unlawful laws . . . fetter men hand and foot, and even a man capable of governing well cannot overcome the handicaps of senseless restraint and suspicion" (de Bary 1993:23).

"Until the end of the Three Dynasties there was Law. Since the Three Dynasties there has been no Law ... It was never laid down solely for the benefit of the ruler himself" (de Bary 1993:97). What passes for law at that juncture, according to Huang, was merely for the benefit of one family. Huang sought to suggest a series of carefully crafted reforms of the basic laws of the country that would overturn the false laws with something more in the spirit of the law of the first three dynasties of sage kings. However, Huang was still enough of a traditional Confucian to yearn for a real sage king to come along to assist in the renovation of the country. As de Bary has noted, Confucians have always been nervous about the grasping of power by the prince. Confucians are more comfortable assisting an able prince than in seeing themselves forming a party to seize power for the people. Nonetheless, Huang's was as great a challenge to established imperial theory as any Ch'ing Confucian would mount until the impact of the West caused the whole Confucian world to crumble.

The School of Evidential Research

Even better known for their philosophical criticism of Sung and Ming philosophy were the train of thinkers who followed Ku Yen-wu (1613–1682) in the School of Evidential Research. Carsun Chang has said that to call Ku the founder of the School of Evidential Research is something of a misnomer. What Ku really wanted was to return to more solid, concrete, and practical learning than was found in late Ming speculative thought. Ku sought this through a combination of his careful study of the ancient texts and his willingness to look at the empirical facts of a situation. As Richard Strassberg (1994) noted in the translation of some of Ku's travel writings, a better term would be "practical studies."

Ku Yen-wu was bothered by the highly abstract nature of Sung and Ming thought. According to Ku, all we have to do is look to see that Confucius and Mencius spent very little time discussing the philosophical nature of human nature but expended a great deal of time on the conditions under which a Confucian scholar ought to serve a ruler as a minister. "Loyalty and integrity may not cover the whole range of *jen*, but one who knows nothing about loyalty and integrity, can never reach *jen*" (Chang 1962:2, 222). When asked about the nature of the Way, Ku answered, "My answer, in accordance to my point of view, is this: For the attainment of *tao* two things are necessary; (1) to widen knowledge as much as possible, (2) to behave with a sense of shame" (Chang 1957–1962:2, 222).

As a leader of the new Ch'ing scholarship, Ku was distinguished by a genuine dedication to the first of his two rules. He infused the study of books with the results of fieldwork. He argued that we could only move on to the elevated discussion of ultimate principles if we base our conversation on the facts of the world. In this regard, Ku actually saw his work as supporting Chu Hsi's admonition to investigate things. In carrying out this investigation, Ku's curiosity carried him into new fields of phonetics, ancient history, archaeology, and classical studies. Late Ch'ing scholars would honor this direction by even more detailed work in these areas of empirical studies.

Another point worth noting about the Evidential Research scholars is that they very much formed their own scholarly world. Benjamin Elman (1984) has chronicled the rise and fall of the movement in the lower Yangtze area in terms of both its philosophical import and its complex social organization. Elman has demonstrated that the movement was a complex of interests and talents. Schools were founded and revived; printing ventures were launched, and new social conditions allowed for the creation of a specialized research community. What started as a movement away from Sung and Ming moral and speculative philosophy became yet another scholarly world. As Elman put it, "These were men trained in a sophisticated body of philological, historical and astronomical methods. They constituted a special community in Kiangnan, one whose informal members were the exclusive audience for, and judges of, each other's work" (Elman 1984:57).

Because of the highly scholastic nature of the mature Evidential Research project, famous scholars such as Tai Chen (1724–1777) and Chang Hsüeh-ch'eng (1738–1801) were often unappreciated for their broader philosophical interests. Tai recognized that he had gained fame for his carefully crafted evidential and philological studies but took more pleasure in his moral and speculative philosophy. Even today, it is impossible to study Chinese thought without making recourse to the best of the work of the Evidential Research scholars. Their erudition and attention to detail is still a marvel of the best kind of detailed textual study of the classical sources.

However, before we leap ahead to the final glories of Ch'ing Confucian thought in scholars such as Chang Hsüeh-ch'eng and Tai Chen, we need to return once again to the beginnings, to the work of Wang Fu-chih (1619–1692). Wang is such an important figure because of his great analytic skill and his sense of intellectual coherence. In the conventional reading of Chinese thought, Wang is often remembered as a reviver of the work of Chang Tsai. This is very true, at least on the surface. On the one hand, Chu Hsi's system seemed prone to collapsing into a kind of dualism of principle and matter-energy, something that the Ch'ing thinkers rejected as a false worldview. But on the other hand, the Ch'ing scholars were equally unimpressed by the Wang Yang-ming followers' radical turn to the subjective. The task of someone like Wang Fu-chih was to reconstruct Confucian philosophy in order to avoid the pitfalls of the Sung and Ming dualism and subjectivism.

As Alison Black wrote of Wang, "What are the issues? the nature of the universe and man's place within it, and, in particular, how things are conceived to change, to come into or go out of existence, both in the universe at large and in the realm of human activity" (Black 1989:5). In order to begin his search for coherence, Wang fastened on a metaphor that Black calls "expressionism." According to Black, expression includes "the factors: the thing unexpressed; the act, event, or relation of expression; and the thing in its expressed form" (Black 1989:14). It is the moving out from something inner to an outer expression of what is essentially within.

Wang's philosophy of expression manifested the typical Confucian love of harmony. According to Wang, the Sung-Ming speculative philosophers went wrong when they, perhaps under the influence of Taoists and Buddhists, stressed too greatly the transcendent reference of this expression. Wang represents a different style of thought wherein the philosopher "resists the idea of a transcendent source and pictures instead a corporate world of being in which what we might roughly call material and immaterial elements are but two aspects of the same things, distinguishable in logic, but not in concrete fact" (Black 1989:34). Wang wanted to retain principle, matter-energy, and the creative powers of the human mind-heart in the synthesis of principle and matter-energy without positing something beyond the concrete cosmos itself.

Wang Fu-chih defended his vision by developing a very sophisticated theory of change or generativity as a philosophical first principle: "The creative principle was located by Wang Fu-chih within the process of change itself. The material force or energy of which everything in the world was composed contained within itself the potential for developing multiple forms, each with its appropriate measure of intelligence (if any)" (Black 1989:48). Of course, at the heart of this cosmology of change was the ceaseless flux of *ch'i*, guided by the interaction of yin and yang. In order to defend his position, Wang returned to a careful exposition of the *Book of Changes*. He argued that creativity itself is not an agent in the sense that any act of creation needs a creator. When the *Book of Changes* seems to talk in this way, it is only metaphorical; hence, "In short, the Supreme Ultimate *is* the Two Modes, the Two Modes *are* the Four Images, and the Four Images *are* the Eight Trigrams" (Black 1989:66). Creativity creates and is not created by anything beyond the creatures that create themselves.

Wang Fu-chih, probably because of his attention to the natural world, did not want to make his system too mechanical or deterministic. In fact, this is the prime area of Wang's criticism of Sung scholars like Shao Yung, who, basing his reasoning on theoretical considerations, found too much order in the empirical world. According to Wang, one "cannot measure" all the intricate patterns of things as they seek their proper harmony and unity. This is why Wang likes to use the term "spirit" to indicate the unpredictable nature of the constant interaction of yin-yang. Or, as Wang phrased it when commenting on the *Chuang Tzu*, "The moving-and-stilling of the inner forces of *ch'i* . . . forms two with the absence of moving-and-stillness as soon as it is distinguished from it; the further distinction between moving and stillness yields three" (Black 1989:78). There again, and perhaps Wang would agree, we find the pattern for form, dynamics, and unification played out again, this time with more attention to the vagaries of spirit and the indeterminacy of natural process than would have been the case for most Sung-Ming speculative philosophers.

Wang Fu-chih walked a fine line between finding order in the human world and pretending that the order he did find was something like an immutable destiny, which he rejected. First of all, Wang notes that "things existing in mutually exclusive, necessary opposition are not to be found in Heaven and Earth, nor in the myriad things, nor in mental conception" (Black 1989:151). From this principle he framed an argument for what he called a theory of "harmonious compliance," or *ho-shun*. Wang meant that we must become adept at weaving our way between the forces of unity and disunity that mark the created order. We need to learn how to adapt ourselves to a world in flux but also to a world where there are provisional patterns to things, a world in which things do achieve their own harmonies and values. There may not be a grand blueprint of the cosmos for Wang as Black has noted, but there is still the need to find what order there is and comply with it. For instance, Wang was exceptional in finding a place for genuine passion as something that we must learn to appreciate. Passion, as a natural human activity, also has its patterns of harmony and to live well is to learn to live with the harmony of passion as well as proper restraint.

Toward the other end of the Ch'ing period, we turn to another of the grand minds of late Confucian thought, Tai Chen (1724–1777). Weng Fang-kang (1733–1818), in a letter to a friend, summarizes why Tai Chen believed that classical study of the ritual texts was so important for returning to the original intent of Confucianism before the detour of the Sung-Ming speculative philosophers.

> (Tai) said, "Moral truth . . . must be grasped in ritual institutions and the knowledge of (ancient) things . . ." This makes sense only if he was referring to one or two things. . . . Is it possible that . . . the principles of loyalty and filial piety can be comprehended from (studying) the birds, animals, grass and trees? . . . Can the *Analects* and the *Mencius* be approached as institutions and knowledge of things? Is it possible to study the *Classic of Filial Piety* as institutions and knowledge of things? What Tai essentially meant is the three ritual Classics. (Chow 1995:180)

Weng argues that Tai Chen wanted to understand ancient history on its own terms because it was only in these specific rituals that we can see the true mind of the sages.

The problem of returning to the truth of the classics, according to Tai, was complicated because of the sedimentation of the great Han and Sung scholars. Tai believed that the Han scholars had understood the system and numerical categories of the classical texts but had not pursued their true moral meaning. Nevertheless, the Sung Confucians were to be commended for realizing the moral import of the classics, but they did not pay attention to the philology and history needed to really comprehend what the sages were trying to teach. Tai wanted to unravel this mystery, and in order to do so, he had to dedicate himself to understanding the phrases and words of the classics: "If through words I were to understand phrases and through phrases the Tao, then I would make progress" (Chin and Freeman 1990:31). Tai is striking for his balanced view of Confucian philosophical history. He refused to take cheap shots at the Han and Sung scholars and tried to take the high road; when the Han and Sung thinkers deserved praise, Tai would give it.

For Tai Chen, what is natural is good because the very nature of the Tao is to create and creation is ultimately good: "What is necessary is goodness; what is natural is nature. To develop into what is necessary is just to complete and perfect what is nature. This is called the utmost of the natural" (Cheng 1971:42). As we see here, although Tai defends his interpretation of these primordial Confucian notions on the basis of the most rigorous scholarship, he is still a Confucian moral philosopher in following Mencius' lead by declaring the essential goodness of human nature and, by extension, human emotions, when they are properly ordered.

If human beings are essentially good, then how does Tai Chen explain that things go wrong? Tai answered that the main problem was that human beings are either selfish or beclouded by external things or both: "In the end, selfishness has its root in the satisfaction of one's private desires and interests. In the other case, (that is), when the mind is beclouded by external things, the mind becomes confused" (Cheng 1971:99). According to Tai, the best way to get rid of selfishness is to develop a sympathetic view of other people, and the best way to begin this process of intersubjective compassion is to reflect on the notions of humaneness, ritual civility, and righteousness. In order to carry this out, Tai provides a curriculum of study based on the *Doctrine of the Mean* and the *Great Learning*.

Typical of the Evidential Research style, it was in Tai Chen's study of the meaning of terms in Mencius that he created his masterpiece. Tai began with an extended meditation on the idea of principle. But it is important to understand that while Tai was working against the false notions of Sung moral philosophy, he was reconstructing his own metaphysics of principle. Actually, Tai went even further and made the claim that the Ch'eng-Chu theory of principle was really an extension of Hsün Tzu's ideas about ritual and righteousness, though this is something that the Sung scholars could not actually admit.

According to Tai Chen, "The word "principle' is a name assigned to the arrangement of the parts of anything which gives the whole its distinctive property or characteristics, and which can be observed by careful examination and analysis of the parts down to the minutest detail" (Chin and Freeman 1990:69). In a long series of articles on principle, Tai hammers away at his central point, namely, that principle is always the pattern of order found within things and not something transcendent in the sense that it is unconnected with mundane human life and things of the world: "The word 'thing' refers to concrete objects and concrete affairs. The word 'principle' refers to its purity and its centrality and correctness. Concrete objects and affairs are what is natural, but by returning to what is necessary, the principles of Heaven, earth, men, things, and affairs are realized" (Chin and Freeman 1990:89). Things might be very complex in this world and they can becloud the selfish person, but this does not mean that such people are without principles. The problem is that the Sung thinkers exalted principle into being something beyond the principles of things and affairs.

Tai Chen believed that the Sung speculative philosophers had followed a wrong turn in accepting too much Taoism and Buddhism into their worldview: "Lao Tzu, Chuang Tzu, and the Buddhists have exalted spirit as transcending the interaction of the yin and yang and the transforming process of the *ch'i*. Ch'eng Tzu and Chu Tzu have exalted principle as transcending the interaction of the yin and yang and the transforming process of the *ch'i*" (Chin and Freeman 1990:99). Nonetheless, "The sage is guided by his physical desires when he formulates the teaching of mutual production and nourishment" (Chin and Freeman 1990:99).

In terms of theories of human emotion, Susan Mann (1997) has taken up the story of the role of women in Confucian history with her detailed study of elite women in the mid-Ch'ing period. Just as with their male relatives, the elite Ch'ing women were more conservative than their late Ming sisters. The great Ch'ing women scholars defended their roles as protectors of the life of the inner chambers and backed away from too grand an appeal to human emotion as a proper theme for women. In fact, the mid-Ch'ing women literary theorists tried to restrain too much emotion, finding it improper for a Confucian lady. And they certainly did not encourage poetry clubs that included educated courtesans. Nonetheless, Ch'ing women did defend their role as proper daughters, sisters, wives, and mothers with a definite role to play in the education of the family.

Tai Chen was a great friend to younger scholars and was an inspiration to the historian-philosopher Chang Hsüeh-ch'eng. Although Chang appreciated the efforts of classical scholars such as Tai, his vision was for a more synoptic view of history. As Ann-ping Chin and Mansfield Freeman noted, "Truth is not the exclusive possession of any single body of knowledge, not even the Classics. It abides in the flow of events over time, and Chang himself intended to become the most scrupulous observer of history's evolution" (1990:20). In this regard, Chang lifts up the sense of piety before facts and exhibits an interest in the evolution of historical forms, traits that we discovered previously in the work of Li Yung.

According to David Nivison (1966), Chang Hsüeh-ch'eng sought a philosophy of history that would make sense of both China's history and philosophy. Chang therefore made a virtue of the disorganized nature of history as the unfolding of principle in the real world of change: "In a sense, what Chang did was to maintain the thesis that all philosophy should be practical and piecemeal, and to work on this thesis till he built it into a system" (Nivison 1966:139). Again as was typical of the creative thinkers of the Ch'ing, Chang rejected any notion that the principles of things were to be found anywhere but in the things themselves. Because the Tao is to be found in the things and the things are myriad and ever new, then there is no way that anyone can state with absolute certainty just what the Tao is perfectly. What we can learn from history is that even the sages were constantly asking questions and learning answers appropriate to their situations. In writing about how Chang differs from Tai Chen, and about Tai's belief that all we can know is to be found in the classics, Nivison commented: "A sage cannot 'create' just anything. What he achieves is strictly limited by the possibilities of the historical moment" (1966:145).

The problem is that the world of Chang Hsüeh-ch'eng, and all his friends and enemies, was becoming a shadow, though the Ch'ing thinkers of the early nineteenth century did not know that yet. Nonetheless, this was a rich time in China's great imperial history. The Manchu dynasty had brought unparalleled prosperity and had expanded the frontiers of the Chinese states beyond places they had ever effectively been before. Tibet and Central Asia were now part of the empire, as was Mongolia and the Far North of Manchuria. The population had grown to something to over 400 million by the middle of the nineteenth century. Great novels were written; poets like Yüan Mei argued with Chang Hsüeh-ch'eng about the relationship of the Tao to history, human institutions, and the passions.

And yet, this entire world was soon to come to an end. The merchant princes, adventurers, and military officials of Victorian England and the other European powers cared nothing for the local histories and the debates about principle and matter-energy. The Manchu empire that in the seventeenth century had defeated the Russians in the North and in the eighteenth century had expanded the empire into new and vast parts of Central Asia could no longer treat the European powers as barbarians who could be bought off with a little trade or a show of force if trade failed. The Confucian world was poised on the brink of a change in reality that it had never faced before. It was confronted by another civilization that was stronger in terms of the flesh and, as regarded philosophy, was little interested in the wisdom of the sages.

❀ 7 ❀

Confucianism in the Modern World

THE BEGINNING OF THE NINETEENTH CENTURY appeared secure to Confucians throughout the cultural region. East Asia was generally at peace and had been so for generations, save for minor civil disturbances and the forceful addition of various territories to China's Central Asian holdings. China was indeed the great dragon, surrounded by a group of successful minidragons. Furthermore, the region had undergone dramatic population growth and economic expansion. Confucian arts and sciences flourished, and more people than ever before took part in the Confucian tradition. In China, Korea, Vietnam, and Japan governments relied on various official or semiofficial Confucian schools, academies, and examinations to staff their civil services. By the end of the century, all of this calm Confucian culture had vanished like a morning mist.

It is an interesting parlor game to speculate on what the states of East Asia could have done to solve their domestic economic and demographic problems if they had been left to their own devices. East Asian intellectuals detest a vision of Asia that depicts the whole region as merely a weak pawn in an European power game. East Asian economic, military, and cultural success at the end of the twentieth century shows how easily images of stagnation and innovation can be recycled. The provocation from the new Western powers had been growing in Asia for three centuries, but by the nineteenth century, what had been a minor rearrangement of traditional trade patterns was transformed into the colonial era. The Western maritime powers no longer humbly petitioned for trade privileges; led by England, the Western countries now dictated the terms of trade and diplomacy. And where they did not trade, they often simply conquered and established their own colonies.

Unfortunately for China, the arrival of a militant West coincided with the dynastic decline and the greatest civil war in Chinese history, the cataclysm of the Taiping Rebellion (1850–1864). Most of central China was devastated, and whole districts and even provinces were depopulated. Although the Ch'ing dynasty survived the Taiping challenge, it did so only by radically changing the balance of power between the central government and regional and provincial powers. The Ch'ing state would never revive effectively during the second half of the nineteenth century, and the foreign powers continued their gradual erosion of Chinese sovereignty, leading to what the Chinese called a state of semicolonization.

The Japanese situation in the 1850s was dramatically different but equally traumatic. After having closed the country to all by minimal trade during the Tokugawa period after 1600, the Japanese were forced to open the country under the guns of a Western fleet commanded by the Americans under Commodore Perry in the 1850s. By the 1860s, the Japanese realized that they needed a radical answer to the Western powers. The great southern lords revolted against the Tokugawa Bakufu in the name of restoring direct rule by the emperor. This began the great Meiji Restoration of 1867. The titular battle cry was to restore the emperor and throw out the barbarians. Although it is true that the emperor was restored to some power compared to the long rule by military governments like the Tokugawa, the Meiji founders astutely understood that they were too weak to expel the foreign powers. The Meiji choice was dramatic. If the Western powers could not be driven from Japan, then the Japanese would have to divine the sources of Western power and develop these technological, social, and scientific skills to defend the nation.

Korea was the last of the northern East Asian Confucian states opened to Western influence. The Koreans resisted as long as they could. By the time they were forced to open their country to Western diplomacy and trade, the Koreans were also faced, in the late nineteenth and early twentieth centuries, with a revived imperial Japan. In Korea, it was not the Western powers that moved in to take control—it was a Japan that had learned how to play the new Western imperial game. The old Japanese dream of control of Korea became reality, and the Koreans were not liberated from Japanese domination until the end of World War II in 1945.

The confrontation with the West had none of the compassionate and protracted give and take of China's encounter with Buddhism. As many shocked missionaries reported, the encounter was unfortunately and literally like a rapid and brutal rape. Western ideas came along with Western opium and guns, and many Westerners had no interest in whether the Chinese understood anything of their Western culture. Of course, there were exceptions to this rule, even in the early period, among religious and secular European visitors to Asia. The Jesuits and some Protestant missionary-scholars evinced a genuine affection and respect for the culture they discovered, but even they were still ultimately bent on converting the Chinese to their form of Christianity. At best, the entire Confucian tradition was perceived to be like the heritage of the Greco-Roman world, a classical pagan culture that needed the Christian gospel in order to find true, Christian salvation.

The East Asian response to the West is a set of tales of different strategies for saving the Confucian world. As Joseph Levenson (1968) pointed out in his great trilogy, *Confucian China and Its Modern Fate*, one of the first and most appealing ways to deal with the Western threat was to employ the traditional category of the *t'i-yung*, or substance-function, contrast. The nineteenth-century Chinese reformers framed a response based on what they took to be the essential core of Chinese traditional values. These were the values of family and Confucian orthodoxy. These values would form the unchanging substance of the dynastic renewal. The *yung* of Western technology could be grafted onto the main trunk of Chinese learning in order to serve Chinese needs without upsetting Chinese tradition. As Levenson demonstrated, this approach did not work.

The great Meiji reformers in Japan, after having abandoned the notion that they could or should expel the foreigners, came to a more radical realization and developed a plan for saving Japan. First, they recognized that if they tried to force the foreigners to leave, Japan would probably simply end up as another European colony. Second, they came to the conclusion that one could not easily separate essence and function in terms of philosophies of life. Social institutions such as technology embody their own worldviews, and once you have adopted a technology, it has an impact on your values. Having accepted the inference that Western technology would bring Western values in its train, some of the more radical Japanese reformers argued for a complete Westernization of Japan in order to save the country. Of course, the Japanese viewed the idea of importing new ideas and technologies with less distaste than did their Chinese and Korean counterparts because they knew that they had been modifying Taoism, Buddhism, and Confucianism for hundreds of years.

However, the death notices of East Asian cultures were premature, even if we accept the critical modern reviews of the tradition based on feminist, Marxist, and developmental perspectives. But even the most impassioned defenders of the possibility of Confucian renewal realize that it is a wounded tradition that has been intellectually and socially challenged as never before in its history. Nonetheless, after the end of the revolutionary convulsions in China, people are beginning to show new signs of interest in the tradition. The Japanese had always continued the study of the tradition, and the same was true of Korea. But with the rise of industrial East Asia, the question is now this: If Confucianism is part of East Asian culture, then what is there in Confucianism that is helping such rapid and effective modernization?

Wm. Theodore de Bary (1991a) has reminded us that in traditional China, the Confucian elite controlled the family through ritual, scholarship through education, and the state through the civil service examinations. However, Confucian rituals no longer dominate, save as an almost genetic form of social civility in the family lives of modern East Asians. Few people consult Chu Hsi's great study of family ritual before they go about marrying each other. Education throughout the region is no longer dominated by great Confucian private academies. Scholars are as likely to study Plato, Aristotle, Hegel, Marx, Wittgenstein, Dewey, Rorty, and Heidegger as they are to reflect on Mencius or Chu Hsi. Nowadays, no Asian civil servant must take examinations based on Chu Hsi's interpretation of the *Four Books*.

Despite the battering Confucianism has taken over the last century, modern Confucians are disinclined to urge a return to a repristinated traditional past. For instance, Confucians are aware of the concerns of women for personal and social freedom and understand that most feminists find Confucianism distasteful because of its patriarchal past. Hence, Confucians realize that they must respond to the criticisms of modern feminist thought in order to rectify basic Confucian claims about the relations between the sexes.

Another case for changing Confucian awareness arises with a willingness to view class conflict and social disharmony in a new light. One of the constant Marxist criticisms is that Confucianism too easily accepted oppressive social harmony at the expense of the social interests of the disadvantaged. A renewed Confucianism must, therefore, find a place for conflict as an inevitable and socially positive part of human life. In this regard, the great early Ch'ing thinker Wang Fu-chih can be reread with profit because he believed that conflict was very much an aspect of human life that needed to be reckoned with.

Just as the Japanese in the Meiji period were more enthusiastic about engaging the West in a positive way, so too were the Japanese the first in East Asia to generate a modern and cross-cultural philosophical school. This is, of course, the justly famous Kyoto school. Although many people immediately assume that the Kyoto school represents Buddhism per se, this is an oversimplification of the history of this multigenerational movement. Steve Odin (1996) has shown that the idea of pure experience, made famous by the school's founder, Nishida Kitaro, owes as much to William James as it does to Zen Buddhism.

The case of Chinese philosophy now more and more resembles the work of the Kyoto school in its ability to fuse the best of Chinese and Western thought. Chinese intellectuals have become as adept at rereading Plato, Hegel, and Marx as they are in reading Chu Hsi and Wang Yang-ming. Of course, the road to social and economic reconstruction has taken longer for Marxist-Maoist China than for capitalist Japan. And last but not least, the whole experience with communism as an ideology and social system has complicated the Chinese response to global philosophy because Chinese intellectuals were forced until very recently to publicly embrace a Marxist-

Maoist form of dialectical materialism as their official philosophy. But as we shall see, ever since the late 1970s the Chinese have returned to the world philosophical stage with a passion to restore what is worth restoring in their traditional worldviews.

The Chaos of First Impressions and Reactions

At first, the Chinese elite sought to manage the Western threat with methods developed over the centuries for dealing with the perennial threats from Central Asian tribal confederacies; needless to say the ruling Manchus understood all of these principles extremely well. These methods did not work, save for the fact that the Taiping Rebellion was finally put down through the largely futile efforts of the Ch'ing central government and the ever more effective efforts of a group of Chinese officials turned military men. The Ch'ing and the Chinese elite viewed the Taiping rebels as an even more difficult problem than the Western threat, which they likened to a disease of the skin rather than of the vital organs. The Westerners were merely a problem for the coastal regions, but the Taiping rebels were a cancer that infected the very middle of China.

The philosophical reaction of two great Confucian generals, Tseng Kuo-fan (1811–1872) and Li Hung-chang (1823–1901), who finally defeated the Taiping Rebellion, was typical of their generation. They sought Chinese categories to deal with the increasing threat to Chinese freedom posed by the Western powers. In the classical dyad of form (t'i) and function (yung), both men found a conceptual way to try to understand what needed to be done in order for the T'ung-Chih Restoration to work. There were actually excellent precedents for such a policy. These skilled administrators were well aware that in the past China had made use of specific kinds of foreign technologies. These could range from the wonderful horses from Central Asia that were so prized by the T'ang elite to the calculations of Muslim and then Jesuit astronomers. Although Tseng and Li had an unshaken belief in the overall excellence of Chinese culture, they realized that in special areas the Western barbarians did have skills useful to China.

The t'i-yung theory of reform was predicated on the hypothesis that technology and science were value-free institutions that could be used without any change or harm to the Chinese way of life. Here again, the Meiji reformers in Japan were more prescient. The Meiji thinkers toyed with the substance-function ideology, but it became very clear to them early on that Western science was an entire worldview and that if you really embraced the method, then your fundamental ways of looking at the world would change too.

However, as the Chinese became more and more exposed to Western thought, they understood that there was a new philosophical worldview embodied in Western science and culture. Facts and values could not be separated even for the noble reason of trying to save China from humiliation at the hands of the Western powers. China was again entering into a period of disunion and chaos that would not end until the Communist victory and reunification in 1949. It was most significant that the Western challenge was unique in being backed by a military and economic power that would not go away.

The Transition to
Modern China and East Asia

The Meiji Reformation was one of the great modernization stories of all time. Japan moved quickly from being completely isolated from the rest of the world to becoming recognized as an international power even by the Western nations in the early part of the twentieth century. First, the Japanese demonstrated that they had mastered Western military science by defeating the Chinese in a short war in 1894–1895. The Japanese decided that a thoroughly modern power on the Western model needed colonies, so one of the outcomes of the Sino-Japanese War was the conquest of Taiwan as part of the Japanese empire. Second, the Japanese became the first Asian power to defeat a major Western power in a contest of arms. In 1905, the Japanese defeated and humiliated the Russian Empire in the Russo-Japanese War, as Japan pursued its course of expanding its grip on Korea and its influence in Manchuria.

Korea's entry into the modern world was even sadder than China's experience. Like Japan, Korea frowned upon any contact with the outside world, save for formal relations with China. In fact, after the Manchu conquest of China in 1644, the Koreans thought of themselves as the last truly Confucian state. Although the Koreans were forced to accept the Manchus and their dynasty, this did not convince the Koreans that they were not really the heirs of Neo-Confucian loyalty. In the end, Korean isolation from the modern world made the country an easy target for colonial adventures. Korea was incorporated into the expanding Japanese empire after the Russo-Japanese War and did not regain independence until 1945.

In the second half of the nineteenth century, there were a growing number of classically trained Chinese intellectuals who were well aware of the fact that the West was not going to disappear like some kind of bad dream and that new ways had to be devised to deal with the threat to the survival of East Asian cultures. One of the participants in this history, Liang Ch'i-ch'ao (1873–1929), even went on to become one of the great historians of late Ch'ing intellectual history. One of Liang's teachers, the scholar-reformer K'ang Yu-wei (1858–1927), was a fascinating visionary of this early attempt at renewal. K'ang was a brilliant scholar of classical Chinese learning. But he also realized that classical Chinese thought must now be integrated with Western thought in order for it to flourish in the modern world.

K'ang Yu-wei, along with a group of younger thinkers and such students of his as Liang Ch'i-ch'ao and T'an Ssu-t'ung (1865–1898), persuaded the young Ch'ing emperor to begin a series of drastic reforms in 1898, often called the One Hundred Day Reform. It was all too clear that China had failed in its program of "self-strengthening" after its humiliating defeat in the brief Sino-Japanese War of 1894–1895. The young emperor turned to K'ang for advice, and during the few heady months of rapid reform, it appeared that K'ang might actually lead a major reform movement. However, this was not to be. The old empress dowager, who was the real power behind the throne, after first allowing the reforms, then moved to crush the whole reform movement with brutal swiftness. She placed the young emperor under what was basically house arrest and scattered the reformers. T'an Ssu-t'ung, one of the brilliant young leaders, refused to flee and gave his short life as a witness to the spirit of reform. The other leaders escaped as best they could to the West, Hong Kong, and Japan to plan for more radical changes.

Even while playing his various revolutionary roles, K'ang Yu-wei created a blueprint for a new, ideal society. If the old Confucian world was not spacious enough, then K'ang set about enlarging that classical worldview so that it would fit modern conditions. K'ang called for an age of peace and equality. Whereas the notion of peace and harmony have been parts of Confucian thought from its beginning, K'ang's emphasis on equality as a concept for the creation of a new Confucian world was unique. As Laurence Thompson (1958) wrote about K'ang's scheme, even marriage as it was known would be transformed. People would be free to form alliances for as long as they were in love and then would end them in order to avoid the pain of an unsuccessful match. Of course, for K'ang, this also meant that there would be complete equality for women in all aspects of public and private life, including free love. Needless to say, these were not quite the kind of family relations that Chu Hsi or even the more radical followers of Wang Yang-ming had had in mind.

K'ang Yu-wei believed that he needed to make use of all the best ideas from Buddhism, classical Chinese thought, and the West. But at the bedrock of his new theories, K'ang affirmed, along with Mencius, that such appeals to utopian theory would work because people have fundamentally good natures. K'ang argues that all people have this compassionate, humane mind-heart and nature because we are all formed from what he calls a spiritual matter-energy, or *ch'i*. K'ang makes his case by adding that matter-energy is like electricity that has awareness. K'ang meant that there is a mutual attraction that comes with the essential polarity of matter-energy, and to be is to have this vital, spiritual nature. Here we can see how K'ang fused classical

Chinese philosophical ideas with what he had learned from Western science. K'ang saw no contradiction between classical *ch'i* theory and modern Western descriptions of the properties and functions of electricity.

Nowhere was K'ang Yu-wei more radical than in his defense of the complete personal and social emancipation of women. In the past, K'ang painted this sorry picture of what happened to women.

> Women, being the private possessions of men, were but men's playthings. Therefore they pierced their ears, bound their feet, compressed their waists, blackened their teeth, shaved their eyebrows, applied mascara, wore rouge, used face powder, (adopted) odd coiffures, walked mincingly. They did not grudge to harm their (own) bodies in order to provide a man one day of pleasure. (Thompson 1958:162)

All of this must change, according to K'ang, so that women can become completely equal partners with men in the world. This equality is based on the complementary nature of yin and yang, and it means that women must be allowed and encouraged to move from the private sphere within the home to take their rightful places in the public world.

One of K'ang's young followers, T'an Ssu-t'ung, provided the reform movement with its greatest martyr. Furthermore, T'an also wrote one of the classics of Chinese thought in this period, entitled *An Exposition of Benevolence*. Typical of the period, T'an's work is eclectic. Although the title of his work, *Jen-hsüeh*, would seem to be standard Confucian fare, there is nothing typical about how T'an argued for benevolence in terms of content and modern practice. For instance, T'an states that "only three persons were able to be the source of benevolence and attained their divineness in nothingness: they were the Buddha (cir. 565–486 B.C.), Confucius (551–479 B.C.) and Jesus" (T'an 1984:55). T'an was so close to Buddhist thought that it makes as much sense to write about him as part of the modern Buddhist revival as it does to include him in the history of Confucianism. T'an represents, in his life and works, the commitment to renewing Chinese thought that was part of this second generation of reformers.

Even the way T'an Ssu-t'ung organized his study of humaneness illustrates the change from the previous generation. T'an begins with a list of twenty-seven explanations or theses about the nature of *jen*. This kind of propositional exposition is borrowed from T'an's understanding of how Western philosophers make their claims for truth value. It is highly instructive to review selectively the opening steps of T'an's argument.

> (1) The most fundamental meaning of benevolence is interconnectedness. The terms ether, electricity, and mental power all indicate the means of interconnection.

(2) Ether and electricity are simply means whose names are borrowed to explain mental power.

(3) The meaning of interconnection is best expressed by "The Way unites all as one by interconnection." . . .

(8) Interconnection is expressed as equality. (T'an 1984:61–62)

One of the things that strikes us is the emphasis K'ang and T'an give to equality as an essential part of humaneness. This in fact becomes one of the essential features of modern New Confucianism. The New Confucians recognize that the tradition was often interpreted as unequal in terms of social relations and gender, and they believe that this is something that must be rectified if Confucianism is to have any relevance for modern women and men.

T'an writes as a very cosmopolitan person interested in Western science and history as much as in classical Chinese lore. T'an's world has opened up dramatically from those of his father and grandfathers. Things are much more relative for him because he cannot and does not want to assume that all beyond China's borders is mere barbarism. T'an is intrigued and stimulated by the facts of world history, and this diversity makes it impossible for him to make simple statements about human nature being of just one kind. For instance, T'an appeals to modern chemistry in order to show how complex life itself is and how difficult it is to find anything truly fixed in nature. He asks, "Where do we see the so-called unalterable nature?" (T'an 1984:89). For T'an the world is a vast creative process, and unlike his Neo-Confucian forebears, who would have agreed about the processive nature of reality, T'an applies this lesson to the moral content of human nature. T'an is consistent in that he not only rejects the Confucian idea of a good human nature but also criticizes Western concepts of the soul.

The Korean Case

However, not all nineteenth-century Confucian encounters with the West were as enthusiastic as K'ang Yu-wei's and T'an Ssu-t'ung's attempts to come to terms with a greatly expanded world. In Korea, Chung Chai-Sik (1995) has written a portrait of a conservative Confucian intellectual, Yi Hang-no (1792–1868), who looked at the West and did not like what he saw. In this regard, Yi agreed with his first-generation Chinese counterparts in rejecting any need to incorporate Western ideas into his thought world. In Yi's case, one of the primary grounds for engagement with the West was with Christianity, as it was beginning to impact Korea through missionary and indigenous efforts and interests.

Yi Hang-no was proudly a scholar of the Chu Hsi tradition and a teacher by inclination. It was only at the end of his life at the age of seventy-three in 1864 that he was called to national service to try to help save his country from foreign intervention. Although Yi did not live to see Korea's subordination to imperial Japan, he believed that the greatest threat to the Confucian order of Korea lay in the West. In one sense he was correct; it was not Confucian Japan that conquered Korea but rather a Westernized Japan that followed the West in carving out an empire in Asia. Whereas K'ang and T'an were rethinking Confucian views toward the economy and human sexuality, Yi rejected any such interest in Western ideas as the worst kind of inhuman perversity: "The calamities of circulating currencies and expressing sexuality would drive us into a barbaric and beastly state without even allowing us any other" (Chung 1995:128).

Yi Hang-no believed that however strong the West might appear, it was a misguided strength because Westerners ultimately did not understand principle. Western power was based on the manipulation of matter-energy without moral principle. There was a grandeur to Yi's view of Korea in the world. He believed that with China falling so rapidly under Western sway, much less Japan, it was only Korea that continued real Confucian teachings. It was Korea's destiny to preserve Asian values in a world being violated by Western military power. Whereas K'ang and T'an were convinced that they would have to find a place for equality (and even women) within a renewed Confucian world, Yi rejected any such notions as violating the Confucian sense of proper order and hierarchy. Ideals like liberty and individuality were without proper principles and would destroy Confucian culture. Of course, Yi was correct—because the West, and most specifically Japan, would do just this to Confucian Korea.

Chinese Revisioning

A Chinese scholar of the next generation, Liang Shu-ming (1893–1988), also struggled with the question of what it meant to be a modern Asian intellectual. There is something poignant and suggestive about Guy S. Alitto's study of Liang called *The Last Confucian*. Alitto has made a good case for the argument that Liang was the last of his generation of Confucians directly linked to the imperial past. However, after Liang there arose a new Confucian reform movement, and it was this third generation of reformers and public scholars that founded what is now called the New Confucian movement.

Liang Shu-ming is a fascinating study in intellectual contrasts. In his own life and thought, he managed to summarize many of the trends of the day in a life dedicated to the reform of China. To grasp Liang's contribution, we need to understand the turbulent world of Chinese thought just after World War I. By that time, many Chinese had studied in Europe and North America and had returned home to teach in the new universities that were being founded around the country, the most famous being Peking

University. Having been betrayed by the Western powers after the war during the signing of the peace treaties, many Chinese called for an even more radical reform than the nationalist revolution that toppled the Ch'ing dynasty and had established the new Chinese republic.

Along with a legendary sense of self-control and personal integrity, Liang Shu-ming also had a refreshingly ironic view of his life: He started out being critical of philosophy and ended being a philosopher who never liked the Confucian schools and yet became a famous Confucian; did not attend a university and yet became a professor in one; and grew up in an urban setting and yet became justly famous for his work in rural reform in the 1930s. He also had the unenviable task of being the object of Mao Tsetung's angry criticism late in life. After the suicide of his father as a protest against China's fate, Liang Shu-ming sought to cure his personal pain through the intense study of Buddhism. Like a number of other Chinese of his generation, he was drawn to the Consciousness Only school because of its idealistic bent. It was not till 1921 that Liang announced that he had returned to the Confucian fold after his Buddhist interlude. He was certainly not the only Confucian who had found solace in Buddhist teachings and meditation during a time of personal crisis.

Liang Shu-ming came to public attention because of a series of public lectures he delivered on the question of Eastern and Western cultures. It was a good time for someone to defend Asian culture. We must remember that many Westernizing Chinese intellectuals had just observed the devastation of World War I. East Asian intellectuals were profoundly disillusioned with what had happened in Europe and were willing to reconsider some aspects of their own cultural heritage. Liang argued that each of these cultures had distinct spirit and that it would be very difficult just to mix them together in order to get the best of both. He came to the conclusion that culture was not merely a supermarket of ideas but was a living reality that could not be changed merely by the whim of a reform movement. If one could not just change culture like a hat in the spring, what should Chinese intellectuals do in order to save China from its present crisis?

Liang agreed with his colleagues at Peking University that the essence of Western culture was the potent combination of science and democracy. He argued that this culture was linked to an epistemology of critical reason and analysis. This was not the path of Chinese culture. Liang discovered the genius of Chinese culture in *I-Ching* and identified intellectual intuition as an alternative epistemological vision (as would Mou Tsung-san as well). The theme of analysis versus intuition is a topic that reverberates throughout the New Confucian movement.

According to Alitto, Liang linked ideas drawn from the *I-Ching* and Bergson together in the following fashion: "The universe is life; life is a ceaseless flux; so the ultimate reality is pure change, and to comprehend change in itself, is to comprehend the essence of reality" (Alitto 1979:99). Liang believed that Confucius was special because he had grasped the essence of this reality as flux and had realized that the basis of this flux was the "harmonization of all elements of existence" (Alitto 1979:99). This ideal of harmony then, of course, found societal expression in the concept of humaneness. Like Bergson, Liang believed that we could know this ultimate harmony only through intuition and not rational or analytic means.

Having made his intellectual breakthrough, Liang decided in the late 1920s that he would need to put his ideas into practice in rural areas. Untold generations of Confucians had functioned as local teachers and administrators with notable success. The next phase of his life was dedicated to rural reform. Whatever the merits of Liang's practical ideas, and they seem to have had good success in local settings, they were swept away by the great war with Japan that began in 1937 and by the victory of the Communist Party after the civil war in 1949. After 1949, Mao Tse-tung was not very interested in listening to a Confucian social activist; Mao had other visions for the reform of China.

The New Confucians

Some of the scholars just discussed here who were writing in the 1920s and 1930s were "new" Confucians in the sense that they were dedicated to the reform and renewal of the tradition from a critical perspective. However, the term "New Confucian" specifies a unique group of scholars, just as the term "speculative moral philosophy" is a way of talking about the more philosophically inclined Confucian intellectuals of the Northern and Southern Sung dynasties. The scholars who make up the three generations of the New Confucian movement trace their origins to the teachings of Hsiung Shih-li (1885–1968), a most remarkable and influential professor of philosophy at Peking University.

Hsiung Shih-li sought to revive the idealistic wing of the Confucian tradition, and in fact was first interested in Yogacara Buddhism before he returned to Confucian scholarship. Most of Hsiung's students followed him in this idealistic direction and identified more with Wang Yang-ming than with Chu Hsi. Perhaps only Fung Yu-lan (1895–1990) truly represented the more rationalistic side of the tradition. Yet Hsiung's Confucianism is highly eclectic, and he tried to make a place in it for the best of traditional Buddhist thought along with modern currents from the West. It is a testimony to his personal stature that he was even allowed to continue to publish works on Confucian thought after the founding of the Communist regime in 1949.

The 1920s, 1930s, and 1940s were not good times in China for any kind of sustained intellectual development. Although China had allied itself with the Western powers during World War I, the Japanese maintained and improved their dominant position in East Asia. As in earlier ages of disunity, there was no effective government for all of China after the founding of the new republic in 1911, and many parts of the country were ruled by independent warlords or were even semicolonies of the Western powers or Japan. This trend toward fragmentation was confronted in the 1920s by the rising power of the Nationalist Party, and their sometime ally, the Chinese Communist Party. But just when it seemed the National Party was poised to reunite the country, defeat the remaining warlords, and destroy the Communist Party, the Japanese struck again. From the early 1930s on, there was a quasiwar going on in North China that spread to the rest of China. The major conflict finally broke out in 1937, putting an end to the attempt of the Nationalist Party to reunify the whole country. Once the war was over in 1945, China immediately plunged back into a protracted civil war that finally ended with the victory of the Communist movement in 1949. The New Confucians suffered during this terrible period of war and civil conflict. However, they never wavered in their belief that there was something noble in the Confucian tradition that needed to be renewed and commended to the world at large. To that end, some of them fled China to work in universities in Taiwan or in Hong Kong. In Hong Kong, this group of scholars helped to found the New Asia College, and later New Asia College joined with other schools to form the new Chinese University of Hong Kong. At New Asia College and then at the Chinese University, the task of reforming the New Confucian movement continued from the 1950s to the present. Scholars from Hong Kong, Taiwan, and elsewhere in the Chinese diaspora did not let Hsiung Shih-li's dream of a revived Confucianism die. In fact, today the New Confucian movement is not only taught and studied in Hong Kong, Singapore, and Taipei, but many younger scholars from China itself are analyzing the philosophical ideas of the first and second generation while working with diaspora Chinese intellectuals in a retrieval of Confucian scholarship.

It is difficult to date precisely the founding of the New Confucian movement. However, in spring 1958, Carsun Chang and a number of his colleagues, including T'ang Chün-i (1909–1978), Mou Tsung-san, and Hsü Fu-kuan (1903–1982) published "A Manifesto for a Re-appraisal of Sinology." This was indeed a manifesto that served to mark the emergence of the New Confucians. In turn, this second generation turned out to be a fine set of teachers, training new generations of Chinese intellectuals dedicated to describing, interpreting, renewing, and then commending the Confucian tradition as something worthy of global attention.

In order to give some idea of the kind of work that the New Confucians did, we will focus on the contribution of Mou Tsung-san (1909–1994). Mou has been recognized as perhaps the most systematic philosopher among the New Confucians. He began his philosophical quest by working in the areas of Western philosophy and logic. He was convinced, as were many Confucians of his generation, that they needed to provide a more logically rigorous defense of the tradition. Mou was acutely aware that compared to modern Western philosophy, Confucian thought looked disorganized and confused, more like poetry than careful argument.

In order to revive the tradition, Mou Tsung-san argued that the true mainline of Chinese thought did not run through the work of Chu Hsi but rather in other lines of descent in the Sung and Ming periods. Mou criticized Chu Hsi for hijacking the tradition through the genius of his work. Mou did not charge that Chu was a Buddhist or Taoist in disguise but rather said that Chu Hsi's intellectual style was more in line with Hsün Tzu in its analytic core than with Mencius and Ch'eng Hao. In short, Ch'eng I and Chu Hsi represented a brilliant side branch of the Neo-Confucian tree that dominated the whole plant, when it should have been pruned back to make room for the more orthodox presentations of Ch'eng Hao and Liu Tsung-chou. According to Mou, Lü Chiu-yuan and Wang Yang-ming were yet another offshoot of the Confucian trunk, and even though they were more in line with Mencius, they too were not the mainline. According to Mou, the last great mainline thinker was Liu Tsung-chou at the end of the Ming.

Mou Tsung-san's revisionist history of the rise of Neo-Confucian discourse is based on his own modern interpretation of what it means to be a Confucian. One thing that distinguished Mou's work was his call to pay attention to questions of epistemology and logic as part of Confucian discourse. For instance, it is in the area of epistemology that Mou made some of his most important points about the reformation of Confucian thought. Mou is not an easy philosopher to read because he moves among three different thought worlds. He has written on all aspects of Chinese thought, including the technical aspects of high T'ang Buddhist philosophy. Furthermore, Mou engaged modern Western philosophy from Descartes to Whitehead, with special attention to the Kantian tradition. Mou was as liable to quote a long section from Kant or Leibniz to make a point about Hu Hung's theory of moral self-cultivation as he was to compare Hu's theory to Ch'eng I. To read Mou is to read the history of classical Chinese thought, Buddhist philosophy, and modern Western metaphysics and ethics.

A good example of Mou's complicated analysis can be found in his critique of Chu Hsi's philosophy. Mou argued that Chu is too committed to the rational analysis of the things and events of the world. Mou does not fault Chu for his interest in the world as an object of reflection. Rather, Mou believed that Chu missed understanding the unique Confucian epistemological stance, a view Mou called moral intuition. Mou then compared Chu with Kant. Mou had the highest regard for both Chu and Kant, even though he believed that they are wrong at one fundamental point. Kant argued that we cannot know things in themselves because we can never get behind the screen of our own world-constituting consciousness. Chu Hsi made the same mistake by focusing on his doctrine of principle, an idea he learned from Ch'eng I. Rather than following Chu and Kant in their endless search for the reasons for things that cannot be analyzed by discursive reason, Mou affirmed that the genius of the Chinese tradition resides in the praxis of moral intuition that does give us access to the things in themselves.

Following Kant's lead, Mou concluded that the best that Kant or Chu Hsi can offer us is a metaphysics of morals, a merely formal rationalism based on the ability of the mind-heart to analyze its principles and the principles of the external world. However, if we follow Ch'eng Hao and Liu Tsung-chou rather than Chu Hsi, we will find a carefully articulated theory of moral intuition that gives access to the world as it is. This allowed Mou to state that the real Confucian philosophical tradition is a moral metaphysics and not a metaphysics of morals that cannot respond to the way things really are because it is always looking at the way things were rather than how they come to be. For Mou, both Chu and Kant have a retrospective view of reason in that they are always looking at the structure of things past rather than using the cultivated mind-heart to intuit reality as a process of ceaseless creativity.

Mou Tsung-san articulated a modern Confucianism as a reformed moral metaphysics. By this he meant that Confucian philosophy is more than just a social ethics, though it is certainly that; Confucian thought is always a fundamental axiology. Confucians are uniformly concerned with human values and occupied with figuring out how these values can lead to human flourishing. Mou often speculated on which single term, if it were possible to find one, could cover this primordial sense of Confucian axiology. The term Mou settled on can be roughly translated as "concern-consciousness." The notion of concern-consciousness describes, for instance, the ceaseless toil and work that the sage kings lavished on their societies. The sage kings never rested until they had done all that they could do for their people. Beyond the images of the sage kings, the notion of concern is another thread that runs through the work of Confucius and Mencius. Both of these sages remind their students that they must be concerned with the cultivation of their moral mind-heart for the sake of serving the world. In these and all other early Confucian writings, Mou found suggestions that a true Confucian has a profound concern for the world. One of the correlates of concern-consciousness is the persistent Confucian affirmation of cosmological realism: The world is real and the values that human beings embrace are real as well.

In order to give concrete examples of what concern-consciousness traditionally meant, Mou suggested that any Confucian philosophical system must consider at least four metaphors, elements, motifs, or traits. Mou knew that this was not "system," but he did believe that the tradition would not be faithful to its past if it did not at least touch on the issues raised by reflection on these traits.

1. *T'ien-ming* as creativity itself, the ceaseless generativity of the Tao as the symbol of all that is or could be.
2. *Jen* as the embodiment of creativity, itself manifested as a primordial concern for others; the Tao made concrete in proper human ethical and social concern.
3. *Hsin* as the mind-heart, functions as the locus of the experiential unity of concern-consciousness within any living human being.
4. *Hsing* as the formal structure of human nature, including the cultivation of the mind-heart so that it actively creates and participates in the cosmic generativity of the Tao.

According to Mou, each one of these traits is related to a specific classical text. For instance, *t'ien-ming*/the Mandate of Heaven as creativity itself is best articulated in the *I-Ching* and the *Doctrine of the Mean*. It is interesting to note that Mou uses the term *t'ien-ming* rather than Tao or *t'ien tao*/the Tao of Heaven to symbolize the profoundly creative aspects of the world. I take this to indicate the normative nature of creativity that Mou was at pains to defend; creativity is not random action without any direction because it is directed toward the good. *Jen,* or humaneness, is, naturally, found as the central thread of Confucius' teachings in the *Analects*.

As for the mind-heart, the obvious canonical text from Mou's point of view is the *Mencius*. For human nature, Mou again selected the *Mencius*, though I would add the *Great Learning* because it provided so many details about the cultivation of human nature for most Confucians over the centuries. Mou's complaint about the *Great Learning* was that it is closer to Hsün Tzu's school than to Mencius. Mou associates the *Great Learning* with Hsün Tzu and Chu Hsi as representing a branch but not the mainline of the Confucian Way. However, in Mou's last public lecture, he argued that modern Confucians ought to find a way to reintegrate Hsün Tzu's defense of ritual action and critical reason into a revived New Confucianism.

Mou's list is suggestive, but it needs to be expanded in light of the contributions of other New Confucians such as Tu Wei-ming, Julia Ching, Liu Shu-hsien, and Cheng Chung-ying. Along with Mou's four basic traits, we need to add the following four:

5. *Tao wen-hsüeh* as pursuing inquiry and study, in order to exhaust principle as a means for critical reason to adjudge the conformity of human conduct with the proper patterns of the Tao
6. *Li* as ritual action or civility, as the methods and agreements human beings propose to deal with each other in a humane manner

7. *Ch'i* as matter-energy, the dynamic force/matrix from which all objects and events are manifested and to which they return
8. *Chih shan,* or *ho,* as the highest good or final harmony of creation.

The fifth trait of inquiry and study in order to exhaust principle is focused on the ideal of the investigation of things (*ko-wu*) made famous by Chu Hsi's commentary on the term in the *Great Learning.* The phrase *tao wen-hsüeh* is taken from the *Doctrine of the Mean,* and Chu Hsi interprets the phrase in light of his commitment to critical reason. Following Cheng Chung-ying's suggestion, Confucian critical reason also originated and was sustained by what the *I-Ching* characterized as broad observation. Chu Hsi agreed that a proper life is a balance between internal *tsun te-hsüeh*/self-cultivation and careful attention to the details of life found in the external world as taught in the *Doctrine of the Mean.*

As for the sixth trait, ritual action/civility, the various early ritual texts such as the *Chou-li* serve to define how humaneness and the other four prime Confucian virtues are understood as ritual conduct and general social intercourse. It is hard to think of Confucianism without making some recourse to ritual action and social ethics. In many respects, the domain of ritual action came to be the most famous part of the Confucian social world when contrasted to Taoist and Buddhist forms of life. However much Confucian literati of the Sung, Ming, or Ch'ing periods might practice Confucian meditation as quiet-sitting, when they arose from such personal cultivation, they were expected to be masters of Confucian ritual. Of course, in the classical period it was Hsün Tzu who most forcefully argued for the centrality of ritual as a means of correcting human perversity and inordinate self-interest.

The seventh trait of *ch'i* as matter-energy is more difficult to specify in terms of classical Confucian texts. Of course, we can always appeal to the *I-Ching,* because that text does indeed provide the locus for many Confucian philosophers' speculations on the nature of matter-energy and the material world. Along with *ch'i* theory, the *I-Ching* also provides the classical Confucian tradition with its understanding of yin and yang and the Five Phases. Chang Li-wen and his colleagues (1991) have devoted a short monograph to *ch'i* as part of a series on key philosophical terms in Chinese philosophy. They begin the *ch'i* section on pre-Ch'in and Han philosophy with selections from the canonical *Tso-chuan* and the *Kuo-yü* and end their section with a more extended discussion of the *Kuan Tzu.* Although the *Kuan Tzu* has never been part of the Confucian canon, traditional and modern scholars have long recognized that the book is highly eclectic and contains materials from all the pre-Han philosophical schools, including sections that certainly have a strong Confucian flavor. It is within the protomedical sections of the *Kuan Tzu* that we see most clearly how *ch'i* becomes the philosophical idea of matter-energy. Although Confucians have never approved of Taoist ritual magic, an interest in medicine was always considered a licit interest for a Confucian gentleman.

One reason that *ch'i* is not mentioned on Mou's shortlist of Confucian traits is historical. Rather like classical Greek thought, Confucian discourse combined cosmological and ethical reflection in diverse patters. The germane point is that the pre-Han Confucians, and especially Confucius in the *Analects*, were not overly concerned with what we call cosmology as it came to be understood and interpreted in the changing patterns of yinyang, the Five Phases and the dynamic energy of *ch'i*. Rather, the early Confucians were concerned with questions of ethical conduct, ritual, good government, education, and self-cultivation. However, as the tradition expanded, later Confucians such as Mencius and Hsün Tzu repeatedly utilized the work of the early cosmologists found in works like the *Kuan Tzu* in order to defend the Confucian Way against other schools.

The notions of the highest good and harmony find their most cogent canonical status defined in the *Doctrine of the Mean*. The first section of the *Doctrine of the Mean* teaches that what follows from the balanced and measured issuance of the emotions in the mind-heart is harmony. It is a state that comes about when the person has achieved not only the inner cultivation of the human nature but also an appropriate encounter with what is in the world beyond the human person. The classic teaches that harmony is the most excellent or perfect functioning of the Way for human flourishing. In the *Analects* (bk. 13, sec. 23) one of the characteristics of the *chüntzu*, or profound person, is that of agreeing with what is good and not merely echoing or accommodating the thoughts of others. Hence, the profound person resides in a state of harmony but not indifferent conformity with the world, *ho erh pu-t'ung*. There are certainly strong grounds to conclude any list of Confucian traits or core teachings by returning to the *Analects* and the ideal of sagely harmony.

New Confucianism is a fresh philosophical movement. None of the second- or third-generation thinkers claim to have perfected a definitive, systematic reformation of the tradition. In fact, thinkers like Mou Tsung-san, Ch'ien Mu, and T'ang Chün-i argued that such grand synthesis would be premature. The present Confucian philosophical task is to sift through the tradition in order to find out what can be saved, what must be modified, and what must be abandoned. For instance, all the New Confucians are aware of the implications of de Bary's (1991a) title, *The Trouble with Confucianism*. If philosophical traditions have distinctive problems, then Confucianism has always had a great problem with its relationship to the state, power, and authority. For instance, de Bary and others have pointed out that Confucians never learned how to form a loyal opposition to the imperial state, often leaving them helpless in the face of a misguided tyrannical emperor. Confucians wanted to serve the state so badly that they were willing to sell their souls for position, power, and money—and sometimes this sale was even more painful because they knew that they were being forced to give up their high moral ideals in the transactions of power.

New Confucians have acknowledged the potent feminist critique of how the patriarchal Confucian tradition denigrated and oppressed women. They further realize that any sustainable New Confucianism will have to deal directly with these critiques and find a way, as all philosophies and religions must, to correct the mistakes of the past. In this regard, some of the work done by Confucian women in the late Ming and mid-Ch'ing is important; it demonstrates that women can find meaning in Confucianism when it is expanded to embrace their concerns and show respect for their issues and scholarship. In short, one of the crucial features of feminism is that women ought—simply and everywhere—to be treated as equals.

The New Confucians have recognized both the critiques of de Bary (1991a) and Metzger (1977) in the realm of political culture and the feminist critiques in gender relations. In terms of response, one of the glories of the tradition was to move from a social system based on birth and social position to one based on achievement and education. A chief outcome was the notion of a career open to talent. One of the ways to expand the tradition's appeal to women is to make the ideal of a career based on talent open to all women as well as all men. But this kind of adjustment does not answer all the questions raised by feminist and other radical social critics of Confucianism. There is still the question of whether Confucianism is essentially an elitist tradition unable to make room for the kind of egalitarian claims made in the name of modernization and democratic institutions. Can such a social philosophy ever get rid of elitist patriarchy?

There are a number of ways Confucians respond to the question of elitism and hierarchy. Scholars like Mou Tsung-san have noted that Confucians have read the Confucian virtues in the most conservative and hierarchical way possible. For instance, humaneness and the other prime virtues were seen as part of the Three Major Relationships, namely those between ruler and subject, father and son, and husband and wife. Mou and others ask, But what would be the situation if the virtues were read in an order that stressed relationships based on the fifth of the great virtues, namely, that of faithfulness in friendship? Mou hinted that the five virtues can be construed quite differently if we take friendship to be the model of social organization rather than the feudal connection between an emperor and a subject. If we read the virtues in the modern world with due respect for the imperatives of the equality of friendship, then there is ample room to create a New Confucianism that is wedded neither to authoritarian government nor to the oppression of women and ethnic minorities.

The question of complete equality is trickier. With careers open to talent and a world of social ethics informed by the faithfulness of friendship, we are still left with the persistent Confucian view that some people simply achieve more than others. Although Confucians affirm the basic equality of chance at the beginning of human endeavor, there is the fact that one cannot always affirm equality of outcome and still have any vision of human excellence. Some people are simply better potential musicians and artists than others; some people are born to be great doctors and scholars; and some people are even good at being politicians and judges. The New Confucians would prefer to see a world wherein careers are truly open to talent and human civility and critical reason are cultivated enough to inculcate deference to talent and achievement for all people. Envy of those who are good at what they achieve ought to be replaced by a recognition that we all benefit when human excellence is encouraged within an open society.

Another area of renovation needed for a New Confucian synthesis is in the Confucian relationship with modern science. As Joseph Needham (1954–) has shown, the classical and Neo-Confucian scholars were often abreast of the best science of their day and rarely saw any reason for conflict between their Confucian commitments and the findings of science. In fact, it is important to remember that China was the most technologically advanced culture in the world for many centuries. The rise of the West to technological and scientific dominance has been recent, and science is one of those very ecumenical exports of human reason that works well no matter where it is found, when practiced by people of talent with the proper training.

The whole question of why "modern" science arose in the West is a hotly debated issue. Suffice it to say that many modern Confucians believe that their vision of a creative universe founded on *ch'i* theory probably works as well as any worldview when contrasted to the empirical teachings of modern science. Confucians, for instance, were always interested in scientific areas such as medicine, astronomy, mathematics, agronomy, and forensics. Although these interests were often pragmatic, driven by the exigencies of being a local or regional administrator, the interests often became objects of genuine curiosity. Here again, New Confucians believe that a modern Confucianism will have no difficulty in dealing with modern science. This is the reason that the notion of matter-energy needs to be included in the shortlist of Confucian traits necessary for the creation of a renewed tradition.

The modern Confucian revival is also a pluralistically international enterprise with developments in China, Korea, and Japan (and perhaps Vietnam). Furthermore, the growing East Asian intellectual diaspora has provided a great deal of the initial impetus for the development of New Confucianism. There are signs of Confucian revival in China signaled by the founding of national and international organizations devoted to Confucian thought sponsored by the government. The reason often given for the official sponsorship of these renewed Confucian organizations is that modern China must decide how to teach its youth about its past. Confucianism is part of this patrimony, a part that needs to be carefully studied and promoted wherever appropriate for the new China in order to encourage a Chinese form of modernization.

To illustrate this diversity, we will briefly look at the work of three modern Confucians. Two are Chinese intellectuals working in the West and represent the third-generation students of teachers such as Mou Tsung-san, Ch'ien Mu, T'ang Chün-i, and Hsü Fu-kuan. The third is a Japanese Confucian concerned with the living practice of Confucian self-cultivation. The Chinese thinkers are Tu Wei-ming and Cheng Chung-ying; the Japanese scholar is Okada Takehiko. All three illustrate the diversity, unity and renewal of the tradition.

The old notions of a rationalistic Chu Hsi school as opposed to an idealistic Wang Yang-ming school make little sense when applied to the work of Cheng Chung-ying and Tu Wei-ming. Nonetheless, Cheng has taken pains to try to show the logical implications of Confucian thought when stated in terms of Western modes of discourse. For instance, Cheng, trained in Western logic and analytic philosophy, explores the ways Confucian philosophers constructed the logic of their arguments. In *New Dimensions of Confucian and Neo-Confucian Philosophy* (1991), Cheng has presented a series of interlocking essays that deal with notions of mind, the special characteristics of Confucian dialectic and philosophy, the role of conscience, and so on. One of Cheng's main tasks is to show how Confucian thought intersects with modern Western thought and how it differs in some of its major conclusions. Cheng's project is profoundly dialogical, as most of the major Eastern responses to Western thought have been.

In terms of its fundamental characteristics, Cheng argues that Confucianism, as a specific case of a larger Chinese worldview, is a form of intrinsic humanism and organic naturalism. Cheng's notion of intrinsic humanism is subtle and is echoed by many New Confucians. Cheng does not want a truncated humanism, a form of reductionism that limits the human to materialism, nor does he think the cosmos is related only to human means and ends. Cheng argues that Confucianism is also a religious humanism in the sense that it is a theory of humanity that is open to the religious dimension of the human experience. It is a form of immanent transcendence wherein the role of human nature is crucial and yet expansive beyond previously achieved values. Cheng defends both the poles of subjective and objective reality in his doctrine of intrinsic humanism: "The philosophic assumption that nature is intrinsic to the existence of man and man intrinsic to the existence of nature, is the foundation of Chinese humanism" (Cheng 1991:81). It is this kind of claim that causes us to link Cheng to Chu Hsi's style of thought. For Cheng, both the world and the mind-heart are fundamentally real and interconnected; there is no bifurcation between humanity and the Tao.

Cheng also holds that Confucianism is a species of organic naturalism: "Organic naturalism in Chinese philosophy is perhaps better described in consideration of the relation between the objective and the subjects and between the physical and mental" (Cheng 1991:84). Here, too, Cheng is at pains to show that Confucian naturalism is not reductionistic in either the direction of a pure idealism and subjectivism or toward a purely objective and physical understanding of the human condition. Actually, none of these claims will seem odd after our studies of Sung, Ming, and Ch'ing thought. Like the more famous Japanese Kyoto school thinkers, Cheng carries on his work dialectically; there is the definition of the Chinese case, a comparison with standard Western ways of looking at these issues, and then the suggestion that the Chinese viewpoint can enrich our global perspective on these questions. A corollary to the enrichment of world philosophy is that Confucian thought now must become a partner in dialogue with Western philosophy and religion.

Cheng presents his material modeled on the best modern Western philosophical scholarship. The arguments are detailed and build upon the presentation of Chinese material in a Western analytic fashion. The effect is cumulative in that once Cheng has presented his case, we see the outlines of a detailed Confucian response to Western philosophical issues. However, as with so many other New Confucians, even Cheng's most detailed essays remain outlines for future elaborations.

One example will have to suffice. Cheng introduces the case that Confucians have a dialectical method of reasoning, yet one that is different from the characteristic Western style made famous by Plato and Hegel. Cheng calls this the dialectics of harmonization. Whereas the characteristic move of Western dialectic is to create some third thing or synthesis in its process of comparison of competing points of view, the Confucian works with a method that does not subsume either poles of the contrast into something completely new. What is created is rather a novel new pattern of the previous poles and not their disappearance into something new. Cheng calls the other model the dialectic of conflict and points out that two good examples are Buddhist Middle Way doctrine and Hegelian-Marxist social and philosophical analysis. Cheng goes back to the *I-Ching* to find the source for the Confucian dialect of harmonization. Cheng's presentation differs from similar Neo-Confucian doctrines in that it is done with an eye toward the critical strength of the dialectic of conflict. Cheng is sensitive to the fact that Confucians, because of their desire for harmonization, do not take conflict sufficiently into their account. Cheng's own attempt to present the dialectic of harmonization is an excellent example of how a New Confucian works both with canonical Confucian texts and within the modern world of global philosophy.

Tu Wei-ming's project is similar, yet distinctively different from Cheng's. Early in his career, Tu was known as a skilled student of Wang Yang-ming's philosophy. In fact, one of Tu's most characteristic contributions to the renewal of Confucian thought has come in his role as a critical intellectual historian. Over the years, Tu has written a large number of illuminating articles on diverse aspects of the development of Confucian thought. Tu's mastery of the Chinese tradition, along with his profound yet critical response to what he has come to call the Western Enlightenment project, allows him to throw new light on famous and minor tales from the Confucian past. Yet there is always an agenda for Tu's scholarship. Tu accomplishes at least four things in his work: (1) there is the task of accurate and faithful description; (2) there is the need to explain the topic in terms of its roots and its modern context; (3) there is the need to understand what this really means not only in its historical context but also as it pertains to modern life; and (4) and there is the need to passionately yet humbly commend what has been found when it is judged to be of value to the modern world.

A perfect example of Tu Wei-ming's craft is found in his essay on Liu Yin's (1249–1293) Confucian eremitism. In the very first sentence, Tu reminds us of an image from Plato's *Republic,* as mediated by Thomas More's reflections on the nature of utopia; Tu then demonstrates how Liu Yin's repeated refusal to serve the new Mongol dynasty has meaning in terms of the historical context of Confucian eremitism and for modern reflections on the nature of public service and personal choices for ethical conduct and self-cultivation. What might have been a study in the history of Yüan thought becomes a parable for any human being forced to think about how to serve the state with integrity. Although there is a specific Confucian context to this debate, the issue is a common one in all large modern societies. Liu's problems and choices are the kinds of choices that we all have to make in a less than perfect world.

Along with being a superb intellectual historian, Tu Wei-ming has also revived the art of writing Confucian commentary. Probably his most influential work in English is his philosophical commentary on the *Doctrine of the Mean.* Here again, Tu begins his exposition by placing his reflections on the *Doctrine of the Mean* within the Confucian tradition as a whole. But Tu argues that this is not enough; we must see what can be recovered within this crucial Confucian text that speaks to the modern condition. One of the most intriguing aspects of his commentary is that it highlights the religious dimension of the Confucian tradition. Like his teacher Mou Tsung-san, Tu does not shy away from the religious elements of the Confucian tradition.

In fact, Tu's discussion of what he calls the religious dimension of the Confucian Way has become something of a modern classic in that it has taught a whole generation of scholars to think anew about a neglected aspect of the modern presentation of the tradition. Once again, Tu makes use of the best classical Chinese scholarship and links it to the best of Western philosophy of religion. One of Tu's basic points is that Confucianism is not a West Asian religion with a sense of absolute transcendence. However, there is a Confucian sense of piety toward the transcendent as immanent; if we overlook it, we fail to understand the real richness of the Confucian vision. Tu finally suggests that within Confucianism we can find an example of an inclusive humanism. Tu (rather like Cheng actually) means by this that Confucians are open to the transcendent within the context of their making a basic affirmation of the value of human life and an effort to create the conditions for its flourishing.

More recently, Tu Wei-ming has added yet a third dimension to his project for the revival of the Confucian tradition. Like generations of Confucians before him, Tu was called upon by the government of Singapore to act as a Confucian adviser in the areas of ethics and education. This problematic excursus into the political realm guided Tu to reflect on the role of the modern Chinese intellectual in China and the expanding Chinese intellectual diaspora. In short, Tu asks, What does it mean to be Chinese today, and what does the Confucian tradition have to do with modern and global Chinese life? Although still very much in the middle of framing this project, Tu constantly points out that what is needed is a Confucian reflection on the Western Enlightenment project. For instance, the Western use of critical reason, in Weber's sense of instrumental reason, needs to be reexamined as the basis for future civilization. Tu challenges the Enlightenment as its heir—but as its Chinese heir, which senses that all is not well with the modern outcomes of instrumental reason and a truncated or reductionistic humanism.

Tu has returned to the classical Confucian question of the role of the intellectual and the state. But in this case, the state is not merely the government of modern China but the much larger emerging New World Order. Tu finds ways for the Confucian tradition to support the Enlightenment project in areas where it deserves support, for instance, in its demands for human freedom, fundamental human rights, and ecological sensitivity. Tu also suggests that the Confucian understanding of the cultivation of the mind-heart probably has something to teach modern philosophy about the human spirit. With Tu's commitment to being a global citizen concerned with human rights and ecology, we have literally moved from the study of the history of philosophy to the front pages of our daily newspapers.

Chu Hsi and Wang Yang-ming, if there is a proper Confucian land of the blessed, must be looking down now with pride on Cheng Chung-ying and Tu Wei-ming as two representatives of the best instincts of the tradition. As their teacher Mou Tsung-san said in his last public lecture, the time has come for modern Confucians to make the best use of their entire tradition. What is important these days is not the continuation of the quarrel, if there really was one, between Chu and Wang, but the mobilization of their thought for the reformation of the Confucian Way. Furthermore, the Confucian tradition needs to and is indeed finding its voice among other religious and philosophical traditions in the modern world.

One ironic thing that Tu Wei-ming points out is that not long ago, scholars were asking why Confucianism played such an important role in slowing down the modernization of China. Now the dynamic has been reversed, and sociologists such as Peter Berger are talking about a second industrialization and even a second complete form of modernization based on the culture of post-Confucian Asia. Confucianism has moved from being an impediment for modernization to becoming one of the engines that is helping to drive the rapid economic growth of the whole region. Tu argues that we need to figure out in what way Confucianism contributes to the modernization of East Asia. But what is more important from Tu's point of view is that East Asia must work to avoid some of the problems of intellectual anomie that have come to plague the North Atlantic world in late modernity. Tu believes that one way to avoid some of these problems of the European and American experience, such as the decay of the family and the lack of respect for age, wisdom, and education, is to reintroduce a serious discussion of Confucian social values. Tu maintains that Confucianism alone cannot solve all of East Asia's problems, but he asserts that a renewed Confucianism must be a key player in Asian development. If the New Confucians are successful in this role, then they will also have a voice in solving the larger questions of intellectual life in the twenty-first century.

Whereas Cheng Chung-ying and Tu Wei-ming have devoted their careers primarily to the refurbishing of the intellectual side of the Confucian Way, Okada Takehiko, as a modern Japanese intellectual, has also been interested in preserving the key meditational practices of the tradition. Although Okada, in the Japanese context, has been just as much concerned with the scholarly description, explanation, and understanding of the roots of the Confucian Way as any Chinese New Confucian, the question of how the intellectual and spiritual relate is a pressing issue for him. One of the marks of the Japanese Confucian tradition has always been its sense of balance between the spiritual cultivation of scholarship and the mind-heart. At least in part, this drive for balance comes from the fact that Japanese Confucians have always been in intimate dialogue with a robust Buddhist tradition. This was historically the case in early modern Japan and continued in the Meiji Reformation and into the modern period.

Whereas, comparatively speaking, Chinese Buddhism entered into a long period of decline after the rise of Sung Neo-Confucianism, Japanese Buddhism has remained a vigorous part of Japanese intellectual life. In fact, the most famous of Japanese philosophical schools, the Kyoto school, is known in the West as a Buddhist-inspired rejoinder to modern Western thought. Of course, even the case of the Kyoto school is more complicated than that, as are most things in modern Japan. As Steve Odin (1996) has shown, there are roots of the Kyoto school that owe as much to William James as they do to Dogen (1200–1253), but the fact remains that most of the Kyoto school scholars are Buddhists. Therefore, any modern Japanese Confucian must grapple with questions dear to the heart of Buddhist intellectuals. One of these is the role of meditation.

The Sung Neo-Confucians had also faced this kind of Buddhist challenge and developed their own unique form of spiritual self-cultivation called quiet-sitting. As both a scholar and teacher of this Confucian form of meditation, Okada Takehiko has presented a detailed historical analysis of the relationship of Buddhist and Confucian meditation. Okada has defended Confucian meditation as something separate from its Buddhist cousins, even if both forms of meditation grew from common roots in the East Asian world. In essence, Okada shows that the Confucian commitment to the world makes for a different kind of spirituality, an active engagement with the governance of the world that leads to a specific kind of meditation.

Okada notes that meditation is important for the Confucian because it encourages the Confucian to settle and calm the mind-heart. It also allows the Confucian to practice a kind of reverence for the fundamental human nature and to nourish the seeds of moral virtue. There is always the risk that the world will set the agenda for the self and that the person will lose direction through not knowing how to react to the demands of the world. Quiet-sitting, when conjoined with real Confucian scholarship, Okada believes, helps the modern Confucian just as much as earlier Confucians to center the self in service to others.

While Rodney L. Taylor (1988) was preparing his translation of Okada's study of quiet-sitting, he had numerous opportunities to talk with Okada about what this practice meant to him personally. It will come as no surprise that Okada views quiet-sitting as just as important for the modern Confucian as it was in the past. According to Okada, all the problems of modern life, from the threat of war to new ethical demands caused by new medical discoveries, need to be considered by a centered mind-heart. Just as New Confucians will have to give thought to what can be learned from the scholarly side of the tradition, Okada shows how quiet-sitting helps us to understand contemporary ethical problems and seek solutions to them. In a very real sense, Okada unites three major aspects of the Confucian tradition in his life: scholarship, correct behavior or ritual action, and quiet-sitting as a way to nourish Confucian spirituality. Okada observes that in the middle of the bustle of modern life, quiet-sitting is just as crucial to New Confucianism as any of the other Confucian arts and virtues.

We have now reached the end of our review of Confucian history by returning to the reality of modern life. The Confucian Way has not only endured for thousands of years but has become an international movement. Modern Confucians such as Cheng Chung-ying, Tu Wei-ming, and Okada Takehiko demonstrate that this is still the case. Confucianism is very much in transition. It is moving out from its East Asian home into the wider world, a world that is now poised on the edge of a new millennium. It is likewise changing from a premodern form of life into a thoroughly modern and vibrant view of the world and in doing so is changing modernity itself. If we live in a postmodern world, as some North Atlantic intellectuals now maintain, part of this new world will be established by what New Confucians teach, say, dream, and do.

Further Readings
and Contentious Issues

The bibliography is arranged in four sections. The first section, on general reference works, deals with comprehensive studies of East Asian culture and history. These books provide a rich background for the specific study of Confucian history and can be consulted when seeking information about the context of the development of Confucianism. The works listed here have been selected with an eye toward their discussion of Confucianism as an integral part of East Asian history and culture. Some deal with other religious traditions such as Taoism and Buddhism, and others are general historical and intellectual studies.

The second section contains works on China; the third, on Korea; and the fourth, on Japan. All of these deal with various facets of the development of the Confucian tradition in a specific country. There has been a revolution in the study of Confucianism over the last three decades, so most of the works cited in the country sections were written after 1960. However, those older works that are still significant have been included.

This is not an exhaustive bibliography of Confucian studies. It is designed to provide the student with access to more detailed information about the topics discussed in the text. Almost all of the works listed also have their own bibliographies, and in some cases these bibliographies are exhaustive of the best modern scholarship.

Nearly all the works listed are in English. But it should be noted that a great deal of this material rests on the shoulders of East Asian research in the Chinese, Korean, and Japanese languages, reaching back to the Han dynasty. The restriction to modern English works was a conscious choice; it is my hope that most college and university libraries will have these books in their own collections, but if they do not, the books ought to be easily obtainable through regional interlibrary loan. If a library does not have these works, the bibliography also provides a good beginning for building a collection in English on Confucian studies.

The Question of Identity

The question of giving one English name, Confucianism, to the *ju* traditions of East Asia is a hotly contested issue. The nineteenth-century taxonomists of religion thought that they could discover and name a variety of independent religious communities, but in the late twentieth century, scholars have grown weary of such searches for easily identifiable abstract entities such as specific religions or cos-

201

mologies with solid, essential sets of definite features. The scholarly mood at the end of the twentieth century is given over to difference, local cultures, deconstruction, and a suspicion about origins, foundations, realities, substances, and essential features. The idea that there might be a way to define the objective characteristics and essential features of something called a religious or philosophic tradition has given way to the more modest claim that we need to study individual history more and taxonomy less. Scholars are aware that the unity of the Confucian tradition may be more in the eye of the beholder than in the facts.

Nonetheless, historians of Chinese intellectual history continue to search for an East Asian way to deal with the plethora of forms and practices that have been identified with the tradition(s) of the *ju* throughout the region for over 2,500 years. For instance, if the Western search for an essential definition of religion, philosophy, and the taxonomy of religious types flounders, perhaps the Chinese penchant for seeking genealogies for the *ju* lineages still throws light on the development of the Confucian Way. The debate about how to define the tradition goes back at least to the great Han historians Ssu-ma T'an and Ssu-ma Ch'ien and before them to the last chapter of the *Chuang Tzu* and to Hsün Tzu. Following the Ssu-mas lead, Pan Ku defined the Confucians as *ju*, or what we might designate as scholars expert about ritual. The defining assumption was that the *ju* were experts in the rituals and the six arts of a Chou dynasty gentleman. When the early Christian missionaries arrived in Asia, they assumed that every people or nation had a religion that could be named. The Western scholar-missionaries, not entirely without reason, called the Ming literati class "Confucians" because of their veneration and study of the Confucian classics. For a fine study of the sense of intellectual genealogy that has informed the tradition, see Thomas A. Wilson (1995).

There has also been a modern debate about the appropriateness of the term "Confucianism" because it has been too tightly bound up with only one school, the later Sung development of what is called Neo-Confucianism, most specifically with the thought of scholars such as Chu Hsi and Wang Yang-ming. However, until and unless something much better is invented to take its place, the term "Confucianism" is broad enough to include all those who would want to be included by a name. It should be pointed out that modern East Asian scholars have adopted the Western point of view in this matter of nomenclature. For the particulars of the debate see L. Jensen, Wm. Theodore de Bary, T. Wilson and H. Tillman.

Furthermore, the task of finding a shortlist of key, ecumenical and historically pervasive themes, motifs, traits, or metaphors for the whole tradition is highly problematical. Mou Tsung-san's initial list of four traits as specifications of concern-consciousness is only one possible reading of the history of the tradition even when supplemented by the four traits I have added from Hsün Tzu and Chu Hsi. I am acutely aware that these thematic claims are what is at issue when we compare and contrast Western categories such as being, nonbeing, human nature, thought, action, mind, emotion, and passion with the equally rich range of Confucian reflections on the cosmos. For a fascinating discussion of these and related issues, see Hall and Ames's (1995) *Anticipating China*. Hall and Ames, following A. C. Graham (1985 and 1989), show that the "one thread" of the whole tradition is what they call correlative, or analogical, thinking. If we accept that such correlative and analogical thinking is always a relational form of life, then what Hall and Ames say does not contravene Mou's and Hsü's notion of concern-consciousness when specified as a constitutive aspect of pan-Chinese cosmological discourse. Both modalities of thought, the concerned and the correlative, can claim the patrimony of the *I-ching* in support of their unique Confucian genealogy. Both traits express what is probably inexpressible in a single phrase even within one culture.

Regional Variations

Linked to the question of the forms and definitions of the development of the Confucian Way are three more problematic questions for further research. The first is the lack of study, as mentioned in the introduction, of the Vietnamese Confucian tradition. I hope that scholars of Vietnamese history will soon fill this void in our understanding of Confucianism in East Asia. As we have seen in our studies of China, Korea, and Japan, each case is both similar to and different from the others. Ideas that originate in China spread throughout the region and were modified to suit the tastes of Korean, Japanese, and Vietnamese cultures. It is also fascinating to observe that new research programs arise in each new cultural instantiation of the Confucian Way. There are always unanticipated developments when a rich tradition moves from one culture to another.

The Role of Women

The second problematic area is the role of women in sustaining and changing Confucianism over the centuries in East Asia. We are just beginning to learn how women saw themselves in the Confucian world. Exciting work is being done to re-call the voices of women in their own right as philosophers and authors. A picture is emerging that confounds easy assumptions about how women understood themselves as part of the Confucian world. Many Asian women reject the idea that their ancestors were powerless objects of the forces of patriarchal history. Contemporary research shows that women changed their opinions over time and were clearly concerned with stating their own interpretation of the Confucian culture whenever they were given the opportunity to do so.

In this regard, I note the research of scholars such as Dorothy Ko (1994), Patricia Ebrey (1991, 1993), and Susan Mann (1997) on China. The work of Ko, Ebrey, and Mann looks at issues of family life and ritual, philosophy, and literary theory and production. For Korea, there is the outstanding study by Martina Deuchler (1992) on the Confucianization process of the whole society. Yet much more needs to be done to reveal what East Asian women thought about the development of the Confucian Way.

Social Relations and Class

The third area has to do with the role of class and ethnicity in the study of Confucian thought. As we have seen, Confucianism has always defined itself in terms of elite culture. Although Confucianism prided itself, especially in late imperial China, on helping worthy students and scholars advance along the path of sage wisdom, it is still the case that its final goal was human excellence defined in terms of intellectual and moral achievement. Traditional Confucians did not believe, for the most part, that everyone in society could become a proper Confucian. What did other classes and ethnic minorities think of the Confucian project? We know that modern Chinese revolutionaries judged Confucius and his disciples harshly. In addition to discovering women's views, it would be salutary to know more about what the less educated thought of the Confucian project. Non-Chinese peoples also had views about Confucianism that need to be taken into account.

Confucians, even if they were near the top of the social hierarchy, were still embedded in the nexus of society. Their ideals and aspirations mirrored their place in society even if they were harsh critics of what society often was. Scholars such as Huang (1981), Mark Elvin (1996), Benjamin Elman (1984, 1990), Najita (1987), Sawada (1993), and Chow (1995) have demonstrated how it is possible, and even crucial, to write the history of Confucianism as social history. These kinds of explorations of the sedimentation of the Confucian Way will help us to better understand the development of Confucian discourse and the way this discourse fits into the broader world of East Asian culture.

Global Connections

Another dimension of the Confucian Way that needs to be explored further is its relationships with other world cultures. The most generous example of this exchange is with Taoism, its Chinese twin, as it were. The second great encounter, and the first with a tradition from beyond East Asia, is Confucianism's vast engagement with Buddhism. We also need to pay even more attention to how Confucianism became a transcultural tradition as it became part of Korean, Vietnamese, and Japanese life.

The dialogue of Confucianism with other civilizations did not end with its encounter with Buddhism or with its spread throughout East Asia. Confucianism has become part of the modern world, and this means that modern Confucians will enter into dialogue with philosophers from other parts of the world. Furthermore, as Ching (1977), Ching and Küng (1989), and Peter Lee (1991) have shown, Confucianism is again engaged in dialogue with Christianity. The dialogue about culture begun so long ago by Confucius continues in worlds and ways he would never have anticipated but would certainly have welcomed as emanating from friends from afar.

Of course, all of these predictions of Confucian dialogue with Western modernity, philosophy, and other communities of faith is predicated on the assumption that there will be Confucians to take part in these dialogues. This is not a self-evident assumption for many careful and even sympathetic scholars of the tradition. For instance, Mark Elvin (1996) chronicles the end of what he calls scriptural Confucianism in the beginning of the twentieth century. Elvin points out that with the end of the imperial examination system, Chinese intellectuals lost their profound commitment to reading and living out of the classical Confucian canon. This is an especially difficult problem for a tradition that depends, at least in part, for its self-definition on a careful reading of the canon. Elvin notes that no other axial age tradition has suffered as much as Confucianism in the twentieth century.

New Confucianism

Paradoxically, along with the demise of imperial scriptural Confucianism, there has been a revival of philosophic Confucianism. This revival has taken the name of New Confucianism in the Chinese-speaking world. The great question for the New Confucians is whether they will be able to move out from their academic posts in order to provide a Confucian interpretation of modern life that will have a real appeal to modern and East Asian peoples. For instance, will there emerge a middle-class Confucianism within the nexus of the changing economic structures of East Asia? Reforming Buddhists in Taiwan have accomplished just this kind of inspired religious marketing by engaging educated lay people in what can only be called socially relevant Buddhism. Will Confucians find a similar key to excite and inspire new generations of students of the Confucian Way?

On the whole, the axial age traditions have proved to be tough customers. As the ravages of time have thrown them in wildly different directions, they have shown an ability to adapt and transform themselves while retaining unmistakable links to their pasts. The great shifts, borrowing Thomas Kuhn's theory of paradigm shifts in science, mark the segmented yet connected visions of ultimate reality unique to each tradition. Whatever else New Confucianism will be, it will be new and transforming, yet linked to the vision that Confucius articulated so long ago in another world.

Unearthing the Past

The scholarly understanding of the development of Confucian intellectual history has been dominated by texts. For the most part, these texts have gone through centuries of editing. However, one of the most exciting areas of research these days has resulted from the tremendous amount of material that is being discovered through controlled archaeological investigations. If anything has a chance of upsetting conventional thinking in the study of early China, it is the richness of the treasures emerging from the Chinese countryside. Older versions of the *Tao Te Ching* and *I-ching* have caused a rethinking of early Taoist origins and the relations with Confucianism and divination. It has been recently reported that an ancient and lost version of the *Analects* has been discovered. These are exciting times for the study of early Chinese culture. These new textual finds will help us understand the intellectual filiations of texts, teachers, and schools in order to better understand the development of early Chinese thought. Forgotten scholars and schools will be discovered and allowed to take their proper place in the history of the Confucian Tao. Perhaps Confucius would not have thought all of this too odd; he, too, lived at the end of an age that was really the beginning of a whole new world.

Wade-Giles to Pinyin Conversion Table

Wade-Giles	Pinyin	Wade-Giles	Pinyin
a	a	ch'ih	chi
ai	ai	chin	jin
an	an	ch'in	qin
ang	ang	ching	jing
ao	ao	ch'ing	qing
		chiu	jiu
cha	zha	ch'iu	qiu
ch'a	cha	chiung	jiong
chai	zhai	ch'iung	qiong
chan	zhan	cho	zhuo
ch'an	chan	ch'o	chuo
chang	zhang	chou	zhou
ch'ang	chang	ch'ou	chou
chao	zhao	chu	zhu
ch'ao	chao	ch'u	chu
che	zhe	chua	zhua
ch'e	che	chuai	zhuai
chei	zhei	ch'uai	chuai
chen	zhen	chuan	zhuan
ch'eng	cheng	ch'uan	chuan
chi	ji	chuang	zhuang
ch'i	qi	ch'uang	chuang
chia	jia	chui	zhui
ch'ia	qia	ch'ui	chui
chiang	jiang	chun	zhun
ch'iang	qiang	ch'un	chun
chiao	jiao	chung	zhong
ch'iao	qiao	ch'ung	chong
chieh	jie	chü	ju
ch'ieh	qie	ch'ü	qu
chien	jian	chüan	juan
ch'ien	qian	ch'üan	quan
chih	zhi	chüeh	jue

continues

continued

Wade-Giles	Pinyin	Wade-Giles	Pinyin
ch'üeh	que	hui	hui
chün	jun	hun	hun
ch'ün	qun	hung	hung
e,o	e	huo	huo
en	en	i,yi	yi
eng	eng	jan	ran
erh	er	jang	rang
fa	fa	jao	rao
fan	fan	je	re
fang	fang	jen	ren
fei	fei	jeng	reng
fen	fen	jih	ri
feng	feng	jo	ruo
fo	fo	jou	rou
fou	fou	ju	ru
fu	fu	juan	ruan
ha	ha	jui	rui
hai	hai	jun	run
han	han	jung	rong
hang	hang	ka	ga
hao	hao	k'a	ka
hei	hei	kai	gai
hen	hen	k'ai	kai
heng	heng	kan	gan
ho	ho	k'an	kan
hou	hou	kang	gang
hsi	xi	k'ang	kang
hsia	xia	kao	gao
hsiang	xiang	k'ao	kao
hsiao	xiao	ke, ko	ge
hsieh	xie	k'e, k'o	ke
hsien	xian	kou	gou
hsin	xin	k'ou	kou
hsing	xing	ku	gu
hsiu	xiu	k'u	ku
hsiung	xiong	kua	gua
hsü	xu	k'ua	kua
hu	hu	kuai	guai
hua	hua	k'uai	kuai
huan	huan	kuan	guan
huang	huang	k'uan	kuan

continues

continued

Wade-Giles	Pinyin	Wade-Giles	Pinyin
kuang	guang	mei	mei
k'uang	kuang	men	men
kuei	gui	meng	meng
k'uei	kui	mi	mi
kun	gun	miao	miao
k'un	kun	mieh	mie
kung	gong	mien	mian
k'ung	kong	min	min
kuo	guo	ming	ming
k'uo	kuo	miu	miu
la	la	mo	mo
lai	lai	mou	mou
lan	lan	mu	mu
lang	lang	na	na
lao	lao	nai	nai
le	le	nan	nan
lei	lei	nang	nag
leng	leng	nao	nao
li	li	nei	nei
lia	lia	nen	nen
liang	liang	neng	neng
liao	liao	ni	ni
lieh	lie	niang	niang
lien	lian	niao	niao
lin	lin	nieh	nie
ling	ling	nien	nian
liu	liu	nin	nin
lo	luo	ning	ning
lou	lou	niu	niu
lu	lu	no	no
luan	luan	nou	nou
lun, lün	lun	nu	nu
lung	long	nuan	nuan
lü	lü	nun	nun
lüan	luan	nung	nong
lüeh	lue	nü	nu
		nüeh	nue
ma	ma	o,e	e
mai	mai	ou	ou
man	man	pa	ba
mang	mang		
mao	mao		

continues

continued

Wade-Giles	Pinyin	Wade-Giles	Pinyin
p'a	pa	shai	shai
pai	bai	shan	shan
p'ai	pai	shang	shang
pan	ban	shao	shao
p'an	pan	she	she
pang	bang	shei	shei
p'ang	pang	shen	shen
pao	bao	sheng	sheng
p'ao	pao	shih	shi
pei	bei	shou	shou
p'ei	pei	shu	shu
pen	ben	shua	shua
p'en	pen	shuai	shuai
peng	beng	shuan	shuan
p'eng	peng	shuang	shuang
pi	bi	shui	shui
p'i	pi	shun	shun
piao	biao	shuo	shuo
p'iao	piao	so	suo
pieh	bie	suo	suo
p'ieh	pie	ssu	si
pien	bian	szu	si
p'ien	pian	su	su
pin	bin	suan	suan
p'in	pin	sui	sui
ping	bing	sun	sun
p'ing	ping	sung	song
po	bo	szu, ssu	si
p'o	po		
pou	bou	ta	da
p'ou	pou	t'a	ta
pu	bu	tai	dai
p'u	pu	t'ai	tai
		tan	dan
sa	sa	t'an	tan
sai	sai	tang	dang
san	san	t'ang	t'ang
sang	sang	tao	dao
sao	sao	te	de
se	se	t'e	te
sen	sen	tei	dei
seng	seng	teng	deng
sha	sha	t'eng	teng

continues

continued

Wade-Giles	Pinyin	Wade-Giles	Pinyin
ti	di	tsun	zun
t'i	ti	ts'uan	cun
tiao	diao	tsung	zong
t'iao	tiao	ts'ung	cong
tieh	die	tu	du
t'ieh	tie	t'u	tu
tien	dian	tuan	duan
t'ien	tian	t'uan	tuan
ting	ding	tui	dui
t'ing	ting	t'ui	tui
tiu	diu	tun	dun
to	duo	t'un	tun
t'o	tuo	tung	dong
tou	duo	t'ung	tong
t'ou	tou	tzu	zi
tsa	za	ts'u	ci
ts'a	ca	wa	wa
tsai	zai	wai	wai
ts'ai	cai	wan	wan
tsan	zan	wang	wang
ts'an	can	wei	wei
tsang	zang	wen	wen
ts'ang	cang	weng	weng
tsao	zao	wo	wo
ts'ao	cao	wu	wu
tse	ze	ya	ya
ts'e	ce	yai	yai
tsei	zei	yang	yang
tsen	zen	yao	yao
ts'en	cen	yeh	ye
tseng	zeng	yen	yan
ts'eng	ceng	yi, i	yi
tso	zuo	yin	yin
ts'o	cuo	ying	ying
tsou	zou	yu	you
ts'ou	cou	yung	yong
tsu	zu	yü	yu
ts'u	cu	yüan	yuan
tsuan	zuan	yüeh	yue
ts'uan	cuan	yün	yun
tsui	zui		
ts'ui	cui		

Glossary

ai 愛
cheng-hsing 正性
cheng-ming 正名
ch'eng 誠
ch'i 愛
chi 幾
chih 知
chih-chueh 知覺
chih 智
chih-chih 至知
chih-ch'eng 至誠
chih-shan 至善
ching 敬
ching 經
ch'ing 清
ch'ing 情
ch'iung 窮
ch'iung-li chin-hsing 窮理盡性
Chou-i 周易
chuan 傳
chün-tzu 君子
chu-ching ch'iung-li 居敬窮理
chung 忠
chung-yung 中庸
fa 發
fa 法
fan-kuan 反觀
han-jen 漢人
hao-jan chih-ch'i 浩然之氣
ho 和
ho er pu-t'ung 和而不同
ho-shun 和順
hsi 習

hsin 信
hsin 心
hsin chi li 心即理
hsin-chih-t'i 心之體
hsin-fa 形罰
hsin-hsüeh 心學
hsing 性
hsing 行
hsing-fa 形罰
hsü 虛
hsüan-hsüeh 玄學
hsüeh 學
hua-nien kuei-hsin 化念歸心
i, yi 易
i 易
i-fa 已發
i-hsin chu-hsing 以心著性
jen 仁
ko-wu 格物
ku-wen 古文
kuan 觀
kuei-shen 鬼神
kung 共
kung-fu 工夫
kung-li 共理
li 理
li-hsüeh 理學
li 禮
liang-chih 良知
ming 名
ming 命
ming-chiao tzu-jan 明覺自然
neng 能

pen 能

pen-mo 本末

p'eng-yu 朋友

po-ai 博愛

ju 儒

shan 善

shen 神

sheng 聲

shih 士

shih 事

shih-wu 事物

shu 恕

so-yi 所以

ssu 思

ta-kung-ming 太極

tang 儻

t'ang-ren 唐人

t'ai-chi 太極

tao 道

tao-hsüeh 道學

tao wen-hsüeh 道文學

te 德

t'ien 天

t'ien-li 天理

t'ien-ming 天命

t'i 體

t'i-yung 體用

ts'ai 材

ts'un te hsing 蹲德性

tuan 端

t'ung 通

tzu-te 自得

tzu-jan 自然

wei-fa 未發

wen 文

wu 物

wu 無

wu-ch'ang 五常

wu-chi 無極

wu-chi er t'ai-chi 無極而太極

wu-hsing 五行

wu-wei 無爲

yu 陰

yu 育

yung 用

yuan 元

yin-yang 陰陽

Bibliography

General Reference Works

Ames, Roger T., Wimal Dissanayake, and Thomas P. Kasulis, eds. 1994. *Self as Person in Asian Theory and Practice*. Albany: State University of New York Press.

Bishop, Donald H., ed. 1985. *Chinese Thought: An Introduction*. New Delhi: Motilal Banarsidass.

Ch'en, Kenneth K. S. 1964. *Buddhism in China: A Historical Survey*. Princeton: Princeton University Press.

_____. 1973. *The Chinese Transformation of Buddhism*. Princeton: Princeton University Press.

Chan, Wing-tsit. 1953. *Religious Trends in Modern China*. New York: Columbia University Press. Reprint, New York: Octagon Books, 1969.

_____. 1963. *A Source Book in Chinese Philosophy*. Princeton: Princeton University Press.

_____. 1967. *Chinese Philosophy, 1949–1963: An Annotated Bibliography of Mainland China Publications*. Honolulu: East-West Center Press, University of Hawaii.

_____. 1969. *An Annotated Bibliography of Chinese Philosophy*. Rev. ed. New Haven: Far Eastern Publications, Yale University.

Ching, Julia. 1993. *Chinese Religions*. Maryknoll, NY: Orbis Books.

Creel, Herrlee G. 1953. *Chinese Thought from Confucius to Mao Tse-tung*. Chicago: University of Chicago Press.

Current Perspectives in the Study of Chinese Religions. History of Religions (special issue), vol. 17, nos. 3 and 4 (February-May 1978).

Dawson, Raymond, ed. 1964. *The Legacy of China*. Oxford: Clarendon Press.

de Bary, Wm. Theodore, Wing-tsit Chan, and Burton Watson, eds. 1964. *Sources of Chinese Tradition*. 2 vols. New York: Columbia University Press.

DeFrancis, John. 1989. *Visible Speech: The Diverse Oneness of Writing Systems*. Honolulu: University of Hawaii Press.

_____, ed. 1996. *ABC Chinese-English Dictionary*. Honolulu: University of Hawaii Press.

Dilworth, David A. 1989. *Philosophy in World Perspective: A Comparative Hermeneutic of the Major Theories*. New Haven: Yale University Press.

Elvin, Mark. 1973. *The Pattern of the Chinese Past*. Stanford: Stanford University Press.

Fairbank, John King. 1992. *China: A New History*. Cambridge: Belknap Press of Harvard University.

Fairbank, John King, and Denis Twitchett, eds. 1986–. *The Cambridge History of China*. 15 vols. Cambridge: Cambridge University Press.

Forke, Alfred. 1964a. *Geschichte der alten chinesischen philosphie*. Hamburg: Cram, de Gruyer and Company.

_____. 1964b. *Geschichte der mittelalterichen chinesischen philosophie*. Hamburg: Cram, de Gruyter and Company.

_____. 1964c. *Geschichte der nueruen chinesischen philosophie*. Hamburg: Cram, de Gryuter and Company.

Fung, Yu-lan. 1947. *The Spirit of Chinese Philosophy*. Translated by E. R. Hughes. Boston: Beacon Press.

_____. 1952–1953. *A History of Chinese Philosophy*. 2 vols. Translated by Derk Bodde. Princeton: Princeton University Press.

_____. 1964. *A Short History of Chinese Philosophy*. Edited by Derk Bodde. New York: Macmillan Company.

Gernet, Jacques. 1982. *A History of Chinese Civilization*. Translated by J. R. Foster. Cambridge: Cambridge University Press.

Jochim, Christian. 1986. *Chinese Religions: A Cultural Perspective*. Englewood Cliffs, NJ: Prentice Hall.

Kalupahana, David J. 1992. *A History of Buddhist Philosophy: Continuities and Discontinuities*. Honolulu: University of Hawaii Press.

Keightley, David N., ed. 1983. *The Origins of Chinese Civilization*. Berkeley: University of California Press.

Lach, Donald F. 1965–. *Asia in the Making of Europe*. Chicago: University of Chicago Press.

Lee, Ki-baik. 1984. *A New History of Korea*. Translated by Edward W. Wagner and Edward J. Schultz. Cambridge: Harvard University Press.

Lee, Peter H. 1993–1996. *Sourcebook of Korean Civilization*. 2 vols. New York: Columbia University Press.

Liu, James T. C., and Tu Wei-ming, eds. 1970. *Traditional China*. Englewood Cliffs, NJ: Prentice Hall.

Liu, Shu-hsien, and Robert E. Allinson, eds. 1988. *Harmony and Strife: Contemporary Perspectives, East and West*. Hong Kong: Chinese University Press.

Loewe, Michael. 1993. *Early Chinese Texts: A Bibliographic Guide*. Early China Special Monograph Series, no. 2. Berkeley: Institute of East Asian Studies.

Lopez, Donald S., Jr. 1996. *Religions of China in Practice*. Princeton: Princeton University Press.

Martinson, Paul Varo. 1987. *A Theology of World Religions: Interpreting God, Self, and World in Semitic, Indian, and Chinese Thought*. Minneapolis: Augsburg Publishing House.

Maspero, Henri. 1978. *China in Antiquity*. Translated by Frank A. Kierman, Jr. Amherst: University of Massachusetts Press.

Moore, Charles A. 1967. *The Chinese Mind: Essentials of Chinese Philosophy and Culture*. Honolulu: University of Hawaii Press.

Mote, Frederick W. 1989. *Intellectual Foundations of China*. 2d ed. New York: McGraw-Hill Publishing Company.

Naes, Arne, and Alastir Hanny, eds. 1972. *Invitation to Chinese Philosophy.* Oslo: Scandinavian University Books.

Nakamura, Hajime. 1965. *Ways of Thinking of Eastern Peoples: India, China, Tibet, and Japan.* Honolulu: East-West Center Press.

_____. 1975. *Parallel Developments: A Comparative History of Ideas.* Tokyo: Kodansha.

Overmeyer, Daniel L. 1986. *Religions of China: The World as Living System.* San Francisco: Harper and Row.

Paper, Jordan. 1995. *The Spirits Are Drunk: Comparative Approaches to Chinese Religion.* Albany: State University of New York Press.

Robinet, Isabelle. 1997. *Taoism: Growth of a Religion.* Translated by Phyllis Brooks. Stanford: Stanford University Press.

Sansom, George. 1962. *Japan: A Short Cultural History.* Rev. ed. New York: Appleton-Century-Crofts.

Scharfstein, Ben-Ami. 1974. *The Mind of China.* New York: Dell.

Schirokauer, Conrad. 1991. *A Brief History of Chinese Civilization.* 2d ed. Forth Worth, TX: Harcourt Brace Publishers.

_____. 1993. *A Brief History of Japanese Civilization.* 2d ed. Forth Worth, TX: Harcourt Brace Publishers.

Shahar, Meir, and Robert P. Weller. 1996. *Unruly Gods: Divinity and Society in China.* Honolulu: University of Hawaii Press.

Smith, Jonathan Z., ed. 1995. *The HarperCollins Dictionary of Religion.* William Scott Green, associate editor with the American Academy of Religion. San Francisco: HarperCollins.

Sommer, Deborah, ed. 1995. *Chinese Religion: An Anthology of Sources.* New York and Oxford: Oxford University Press.

Spence, Jonathan D. 1990. *The Search for Modern China.* New York: W. W. Norton and Company.

Thompson, Laurence. 1989. *Chinese Religion.* 4th ed. Belmond, CA: Wadsworth Publishing.

Tsunoda, Ryusaku, ed. 1958. *Sources of the Japanese Tradition.* New York: Columbia University Press.

Tu, Wei-ming, ed. 1996. *Confucian Traditions in East Asian Modernity: Moral Education and Economic Culture in Japan and the Four Mini-Dragons.* Cambridge: Harvard University Press.

Tuan, Yi Fu. 1982. *Segmented Worlds and Self: Group Life and Individual Consciousness.* Minneapolis: University of Minnesota Press.

_____. 1990. *Topophila: A Study of Environmental Perceptions, Attitudes, and Values.* New York: Columbia University Press.

Verdu, Alfonso. 1981. *The Philosophy of Buddhism: A "Totalistic" System.* The Hague: Martinus Nijhoff Publishers.

Watson, Walter. 1993. *The Architectonics of Meaning: Foundations of the New Pluralism.* Chicago: University of Chicago Press.

Weller, Robert P. 1987. *Unities and Diversities in Chinese Religion.* Seattle: University of Washington Press.

Williams, Paul. 1989. *Mahayana Buddhism: The Doctrinal Foundations.* London: Routledge.

Yang, C. K. 1967. *Religion in Chinese Society.* Berkeley: University of California Press.
Yates, Robin D. 1997. *Five Lost Classics: Tao, Huang-Lao, and Yin-Yang in Han China.* New York: Ballantine Books.
Yu, David C. 1994. *Religion in Postwar China: A Critical Analysis and Annotated Bibliography.* Westport, CT: Greenwood Press.
Zürcher, Eric. 1959. *The Buddhist Conquest of China: The Spread and Adaptation of Buddhism in Early Medieval China.* 2 vols. Leiden: E. J. Brill.

Monographs: China

Alitto, Guy S. 1979. *The Last Confucian: Liang Shu-ming and the Chinese Dilemma of Modernity.* Berkeley: University of California Press.
Allan, Sarah. 1991. *The Shape of the Turtle: Myth, Art, and Cosmos in Early China.* Albany: State University of New York Press.
Alley, Rewi, trans. 1964. *Tu Fu: Selected Poems.* Compiled by Feng Chih. Peking: Foreign Languages Press.
Allinson, Robert E., ed. 1989. *Understanding the Chinese Mind: The Philosophic Roots.* Oxford: Oxford University Press.
Ariel, Yoav. 1989. *K'ung Tsung-tzu: The K'ung Family Masters' Anthology.* Princeton: Princeton University Press.
Balazs, Etienne. 1964. *Chinese Civilization and Bureaucracy: Variations on a Theme.* Translated by H. M. Wright and edited by Arthur F. Wright. New Haven: Yale University Press.
Barfield, Thomas J. 1989. *The Perilous Frontier: Nomadic Empires and China.* Cambridge, MA, and Oxford: Blackwell Publishers.
Barrett, T. H. 1992. *Li Ao: Buddhist, Taoist, or Neo-Confucian?* Oxford: Oxford University Press.
Bauer, Wolfgang. 1976. *China and the Search for Happiness: Recurring Themes in Four Thousand Years of Chinese Cultural History.* Translated by Michael Shaw. New York: Seabury Press.
Berling, Judith A. 1980. *The Syncretic Religion of Lin Chao-en.* New York: Columbia University Press.
Berthrong, John H. 1993. "Master Chu's Self-Realization: The Role of Ch'eng." *Philosophy East and West* 43 (January):39–64.
_____. 1994. *All Under Heaven: Transforming Paradigms in Confucian-Christian Dialogue.* Albany: State University of New York Press.
Billeter, Jean-François. 1979. *Li Zhi: Philosophie maudit (1527–1602).* Genève: Librairie Droz.
Biot, Edouard. 1969. *Le Tcheou-Li: Rites des Tcheou.* 3 vols. Reprint, Taipei: Ch'eng Wen Publishing Company.
Birdwhistell, Anne D. 1989. *Transition to Neo-Confucianism: Shao Yung on Knowledge and Symbols of Reality.* Stanford: Stanford University Press.
_____. 1996. *Li Yong (1627–1705) and Epistemological Dimensions of Confucian Philosophy.* Stanford: Stanford University Press.
Black, Alison Harley. 1989. *Man and Nature in the Philosophical Thought of Wang Fu-chih.* Seattle: University of Washington Press.

Bloom, Irene. 1987. *Knowledge Painfully Acquired: The K'un-chih chi by Lo Ch'in-shun*. New York: Columbia University Press.

Bloom, Irene, and Joshua A. Fogel, eds. 1996. *Meetings of Minds: Intellectual and Religious Interaction in East Asian Traditions of Thought*. New York: Columbia University Press.

Bodde, Derk. 1981. *Essays on Chinese Civilization*. Edited by Charles Le Blanc and Dorthy Borei. Princeton: Princeton University Press.

————. 1991. *Chinese Thought, Society, and Science: The Intellectual and Social Background of Science and Technology in Pre-Modern China*. Honolulu: University of Hawaii Press.

Bol, Peter K. 1992. *"This Culture of Ours": Intellectual Transition in T'ang and Sung China*. Stanford: Stanford University Press.

Brière, O.S.J. 1956. *Fifty Years of Chinese Philosophy, 1898–1950*. Translated by Laurence G. Thompson. London: George Allen and Unwin.

Brokaw, Cynthia J. 1991. *The Ledgers of Merit and Demerit: Social Change and Moral Order in Late Imperial China*. Princeton: Princeton University Press.

Bruce, J. Percy. 1973. *Chu Hsi and His Masters: An Introduction to Chu Hsi and the Sung School of Chinese Philosophy*. New York: AMS Press Edition; London: Pobsthain and Company, 1923.

Chaffee, John W. 1995. *The Thorny Gates of Learning in Sung China*. Albany: State University of New York Press.

Chai, Ch'u, and Winberg Chai. 1973. *Confucianism*. New York: Barron's Educational Series.

Chan, Alan K. L. 1991. *Two Visions of the Way: A Study of Wang Pi and the Ho-shang Kung Commentaries on the Lao Tzu*. Albany: State University of New York Press.

Chan, Albert. 1982. *The Glory and Fall of the Ming Dynasty*. Norman: University of Oklahoma Press.

Chan, Hok-lam. 1980. *Li Chih (1527–1602) in Contemporary Chinese Historiography: New Light on His Life and Works*. White Plains, NY: M. E. Sharpe.

Chan, Hok-lam, and Wm. Theodore de Bary, eds. 1982. *Yüan Thought: Chinese Thought and Religion Under the Mongols*. New York: Columbia University Press.

Chan, Sin-wai. 1985. *Buddhism in Late Ch'ing Political Thought*. Hong Kong: Chinese University Press.

Chan, Wing-tsit. 1986. *Chu Hsi and Neo-Confucianism*. Honolulu: University of Hawaii Press.

————. 1987. *Chu Hsi: Life and Thought*. Hong Kong: Chinese University Press.

————. 1989. *Chu Hsi: New Studies*. Honolulu: University of Hawaii Press.

Chang, Carsun. 1957–1962. *The Development of Neo-Confucian Thought*. 2 vols. New York: Bookman Associates.

————. 1970. *Wang Yang-ming: Idealist Philosopher of Sixteenth-Century China*. New York: St. John's University Press.

Chang, Hao. 1971. *Liang Ch'i-ch'ao and Intellectual Transition in China (1890–1907)*. Cambridge: Harvard University Press.

Chang, Li-wen et al. 1991. *Ch'i*. Beijing: Chung-kuo jen-min ta-hsüeh ch'u-pan she.

Chang, K. C. 1983. *Art, Myth, and Ritual: The Path to Political Authority in Ancient China.* Cambridge: Harvard University Press.

_____. 1986. *The Archaeology of Ancient China.* 4th ed., rev. and enl. New Haven: Yale University Press.

Chappell, David W., ed. 1983. *T'ien-t'ai Buddhism: An Outline of the Fourfold Teachings.* Tokyo: Daiichi-Shobo. Distributed by the University of Hawaii Press.

Chaves, Jonathan. 1993. *Sing of the Source: Nature and Gospel in the Poetry of the Chinese Painter Wu Li.* Honolulu: SHAPS Library of Translations, University of Hawaii Press.

Chen, Charles K. H., comp. 1969. *Neo-Confucianism, Etc.: Essays by Wing-tsit Chan.* Hanover, NH: Oriental Society.

Chen, Jingpan. 1993. *Confucius as a Teacher: Philosophy of Confucius with Special Reference to Its Educational Implications.* Petaling Jaya Malaysia: Delta Publishing Group; Beijing: Foreign Languages Press, 1990.

Chen, Jo-shui. 1992. *Liu Tsung-yüan and Intellectual Change in T'ang China, 773–819.* Cambridge: Cambridge University Press.

Chen, Li-Fu. 1948. *Philosophy of Life.* New York: Philosophical Library.

_____. 1972. *The Confucian Way: A New and Systematic Study of the "Four Books."* Translated by Liu Shih Shun. Taipei: Commercial Press.

Ch'en, Ch'i-yun. 1980. *Hsün Yüeh and the Mind of Late Han Chin: A Translation of the Shen-ching with Introductions and Annotations.* Princeton: Princeton University Press.

Cheng, Chung-ying, trans. 1971. *Tai Chin's Inquiry into Goodness.* Honolulu: East-West Center Press.

_____. 1991. *New Dimensions of Confucian and Neo-Confucian Philosophy.* Albany: State University of New York Press.

Ch'ien, Edward T. 1986. *Chiao Hung and the Restructuring of Neo-Confucianism in the Late Ming.* New York: Columbia University Press.

Chin, Ann-ping, and Mansfield Freeman. 1990. *Tai Chen on Mencius: Explorations in Words and Meaning.* New Haven: Yale University Press.

Ching, Julia. 1972–1973. "Neo-Confucian Utopia Theories and Political Ethics." *Monumenta Serica* 30 (1972–1973):1–56.

_____. 1976. *To Acquire Wisdom: The Way of Wang Yang-ming.* New York: Columbia University Press.

_____. 1977. *Confucianism and Christianity: A Comparative Study.* Tokyo: Kodansha International.

_____, trans. 1972. *The Philosophical Letters of Wang Yang-ming.* Columbia: University of South Carolina Press.

Ching, Julia, and Hans Küng. 1989. *Christianity and Chinese Religion.* New York: Doubleday.

_____. 1990. *Probing China's Soul: Religion, Politics, and Protest in the People's Republic.* San Francisco: Harper and Row, Publishers.

Ching, Julia, and R.W.L. Guisso, eds. 1991. *Sages and Filial Sons: Mythology and Archaeology in Ancient China.* Hong Kong: Chinese University of Hong Kong Press.

Ching, Julia, and Willard G. Oxtoby. 1992a. *Moral Enlightenment: Leibniz and Wolff on China.* Nettetal: Steyler Verlag.

Ching, Julia, and Willard G. Oxtoby, eds. 1992b. *Discovering China: European Interpretations in the Enlightenment.* Rochester: University of Rochester Press.

Chow, Kai-wing. 1995. *The Rise of Confucian Ritualism in Late Imperial China: Ethics, Classics, and Lineage Discourse.* Stanford: Stanford University Press.

Chow, Rey. 1991. *Woman and Chinese Modernity: The Poetics of Reading Between West and East.* Minneapolis: University of Minnesota Press.

Chow, Tse-tsung. 1960. *The May Fourth Movement: Intellectual Revolution in Modern China.* Stanford: Stanford University Press.

Chow, Yih-Ching. 1954. *La philosophie morale dans le Neo-Confucianisme (Tcheou Touen-Yi).* Paris: Presses Universitaires de France.

Chu, Hsi. 1973. *The Philosophy of Human Nature.* Translated by J. Percy Bruce. New York: AMS Press Edition; London: Probsthain and Company, 1922.

Chu, Hsi, and Lü Tsu-ch'ien. 1967. *Reflections on Things at Hand: The Neo-Confucian Anthology.* Translated by Wing-tsit Chan. New York: Columbia University Press.

_____. 1991. *Chu Hsi's Family Rituals: A Twelfth-Century Chinese Manual for the Performance of Cappings, Weddings, Funerals, and Ancestral Rites.* Translated and edited by Patricia Buckley Ebrey. Princeton: Princeton University Press.

Chu, Sin-jan. 1995. *Wu Leichuan: A Confucian-Christian in Republican China.* New York: Peter Lang.

Cleary, J. C., trans. and ed. 1991. *Worldly Wisdom: Confucian Teachings of the Ming Dynasty.* Boston and London: Shambhala.

Colvell, Ralph R. 1986. *Confucius, the Buddha, and Christ.* Maryknoll, NY: Orbis Books.

Confucius. 1992. *Confucius: The Analects (Lun yü).* Translated by D. C. Lau. Hong Kong: Chinese University Press.

Couvreur, Seraphin. 1949. *Les quarte livres.* Leiden: E. J. Brill.

Creel, H. G. 1949. *Confucius and the Chinese Way.* New York: Harper and Row, Publishers.

_____. 1970. *What Is Taoism? And Other Studies in Chinese Cultural History.* Chicago: University of Chicago Press.

_____. 1974. *Shen Pu-hai: A Chinese Political Philosopher of the Fourth Century B.C.* Chicago: University of Chicago Press.

Cua, A. S. 1978. *Dimensions of Moral Creativity: Paradigms, Principles, and Ideals.* University Park: Pennsylvania State University Press.

_____. 1982. *The Unity of Knowledge and Action: A Study of Wang Yang-ming's Moral Psychology.* Honolulu: University Press of Hawaii.

_____. 1985. *Ethical Argumentation: A Study in Hsün Tzu's Moral Epistemology.* Honolulu: University Press of Hawaii.

Dardess, John W. 1973. *Conquerors and Confucians: Aspects of Political Change in Late Yüan China.* New York: Columbia University Press.

_____. 1983. *Confucianism and Autocracy: Professional Elites in the Founding of the Ming Dynasty.* Berkeley: University of California Press.

Davis, Richard L. 1986. *Court and Family in Sung China, 960–1279: Bureaucratic Success and Kinship Fortunes for the Shih of Ming-chou.* Durham, NC: Duke University Press.

de Bary, Wm. Theodore. 1975. *The Unfolding of Neo-Confucianism*. New York: Columbia University Press.

_____. 1981. *Neo-Confucian Orthodoxy and the Learning of the Mind-and-Heart*. New York: Columbia University Press.

_____. 1983. *The Liberal Tradition in China*. New York: Columbia University Press.

_____. 1988. *East Asian Civilizations: A Dialogue in Five Stages*. Cambridge: Harvard University Press.

_____. 1989. *The Message of the Mind in Neo-Confucianism*. New York: Columbia University Press.

_____. 1991a. *Learning for One's Self: Essays on the Individual in Neo-Confucian Thought*. New York: Columbia University Press.

_____. 1991b. *The Trouble with Confucianism*. Cambridge: Harvard University Press.

_____, ed. 1970. *Self and Society in Ming Thought*. New York: Columbia University Press.

_____, trans. 1993. *Waiting for the Dawn: A Plan for the Prince*. New York: Columbia University Press.

de Bary, Wm. Theodore, and Irene Bloom, eds. 1979. *Principle and Practicality: Essays in Neo-Confucianism and Practical Learning*. New York: Columbia University Press.

de Bary, Wm. Theodore, and John W. Chaffee, eds. 1989. *Neo-Confucian Education: The Formative Stage*. Berkeley: University of California Press.

DeFoort, Carine. 1997. *The Pheasant Cap Master (He guan zi): A Rhetorical Reading*. Albany: The State University of New York Press.

Dennerline, Jerry. 1981. *The Chia-ting Loyalists: Confucian Leadership and Social Change in Seventeenth-Century China*. New Haven: Yale University Press.

_____. 1988. *Qian Mu and the World of Seven Mansions*. New Haven: Yale University Press.

Dimberg, Ronald G. 1974. *The Sage and Society: The Life and Thought of Ho Hsin-yin*. Honolulu: University of Hawaii Press.

Dubs, Homer H. 1966a. *Hsüntze: The Molder of Ancient Confucianism*. Taipei: Ch'eng-Wen Publishing Company.

_____, trans. 1966b. *The Works of Hsüntze*. Taipei: Ch'eng-Wen Publishing Company.

Eber, Irene, ed. 1986. *Confucianism: The Dynamics of Tradition*. New York: Macmillan Publishing Company.

Ebrey, Patricia Buckley. 1991. *Confucianism and Family Rituals in Imperial China: A Social History of Writing About Rites*. Princeton: Princeton University Press.

_____. 1993. *The Inner Quarters: Marriage and the Lives of Chinese Women in the Sung Period*. Berkeley: University of California Press.

Egan, Ronald C. 1994. *Word, Image, and Deed in the Life of Su Shi*. Cambridge: Harvard University Press.

Elman, Benjamin A. 1984. *From Philosophy to Philology: Intellectual and Social Aspects of Change in Late Imperial China*. Cambridge: Harvard University Press.

_____. 1990. *Classicism, Politics, and Kinship: The Ch'ang-Chou School of New Test Confucianism in Later Imperial China*. Berkeley: University of California Press.

Elvin, Mark. 1996. *Another History: Essays on China from a European Perspective.* Sydney: Wild Peony.

Eno, Robert. 1990. *The Confucian Creation of Heaven: Philosophy and the Defense of Ritual Mastery.* Albany: State University of New York Press.

Fairbank, John K., ed. 1957. *Chinese Thought and Institutions.* Chicago: University of Chicago Press.

Fang, Thome H. N.d. *The Chinese View of Life: The Philosophy of Comprehensive Harmony.* Hong Kong: Union Press.

Fehl, Noah Edward. 1971. *Rites and Propriety in Literature and Life: A Perspective for a Cultural History of Ancient China.* Hong Kong: Chinese University of Hong Kong.

Fingarette, Herbert. 1972. *Confucius—The Secular as Sacred.* New York: Harper and Row, Publishers.

Forke, Alfred. 1925. *The World Concept of the Chinese.* London: Arthur Probsthain.

Franklin, Ursula Martius. 1983. "On Bronze and Other Metals in Early China." In *The Origins of Chinese Civilization,* edited by David N. Keightley. Berkeley: University of California Press.

_____. 1985. "Metallurgy, Cosmology and Knowledge: The Chinese Experience." *Journal of Chinese Philosophy* 12, no. 4 (December):333–370.

Furth, Charlotte. 1970. *Ting Wen-chiang: Science and China's New Culture.* Cambridge: Cambridge University Press.

_____, ed. 1976. *The Limits of Change: Essays in Conservative Alternatives in Republican China.* Cambridge: Harvard University Press.

Gale, Esson M. 1973. *Discourses on Salt and Iron: A Debate on State Control of Commerce and Industry in Ancient China.* Reprint edition, Taipei: Ch'eng Wen Publishing Company.

Gardner, Daniel K. 1986. *Chu Hsi and the Ta-hsüeh: Neo-Confucian Reflection on the Confucian Canon.* Cambridge: Harvard University Press.

_____, trans. 1990. *Learning to Be a Sage: Selections from the Conversations of Master Chu, Arranged Topically.* Berkeley: University of California Press.

Gedalecia, David. 1971. "Wu Ch'eng: A Neo-Confucian of the Yüan." Ph.D. diss., Harvard University.

_____. 1974. "Excursion into Substance and Function: The Development of the *T'i-yung* Paradigm in Chu Hsi." *Philosophy East and West* 24 (October):443–451.

Gernet, Jacques. 1985. *China and the Christian Impact.* Translated by Janet Lloyd. Cambridge: Cambridge University Press.

Gilmartin, Christina K., G. Hershatter, L. Rofel, and T. White, eds. 1994. *Engendering China: Women, Culture, and the State.* Cambridge: Harvard University Press.

Graf, Olaf. 1970. *Tao und Jen: Sein und Sollen in Sungchinesischen Monismus.* Wiesbaden: Otto Harrassowitz.

Graham, A. C. 1985. *Reason and Spontaneity: A New Solution to the Problem of Fact and Value.* London: Curzon Press.

_____. 1986a. *Studies in Chinese Philosophy and Philosophical Literature.* Singapore: Institute of East Asian Philosophy.

_____. 1986b. *Yin-yang and the Nature of Correlative Thinking.* Singapore: Institute of East Asian Philosophy.

_____. 1989. *Disputers of the Tao: Philosophical Argument in Ancient China.* La Salle, IL: Open Court.

_____. 1992a. *Two Chinese Philosophers: The Metaphysics of the Brothers Ch'eng.* La Salle, IL: Open Court.

_____. 1992b. *Unreason Within Reason: Essays on the Outskirts of Rationality.* La Salle, IL: Open Court.

Granet, Marcel. 1968. *La pensée Chinoise.* Paris: Editions Albin Michel.

_____. 1975. *The Religion of the Chinese People.* Translated by Maurice Freedman. New York: Harper and Row.

Grant, Beata. 1994. *Mount Lu Revisited: Buddhism in the Life of Su Shih.* Honolulu: University of Hawaii Press.

Gregory, Peter N. 1991. *Tsung-mi and the Sinification of Buddhism.* Princeton: Princeton University Press.

_____, trans. 1995. *Inquiry in the Origin of Humanity: An Annotated Translation of Tsung-mi's Yüan jen lun with a Modern Commentary.* Honolulu: University of Hawaii Press.

Grieder, Jerome B. 1970. *Hu Shih and the Chinese Renaissance: Liberalism in the Chinese Revolution, 1917–1937.* Cambridge: Harvard University Press.

Haeger, John Winthrop. 1972. "The Intellectual Context of Neo-Confucianism Syncretism." *Journal of Asian Studies* 31 (May):499–513.

Hall, David L. 1973. *The Civilization of Experience: A Whiteheadian Theory of Culture.* New York: Fordham University Press.

Hall, David L., and Roger T. Ames. 1987. *Thinking Through Confucius.* Albany: State University of New York Press.

_____. 1995. *Anticipating China: Thinking Through the Narratives of Chinese and Western Culture.* Albany: State University of New York Press.

Handlin, Joanna F. 1983. *Action in Late Ming Thought: The Reorientation of Lü K'un and Other Scholar-Officials.* Berkeley: University of California Press.

Hansen, Chad. 1983. *Language and Logic in Ancient China.* Ann Arbor: University of Michigan Press.

_____. 1992. *A Daoist Theory of Chinese Thought: A Philosophic Interpretation.* Oxford: Oxford University Press.

Hartman, Charles. 1986. *Han Yü and the T'ang Search for Unity.* Princeton: Princeton University Press.

Hatton, Russell. 1982. "*Ch'i*'s Role Within the Psychology of Chu Hsi." *Journal of Chinese Philosophy* 9, no. 4:441–469.

Hegel, Robert E., and Richard C. Hessney, eds. 1985. *Expressions of Self in Chinese Literature.* New York: Columbia University Press.

Henderson, John B. 1984. *The Development and Decline of Chinese Cosmology.* New York: Columbia University Press.

_____. 1991. *Scripture, Canon, and Commentary: A Comparison of Confucian and Western Exegesis.* Princeton: Princeton University Press.

Henke, Frederick Goodrich. 1964. *The Philosophy of Wang Yang-ming.* 2d ed. New York: Paragon Boo Reprint Company.

Henricks, Robert G. 1983. *Philosophy and Argument in Third-Century China: The Essays of Hsi K'ang.* Princeton: Princeton University Press.

Ho, Peng Yoke. 1985. *Li, Qi, and Shu: An Introduction to Science and Civilization in China.* Hong Kong: Hong Kong University Press.

Ho, Ping-ti. 1962. *The Ladder of Success in Imperial China: Aspects of Social Mobility, 1386–1911.* New York: Columbia University Press.

———. 1975. *The Cradle of the East: An Inquiry into the Indigenous Origins of Techniques and Ideas of Neolithic and Early Historic China, 5000–1000 B.C.* Hong Kong: Chinese University of Hong Kong.

Hocking, William Ernest. 1936. "Chu Hsi's Theory of Knowledge." *Harvard Journal of Asiatic Studies* 1:109–127.

Hoobler, Thomas, and Dorthy Hoobler. 1993. *Confucianism: World Religions.* New York: Facts on File.

Hsieh, Shan-yuan. 1979. *The Life and Thought of Li Kou (1009–1069).* San Francisco: Chinese Materials Center.

Hsiao, Kung-chuan. 1975. *A Modern China and New World: K'ang Yu-wei, Reformer and Utopian, 1854–1927.* Seattle: University of Washington Press.

———. 1979. *A History of Chinese Political Thought. Vol. 1: From the Beginnings to the Sixth Century A.D.* Translated by F. W. Mote. Princeton: Princeton University Press.

Hsu, Cho-yun. 1965. *Ancient China in Transition: An Analysis of Social Mobility, 722–222 B.C.* Stanford: Stanford University Press.

Hsü, Leonard Shihlien. 1932. *The Political Philosophy of Confucianism.* London: Curzon Press.

Hu, Shih. 1928. *The Development of the Logical Method in Ancient China.* Shanghai: Oriental Book Company.

Huang, Chichung. 1997. *The Analects of Confucius.* New York: Oxford University Press.

Huang, Chin-shing. 1995. *Philosophy, Philology, and Politics in Eighteenth-Century China: Li Fu and the Lu-Wang School Under the Ch'ing.* Cambridge: Cambridge University Press.

Huang, Ray. 1981. *1587: A Year of No Significance: The Ming Dynasty in Decline.* New Haven: Yale University Press.

Huang, Siu-chi. 1968. "Chang Tsai's Concept of *Ch'i.*" *Philosophy East and West* 18 (October):247–260.

———. 1971. "The Moral Point of View of Chang Tsai." *Philosophy East and West* 21 (April):141–156.

———. 1977. *Lu Hsiang-shan: A Twelfth-Century Chinese Idealist Philosophy.* Westport, CT: Hyperion Press.

Huang, Tsung-hsi. 1987. *The Records of Ming Scholars.* Edited by Julia Ching, with the collaboration of Chaoying Fang. Honolulu: University of Hawaii Press.

Hughes, E. R. 1943. *The Great Learning and the Mean-in-Action.* New York: E. P. Dutton and Company.

Hurvitz, Leon. 1962. "Chih-I (538–597): An Introduction to the Life and Ideas of a Chinese Buddhist Monk." *Mélanges Chinois et Bouddhiques* 12 (1960–1962).

Hymes, Robert P. 1986. *Statesmen and Gentlemen: The Elite of Fu-Chou, Chiang-Hsi, in Northern and Southern Sung.* Cambridge: Cambridge University Press.

Ivanhoe, Philip J. 1990. *Ethics in the Confucian Tradition: The Thought of Mencius and Wang Yang-ming.* Atlanta: Scholars Press.

_____. 1991. "A Happy Symmetry: Xunzi's Ethical Thought." *Journal of the American Academy of Religion* 59, no. 2 (Summer):309–322.

_____. 1993a. "Confucian Moral Self-Cultivation." *Journal of the American Academy of Religion* 59, no. 2 (Summer):309–322.

_____. 1993b. *Confucian Moral Self-Cultivation.* New York: Peter Lang.

_____, ed. 1996. *Chinese Language, Thought, and Culture: Nivison and His Critics.* Chicago, IL: Open Court.

Jen, Yu-wen. 1970. "Ch'en Hsien-chang's Philosophy." In *Self and Society in Ming Thought,* edited by Wm. Theodore de Bary. New York: Columbia University Press.

Jensen, Lionel M. 1993. "The Invention of 'Confucius' and His Chinese Other, 'Kong Fuzi.'" *Positions* 1, no. 2 (Fall):414–449.

Jiang, Paul Yun-ming. 1980. *The Search for Mind: Ch'en Pai-sha, Philosopher-Poet.* Singapore: Singapore University Press.

Johnson, David, Andrew J. Nathan, and Evelyn S. Rawski, eds. 1985. *Popular Culture in Late Imperial China.* Berkeley: University of California Press.

Kahn, Harold L. 1971. *Monarchy in the Emperor's Eyes: Image and Reality in the Ch'ien-lung Reign.* Cambridge: Harvard University Press.

Kasoff, Ira E. 1984. *The Thought of Chang Tsai.* Cambridge: Cambridge University Press.

Kim, Sung-Hae. 1985. *The Righteous and the Sage: A Comparative Study on the Ideal Images of Man in Biblical Israel and Classical China.* Seoul: Sogang University Press.

Kim, Yung Sik. 1980. "The World-view of Chu Hsi (1130–1200): Knowledge About the Natural World in *Chu-tzu ch'üan-shu.*" Ph.D. diss., Princeton University.

Knoblock, John. 1988–1994. *Xunzi: A Translation and Study of the Complete Works.* 3 vols. Stanford: Stanford University Press.

Ko, Dorothy. 1994. *Teachers of the Inner Chambers: Women and Culture in Seventeenth-Century China.* Stanford: Stanford University Press.

Kohn, Livia. 1991. *Early Chinese Mysticism: Philosophy and Soteriology in the Taoist Tradition.* Princeton: Princeton University Press.

_____. 1995. *Laughing at the Tao: Debates Among Buddhists and Taoists in Medieval China.* Princeton: Princeton University Press.

Kracke, E. A., Jr. 1953. *Civil Service in Early Sung China.* Cambridge: Harvard University Press.

Kuhn, Philip A. 1990. *Soulstealers: The Chinese Sorcery Scare of 1768.* Cambridge: Harvard University Press.

Lach, Donald F., trans. and ed. 1957. *The Preface to Leibniz' Novissima Sinica.* Honolulu: University of Hawaii Press.

LaFargue, Michael. 1994. *Tao and Method: A Reasoned Approach to the Tao Te Ching.* Albany: State University of New York Press.

Lamont, H. G. 1973–1974. "An Early Ninth-Century Debate on Heaven: Liu Tsung-yüan's *T'ien-Shou* and Liu Yü-hsi's *T'ien-Lun.*" *Asia Major* 18:181–209, 37–85.

Langlois, John D., Jr., ed. 1981. *China Under Mongol Rule.* Princeton: Princeton University Press.

Lau, D. C., trans. 1989. *Tao Te Ching*. Rev. ed. Hong Kong: Chinese University Press.

Lee, Peter K. H., ed. 1991. *Confucian-Christian Encounter in Historical and Contemporary Perspective*. Lewiston, NY: Edwin Mellen Press.

Lee, Thomas H. C. 1985. *Government Education and Examinations in Sung China*. Hong Kong: Chinese University Press.

_____. 1991. "Christianity and Chinese Intellectuals: From the Chinese Point of View." In *China and Europe: Images and Influences in the Sixteenth to Eighteenth Centuries*, edited by Thomas H. C. Lee. Hong Kong: Chinese University Press.

Legge, James, trans. 1960. *The Chinese Classics*. 5 vols. Hong Kong: Hong Kong University Press.

_____, trans. 1968. *The Li Ki*. 2 Vols. Delhi: Motilal Barnarsidass.

Leibniz, Gottfried Wilhelm. 1977. *Discourse on the Natural Theology of the Chinese*. Translated by Henry Rosemont Jr. and Daniel J. Cook. Honolulu: University of Hawaii Press.

_____. 1994. *Writings on China*. Translated by Daniel J. Cook and Henry Rosemont Jr. Chicago: Open Court.

Levenson, Joseph R. 1968. *Confucian China and Its Modern Faith: A Trilogy*. 3 vols. Berkeley: University of California Press.

Levenson, Joseph R., and Franz Schurmann. 1969. *China: An Interpretive History from the Beginnings to the Fall of Han*. Berkeley: University of California Press.

Lewis, Mark Edward. 1990. *Sanctioned Violence in Early China*. Albany: State University of New York Press.

Leys, Simon, trans. 1997. *The Analects of Confucius*. New York: W. W. Norton and Company.

Liang, Ch'i-ch'ao. 1959. *Intellectual Trends in the Ch'ing Period*. Translated by Immanuel C. Y. Hsü. Cambridge: Harvard University Press.

Lin, Tongqi, Henry Rosemont, Jr., and Roger T. Ames. 1995. "Chinese Philosophy: A Philosophical Essay on the 'State of the Art.'" *Journal of Asian Studies* 54, no. 3 (August):727–758.

Lin, Yü-sheng. 1979. *The Crisis of Chinese Consciousness: Radical Antitraditionalism in the May Fourth Era*. Madison: University of Wisconsin Press.

Liu, I-ch'ing. 1976. *Shih-shuo Hsin-yü: A New Account of Tales of the World*. Translated by Richard B. Mather. Minneapolis: University of Minnesota Press.

Liu, James J. Y. 1975. *Chinese Theories of Literature*. Chicago: University of Chicago Press.

Liu, James T. C. 1959. *Reform in Sung China: Wang An-shih (1021–1086) and His New Policies*. Cambridge: Harvard University Press.

_____. 1967. *Ou-yang Hsiu: An Eleventh-Century Neo-Confucianist*. Palo Alto, CA: Stanford University Press.

_____. 1988. *China Turning Inward: Intellectual Changes in the Early Twelfth Century*. Cambridge: Harvard University Press.

Liu, James T. C., and Peter J. Golas, eds. 1969. *Change in Sung China: Innovation or Renovation?* Lexington, MA: B. C. Heath and Co.

Liu, Shu-hsien. 1971. "The Religious Import of Confucian Philosophy: Its Traditional Outlook and Contemporary Significance." *Philosophy East and West* 21 (April):157–175.

_____. 1978. "The Functions of the Mind in Chu Hsi's Philosophy." *Journal of Chinese Philosophy* 5:204.

_____. 1989. "Postwar Neo-Confucian Philosophy: Its Development and Issues." In *Religious Issues and Interreligious Dialogues,* edited by Charles Wei-hsun Fu and Gerhard E. Spiegler. New York: Greenwood Press.

_____. 1990. "Some Reflections on the Sung-Ming Understanding of Mind, Nature, and Reason." *Journal of the Institute of Chinese Studies of the Chinese University of Hong Kong* 21:331–343.

Liu, Wu-chi. 1955. *A Short History of Confucian Philosophy.* New York: Dell Publishing Company.

Lo, Jung-pang, ed. 1967. *K'ang Yu-wei: A Biography and a Symposium.* Tucson: University of Arizona Press.

Lo, Winston Wan. 1974. *The Life and Thought of Yeh Shih.* Hong Kong: Chinese University of Hong Kong.

Loden, Torbjon, trans. 1988. "Dai Zhen's Evidential Commentary on the Meaning of the Words of Mencius." *Bulletin of the Museum of Far Eastern Antiquities,* no. 60 (Stockholm):165–313.

Loewe, Michael. 1979. *Ways to Paradise: The Chinese Quest for Immortality.* London: George Allen and Unwin.

_____. 1982. *Chinese Ideas of Life and Death: Faith, Myth, and Reason in the Han Period (202 B.C.–A.D. 220).* London: George Allen and Unwin.

_____. 1994. *Divination, Mythology, and Monarch in Han China.* Cambridge: Cambridge University Press.

Lynn, Richard John, trans. 1994. *The Classic of Changes: A New Translation of the I Ching as Interpreted by Wang Bi.* New York: Columbia University Press.

Machle, Edward J. 1993. *Nature and Heaven in the Xunzi: A Study of Tien Lun.* Albany: State University of New York Press.

McKight, Brian. 1981. *The Washing Away of Wrongs: Forensic Medicine in Thirteenth-Century China.* Ann Arbor: University of Michigan Center for Chinese Studies.

_____. 1992. *Law and Order in Sung China.* Cambridge: Cambridge University Press.

McMullen, David. 1988. *State and Scholars in T'ang China.* Cambridge: Cambridge University Press.

Makeham, John. 1995. *Name and Actuality in Early Chinese Thought.* Albany: State University of New York Press.

Malebranche, Nicolas. 1980. *Dialogue Between a Christian Philosopher and a Chinese Philosopher on the Existence and Nature of God.* Translated by Dominick A. Iorio. Washington, DC: University Press of America.

Mann, Susan. 1997. *Precious Records: Women in China's Long Eighteenth Century.* Stanford: Stanford University Press.

Maspero, Henri. 1978. *China in Antiquity.* Translated by Frank A. Kierman, Jr. Amherst: University of Massachusetts Press.

Mencius. 1963. *Mencius.* Translated by W.A.C. Dobson. Toronto: University of Toronto Press.

Mencius. 1984. *Mencius.* Translated by D. C. Lau. 2 vols. Hong Kong: Chinese University Press.

Meskill, John. 1982. *Academies in Ming China: A Historical Essay.* Tucson: University of Arizona Press, published for the Association of Asian Studies.

Metzger, Thomas A. 1977. *Escape from Predicament: Neo-Confucianism and China's Evolving Political Culture.* New York: Columbia University Press.

Minamiki, George S. J. 1985. *The Chinese Rites Controversy from Its Beginning to Modern Times.* Chicago: Loyola University Press.

Miyazaki, Ichisada. 1976. *China's Examination Hell: The Civil Service Examinations of Imperial China.* Translated by Conrad Schirokauer. New York and Tokyo: Weatherhill.

Mo, Yi-moh. 1985. *La personne dans l'éthique du Confucianisme ancien.* Taipei: Ch'eng Wen Publishing Company.

Moran, Patrick Edwin. 1993. *Three Smaller Wisdom Books: Lao Zi's Dao De Jing, The Great Learning (Da Xue), and the Doctrine of the Mean (Zhong Yong).* Lanham, MD: University Press of America.

Mungello, David E. 1977. *Leibniz and Confucianism: The Search for Accord.* Honolulu: University of Hawaii Press.

_____. 1985. *Curious Land: Jesuit Accommodation and the Origins of Sinology.* Stuttgart: Franz Steiner Verlag Wiesdbaden GMBH.

Munro, Donald J. 1969. *The Concept of Man in Early China.* Stanford: Stanford University Press.

_____. 1977. *The Concept of Man in Contemporary China.* Ann Arbor: University of Michigan Press.

_____. 1988. *Images of Human Nature: A Sung Portrait.* Princeton: Princeton University Press.

Needham, Joseph. 1954–. *Science and Civilisation in China.* 8 vols. Cambridge: Cambridge University Press.

Neville, Robert C. 1982. *The Tao and the Daimon: Segments of a Religious Inquiry.* Albany: State University of New York Press.

_____. 1987. *The Puritan Smile: A Look Toward Moral Reflection.* Albany: State University of New York Press.

_____. 1991. *Behind the Masks of God: An Essay Toward Comparative Theology.* Albany: State University of New York Press.

Nivison, David S. 1966. *The Life and Thought of Chang Hsüeh-ch'eng (1738–1801).* Stanford: Stanford University Press.

_____. 1996. *The Ways of Confucianism: Investigations in Chinese Philosophy.* Edited by Bryan W. Van Norden. Chicago and La Salle, IL: Open Court.

Nivison, David S., and Arthur F. Wright, eds. 1959. *Confucianism in Action.* Stanford: Stanford University Press.

Ng, On-cho. 1986. "Tests in Context: *Chin-wen* Learning in Ch'ing Thought." Ph.D. diss., University of Hawaii.

Obenchain, Diane B., ed. 1994. "Feng Youlan: Something Happens." *Journal of Chinese Philosophy* (sepcial issue) 21, nos. 3/4 (September-December):1–574.

Pang, Ching-jen. 1942. *L'idée de Dieu chez Malebrance et l'idée de Li chez Tchou Hi.* Paris: Librarie Philosophique.

Paper, Jordan. 1987. *The Fu-Tzu: A Post-Han Confucian Text.* Leiden: E. J. Brill.

Peterson, Willard J. 1979. *Bitter Gourd: Fan I-chih and the Impetus for Intellectual Change.* New Haven: Yale University Press.

Pokora, Timotheus, trans. 1975. *Hsin-lun (New Treatise) and Other Writings of Huan T'an (43 B.C.–28 A.D.)*. Ann Arbor: Center for Chinese Studies, University of Michigan.

Prazniak, Roxann. 1996. *Dialogues Across Civilizations: Sketches in World History from the Chinese and European Experiences*. Boulder: Westview Press.

Queen, Sarah A. 1996. *From Chronicle to Canon: The Hermeneutics of the Spring and Autumn, According to Tung Chung-shu*. Cambridge: Cambridge University Press.

Raphals, Lisa. 1992. *Knowing Words: Wisdom and Cunning in the Classical Traditions of China and Greece*. Ithaca and London: Cornell University Press.

Ricci, Matteo, S. J. 1985. *The True Meaning of the Lord of Heaven (T'ien-chu Shih-i)*. Translated by Douglas Lancashire and Peter Hu Kuo-chen, S.J. Taipei: Ricci Institute.

Richards, I. A. 1932. *Mencius on the Mind: Experiments in Multiple Definition*. London: Kegan Paul, Trench, Trubner and Company.

Roetz, Heiner. 1993. *Confucian Ethics of the Axial Age: A Reconstruction Under the Aspect of the Breakthrough Toward Postconventional Thinking*. Albany: State University of New York Press.

Ropp, Paul S., ed. 1990. *Heritage of China: Contemporary Perspectives on Chinese Civilization*. Berkeley: University of California Press.

Rosemont, Henry, Jr., ed. 1984. *Explorations in Early Chinese Cosmology*. Chico, CA: Scholars Press.

_____. 1991a. *A Chinese Mirror: Moral Reflections on Political Economy and Society*. La Salle, IL: Open Court.

_____, ed. 1991b. *Chinese Texts and Philosophical Contexts: Essays Dedicated to Angus C. Graham*. La Salle, IL: Open Court.

Rowley, Harold Henry. 1956. *Prophecy and Religion in Ancient China and Israel*. London: University of London, Athlone Press.

Rozman, Gilbert, ed. 1991. *The East Asian Region: Confucian Heritage and Its Modern Adaptation*. Princeton: Princeton University Press.

Rubin, Vitaly A. 1976. *Individual and State in Ancient China: Essays on Four Chinese Philosophers*. Translated by Steven I. Levine. New York: Columbia University Press.

Sargent, Galen Eugene. 1955. "Les débats personnels de Tchou Hi en matière de méthodologie." *Journal Asiatique* 243:213–228.

Saussy, Haun. 1993. *The Problem of a Chinese Aesthetic*. Stanford: Stanford University Press.

Schirokauer, Conrad. 1960. "The Political Thought and Behavior of Chu Hsi." Ph.D. diss., Stanford University.

Schneider, Laurence A. 1971. *Ku Chieh-kang and China's New History: Nationalism and the Quest for Alternative Traditions*. Berkeley: University of California Press.

Schwarcz, Vera. 1986. *The Chinese Enlightenment: Intellectuals and the Legacy of the May Fourth Movement of 1919*. Berkeley: University of California Press.

Schwartz, Benjamin I. 1964. *In Search of Wealth and Power: Yen Fu and the West*. Cambridge: Belknap Press of Harvard University.

_____. 1985. *The World of Thought in Ancient China*. Cambridge: Belknap Press of Harvard University.

Shao, Yung. 1986. *Dialogue Between a Fisherman and a Wood-Cutter*. Translated by Knud Lundbaek. Hamburg: C. Bell Verlag.

Shaughnessy, Edward L. 1996. *I Ching: The Classic of Changes*. New York: Ballantine Books.

_____. 1997. *Before Confucius: Studies in the Creation of the Chinese Classics*. Albany: State University of New York Press.

Shih, Vincent Y. C. 1963. "Metaphysical Tendencies in Mencius." *Philosophy East and West* 12 (January):319–341.

Shryock, J. K. 1937. *The Study of Human Abilities: The Jen wu chih of Liu Shao*. New Haven: American Oriental Society.

Shun, Kwong-loi. 1997. *Mencius and Early Chinese Thought*. Stanford: Stanford University Press.

Smith, D. Howard. 1968. *Chinese Religions*. New York: Holt, Rinehart and Winston.

_____. 1973. *Confucius*. New York: Charles Scribner's Sons.

Smith, Kidder, Jr. et al. 1990. *Sung Dynasty Uses of the I Ching*. Princeton: Princeton University Press.

Smith, Richard J. 1991. *Fortune-Tellers and Philosophers: Divination in Traditional Chinese Society*. Boulder: Westview Press.

_____. 1994. *China's Cultural Heritage: The Ch'ing Dynasty, 1644–1912*. 2d ed. Boulder: Westview Press.

Smith, Richard J., and D.W.Y. Kwok, eds. 1993. *Cosmology, Ontology, and Human Efficacy*. Honolulu: University of Hawaii Press.

Som, Tjan Tjoe. 1973. *The Comprehensive Discussions in the White Tiger Hall*. 2 vols. Westport, CT: Hyperion Press; E. J. Brill, Leiden, 1949.

Spence, Jonathan D. 1974. *Emperor of China: Self-portrait of K'ang-hsi*. New York: Alfred A. Knopf.

_____. 1984. *The Memory Palace of Matteo Ricci*. New York: Viking.

Standaert, N. 1988. *Yang Tingyun, Confucian and Christian in Late Ming China*. Leiden: E. J. Brill.

Steele, John. 1966. *The I-Li, or Book of Etiquette and Ceremonial*. Taipei: Ch'eng-wen Publishing Company.

Strassberg, Richard E. 1983. *The World of K'ung Shang-jen: A Man of Letters in Early Ch'ing China*. New York: Columbia University Press.

_____. 1994. *Inscribed Landscapes: Travel Writing from Imperial China*. Berkeley: University of California Press.

Struve, Lynn A. 1988. "The Early Ch'ing Legacy of Huang Tsung-hsi: A Reexamination." *Asia Major*, 3d ser., no. 1, pt. 1.

Sun, Stanislaus, S. J. 1966. "The Doctrine of *Li* in the Philosophy of Chu Hsi." *International Philosophic Quarterly* 6:153–188.

Swann, Nancy Lee. 1968. *Pan Chao: Foremost Woman Scholar of China*. New York: Russell and Russell.

T'an, Ssu-t'ung. 1984. *An Exposition of Benevolence: The Jen-hsüeh of T'an Ssu-t'ung*. Translated by Chan Sin-wai. Hong Kong: Chinese University of Hong Kong Press.

T'ang, Chün-i. 1956. "Chang Tsai's Theory of Mind and Its Metaphysical Basis." *Philosophy East and West* 6:113–136.

_____. 1962. "The *T'ien Ming* (Heavenly Ordinance) in pre-Ch'in China." *Philosophy East and West* 11 (January):195–218.

_____. 1974. "The Spirit and Development of Neo-Confucianism." In *Invitation to Chinese Philosophy*, edited by A. Naess and A. Hanny. Oslo: Scandinavian University Press.

Taylor, Rodney L. 1978. *The Cultivation of Sagehood as a Religious Goal in Neo-Confucianism: A Study of Selected Writings of Kao P'an-lung, 1562–1626.* Missoula, MT: Scholars Press.

_____. 1990. *The Religious Dimensions of Confucianism.* Albany: State University of New York Press.

Thompson, Laurence G. 1958. *The One-World Philosophy of K'ang Yu-wei.* London: George Allen and Unwin.

Tillman, Hoyt Cleveland. 1982. *Utilitarian Confucianism: Ch'en Liang's Challenge to Chu Hsi.* Cambridge: Harvard University Press.

_____. 1992a. *Confucian Discourse and Chu Hsi's Ascendancy.* Honolulu: University of Hawaii Press.

_____. 1992b. "A New Direction in Confucian Scholarship: Approaches to Examining the Differences Between Neo-Confucianism and *Tao-hsüeh*." *Philosophy East and West* 42 (July):455–474.

_____. 1994. *Ch'en Liang on Public Interest and the Law.* Honolulu: University of Hawaii Press.

Tillman, Hoyt Cleveland, and Stephen H. West, eds. 1994. *China Under Jurchen Rule: Essays on Chin Intellectual and Cultural History.* Albany: State University of New York Press.

Ts'ai, Y. C. 1950. "The Philosophy of Ch'eng I: A Selection from the Complete Works." Ph.D. diss., Columbia University.

Tsai, Yen-zen. 1994. "*Ching* and *Chuan*: Towards Defining the Confucian Scriptures in Han China (206 B.C.E.–220 C.E.)." National Chengchi University, Taipei, Taiwan.

Tu, Wei-ming. 1971. "Review of *Hsin-t'i yü hsing-t'i* (Mind and Nature), by Mou Tsung-san." *Journal of Asian Studies* 30 (May):642–647.

_____. 1974. "Reconstituting the Confucian Tradition." *Journal of Asian Studies* 33 (May):441–454.

_____. 1976. *Neo-Confucian Thought in Action: Wang Yang-ming's Youth (1472–1509).* Berkeley: University of California Press.

_____. 1979. *Humanity and Self-Cultivation: Essays in Confucian Thought.* Berkeley: Asian Humanities Press.

_____. 1985. *Confucian Thought: Selfhood as Creative Transformation.* Albany: State University of New York Press.

_____. 1989. *Centrality and Commonality: An Essay on Confucian Religiousness.* Albany: State University of New York Press.

_____. 1993. *Way, Learning, and Politics: Essays on the Confucian Intellectual.* Albany: State University of New York Press.

_____, ed. 1994. *China in Transformation.* Cambridge: Harvard University Press.

Tu, Wei-ming, Milan Hejtmanek, and Alan Wachman, eds. 1992. *The Confucian World Observed: A Contemporary Discussion of Confucian Humanism in East Asia.* Honolulu: University of Hawaii Press.

Twitchett, Denis. 1959. "The Fan Clan's Charitable Estate, 1050–1760." In David S. Nivison and Arthur F. Wright, eds. *Confucianism in Action.* Stanford: Stanford University Press.

Van Zoeren, Steven. 1991. *Poetry and Personality: Reading, Exegesis, and Hermeneutics in Traditional China.* Stanford: Stanford University Press.

Verdu, Alfonso. 1981. *The Philosophy of Buddhism: A "Totalistic" Synthesis.* The Hague: Martinus Nijhoff Publishers.

Wakeman, Frederick, Jr. 1966. *Strangers at the Gate: Social Disorder in South China, 1839–1861.* Berkeley: University of California Press.

_____. 1970. *"Nothing Concealed": Essays in Honor of Liu Yü-yün.* Taipei: Chinese Materials and Research Aids Service Center.

Waley, Arthur. 1938. *The Analects of Confucius.* London: George Allen and Unwin.

_____. 1939. *Three Ways of Thought in Ancient China.* Garden City, NY: Doubleday.

_____. 1970. *Yuan Mei: Eighteenth-Century Chinese Poet.* Stanford: Stanford University Press.

Wang, Y. C. 1966. *Chinese Intellectuals and the West: 1872–1949.* Chapel Hill: University of North Carolina Press.

Wang, Yang-ming. 1963. *Instructions for Practical Living and Other Neo-Confucian Writings.* Translated by Wing Tsit-chan. New York: Columbia University Press.

Watson, Burton, trans. 1967. *Basic Writings of Mo Tzu, Hsün Tzu, and Han Fei Tzu.* New York: Columbia University Press.

Weber, Max. 1951. *The Religion of China: Confucianism and Taoism.* Translated by Hans H. Gerth. New York: Macmillan.

Wechsler, Howard J. 1985. *Offerings of Jade and Silk: Ritual and Symbol in the Legitimization of the T'ang Dynasty.* New Haven: Yale University Press.

Wieger, P. Leon, S.J. 1930. *Textes philosophiques: Confucianisme, Taoism, Buddhisme.* Hien-hien: N.p.

Wilhelm, Richard. 1931. *Confucius and Confucianism.* Translated by George H. Danton and Annina Periam Danton. New York: Harcourt Brace Jovanovich.

Williamson, H. R. 1973. *Wang An Shih: A Chinese Statesman and Educationalist of the Sung Dynasty.* 2 vols. Westport, CT: Hyperion Press.

Wilson, Thomas A. 1995. *Genealogy of the Way: The Construction and Uses of the Confucian Tradition in Late Imperial China.* Stanford: Stanford University Press.

Wittenborn, Allen, trans. 1991. *Further Reflections on Things at Hand: A Reader, Chu Hsi.* Lanham, MD: University Press of America.

Wood, Alan T. 1995. *Limits to Autocracy: From Sung Neo-Confucianism to a Doctrine of Political Rights.* Honolulu: University of Hawaii Press.

Wright, Arthur F., ed. 1953. *Studies in Chinese Thought.* Chicago: University of Chicago Press.

_____, ed. 1960. *The Confucian Persuasion.* Stanford: Stanford University Press.

Wright, Arthur F., and Denis Twichett, eds. 1962. *Confucian Personalities.* Stanford: Stanford University Press.

Wright, Mary C. 1966. *The Last Stand of Chinese Conservatism: The T'ung-Chih Restoration, 1862–1874.* New York: Atheneum.

Wu, Pei-yi. 1990. *The Confucian's Progress: Autobiographical Writings in Traditional China.* Princeton: Princeton University Press.

Wyatt, Don J. 1996. *The Recluse of Loyang: Shao Yung and the Moral Evolution of Early Sung Thought.* Honolulu: University of Hawaii Press.

Yang, Hsiung. 1993. *The Canon of Supreme Mystery: A Translation with Commentary of the T'ai Hsüan Ching.* Translated and edited by Michael Nylan. Albany: State University of New York Press.

_____. 1994. *The Elemental Changes: The Ancient Chinese Companion to the I Ching, The T'ai Hsüan Ching of Master Yang Hsiung.* Translated and edited by Michael Nylan. Albany: State University of New York Press.

Yang, Lien-sheng. 1957. "The Concept of *Pao* as a Basis for Social Relations in China." In *Chinese Thought and Institutions,* edited by J. K. Fairbank. Chicago: University of Chicago Press.

Yearley, Lee H. 1990. *Mencius and Aquinas: Theories of Virtue and Conceptions of Courage.* Albany: State University of New York Press.

Yeh, Theodore T. Y. 1969. *Confucianism, Christianity, and China.* New York: Philosophical Library.

Yen, Yüan. 1972. *Preservation of Learning.* Translated by Maurice Freeman. Los Angles: Monumenta Serica.

Young, John D. 1983. *Confucianism and Christianity: The First Encounter.* Hong Kong: Hong Kong University Press.

Yu, David. 1959. "A Comparative Study of the Metaphysics of Chu Hsi and A. N. Whitehead." Ph.D. diss., University of Chicago.

_____. 1969. "Chu Hsi's Approach to Knowledge." *Chinese Culture* (December): 1–14.

Yü, Chün-fang. 1981. *The Renewal of Buddhism in China: Chu-hung and the Late Ming Synthesis.* New York: Columbia University Press.

Zaehner, R. C. 1970. *Concordant Discord: The Interdependence of Faiths.* Oxford: Oxford University Press.

Monographs: Korea

Choe, Ching-young. 1972. *The Rule of the Taewon'gun, 1864–1873: Restoration in Yi Korea.* Cambridge: East Asia Study Research Center, Harvard University.

Choi, Ming-hong. 1980. *A Modern History of Korean Philosophy.* Seoul: Seong Moon Sa.

Choung, Haechang, and Han Hyong-jo, eds. 1996. *Confucian Philosophy in Korea.* Kyonggi-do: Academy of Korean Studies.

Chung, Chai-Sik. 1995. *A Korean Confucian Encounter with the Modern World: Yi Hang-no and the West.* Berkeley: Institute of East Asian Studies, University of California Press.

Chung, Edward Y. J. 1995. *The Korean Neo-Confucianism of Yi T'oegye and Yi Yulgok: A Reappraisal of the "Four-Seven Thesis" and Its Practical Implications for Self-Cultivation.* Albany: State University of New York Press.

de Bary, Wm. Theodore, and JaHyun Kim Haboush, eds. 1985. *The Rise of Neo-Confucianism in Korea.* New York: Columbia University Press.

Deuchler, Martina. 1992. *The Confucian Transformation of Korea: A Study of Society and Ideology.* New York: Columbia University Press.

Grayson, James Huntley. 1989. *Korea: A Religious History.* Oxford: Clarendon Press.

Haboush, JaHyun Kim. 1988. *A Heritage of Kings: One Man's Monarchy in the Confucian World*. New York: Columbia University Press.

_____. 1996. *The Memoirs of Lady Hyegyong: The Autobiographical Writings of a Crown Princess of Eighteenth-Century Korea*. Berkeley: University of California Press.

Kalton, Michael C., trans. 1988. *To Become a Sage: The Ten Diagrams on Sage Learning by Yi T'oegye*. New York: Columbia University Press.

Kalton, Michael et al. 1994. *The Four Seven Debate: An Annotated Translation of the Most Famous Controversy in Korean Neo-Confucian Thought*. Albany: State University of New York Press.

Kang, Hugh H. W., ed. 1975. *The Traditional Culture and Society of Korea: Thought and Institutions*. Honolulu: Center for Korean Studies, University of Hawaii Press.

Kendall, Laurel, and Griffin Dix, eds. 1987. *Ritual and Religion in Korean Society*. Berkeley: Institute of East Asian Studies, University of California, Berkeley Center for Korean Studies.

Kim, Sung-Hae. 1985. *The Righteous and the Sage: A Comparative Study on the Ideal Images of Man in Biblical Israel and Classical China*. Seoul: Sogang University Press.

_____. 1990. "Liberation Through Humanization: With a Focus on Korean Confucianism." *Ching Feng* 33, nos. 1 and 2 (April):20–46.

Kim, Sung-Wan. 1994. "A Model of Moral Metaphysics Based on Yi T'oegye's Theory of Principle." Ph.D. diss., Boston University.

Nelson, M. Frederick. 1945. *Korea and the Old Orders in East Asia*. Baton Rouge: Louisiana State University Press.

Palais, James B. 1975. *Politics and Policy in Traditional Korea*. Cambridge: Harvard University Press.

_____. 1984. "Confucianism and the Aristocractic/Bureaucractic Balance in Korea." *Harvard Journal of Asiatic Studies* 44, no. 2 (December):427–468.

_____. 1996. *Confucian Statescraft and Korean Institutions: Yu Hyongwon and the Late Chosen Dynasty*. Seattle: University of Washington Press.

Peterson, Mark A. 1996. *Korean Adoption and Inheritance: Case Studies in the Creation of a Classic Confucian Society*. Ithaca: East Asian Studies Program, Cornell University.

Phillips, Earl H., and Eui-young Yu, eds. 1982. *Religions in Korea: Beliefs and Cultural Values*. Los Angeles: Center for Korean-American and Korean Studies, California State University.

Ro, Young-chan. 1989. *The Korean Neo-Confucianism of Yi Yulgok*. Albany: State University of New York Press.

Setton, Mark. 1997. *Chong Yagyong: Korea's Challenge to Orthodox Neo-Confucianism*. Albany: State University of New York Press.

Smith, Warren William, Jr. 1971. "The Rise of the *Sowon*: Literary Academies in Sixteenth-Century Korea." Ph.D. diss., University of California, Berkeley.

Wagner, Edward Willett. 1974. *The Literati Purges: Political Conflict in Yi Korea*. Cambridge: Harvard University Press.

Weems, Benjamin B. 1966. *Reform, Rebellion, and the Heavenly Way*. Tucson: University of Arizona Press.

Monographs: Japan

Backus, Robert L. 1979a. "The Kansei Prohibition of Heterodoxy." *Harvard Journal of Asiatic Studies* 39, no. 1:55–106.

_____. 1979b. "The Motivation of Confucian Orthodoxy in Tokugawa Japan." *Harvard Journal of Asiatic Studies* 39, no. 1:275–338.

Bellah, Robert N. 1957. *Tokugawa Religion: The Values of Pre-Industrial Japan.* Boston: Beacon Press.

Bolitho, Harold. 1974. *Treasures Among Men: The Fudai Daimyo in Tokugawa Japan.* New Haven: Yale University Press.

Boot, Willem Jan. 1982. "The Adoption and Adaptation of Neo-Confucianism in Japan: The Role of Fujiwara Seika and Hayashi Razan." Ph.D. diss., University of Leiden.

Craig, Albert, and Donald Shively, eds. 1970. *Personality in Japanese History.* Berkeley: University of California Press.

Davis, Winston. 1992. *Japanese Religion and Society: Paradigms of Structure and Change.* Albany: State University of New York Press.

Dore, Ronald P. 1965. *Education in Tokugawa Japan.* Berkeley: University of California Press.

_____. 1987. *Taking Japan Seriously: A Confucian Perspective on Economic Issues.* Stanford: Stanford University Press.

Earl, David M. 1964. *Emperor and Nation in Japan: Political Thinkers of the Tokugawa Period.* Seattle: University of Washington Press.

Elison, George. 1973. *Deus Destroyed: The Image of Christianity in Early Modern Japan.* Cambridge: Harvard University Press.

Gluck, Carol. 1985. *Japan's Modern Myths: Ideology in the Late Meiji Period.* Princeton: Princeton University Press.

Harootunian, Harry. 1970. *Toward Restoration: The Growth of Political Consciousness in Tokugawa Japan.* Berkeley: University of California Press.

_____. 1988. *Things Seen and Unseen: Discourse and Ideology in Tokugawa Nativism.* Chicago: University of Chicago Press.

Iriye, Akira, ed. 1980. *The Chinese and the Japanese: Essays in Political and Cultural Interactions.* Princeton: Princeton University Press.

Irokawa, Daikichi. 1985. *The Culture of the Meiji Period.* Translation edited by Marius B. Jansen. Princeton: Princeton University Press.

Jansen, Marius B. 1992. *China in the Tokugawa World.* Cambridge: Harvard University Press.

Kang, Thomas. 1971. "The Making of Confucian Societies in Tokugawa Japan and Yi Korea." Ph.D. diss., American University.

Kassel, Marleen. 1996. *Tokugawa Confucian Education: The Kangien Academy of Hirose Tanso (1782–1856).* Albany: State University of New York Press.

Kitagawa, Joseph M. 1987. *On Understanding Japanese Religion.* Princeton: Princeton University Press.

Koschmann, Victor. 1987. *The Mito Ideology: Discourse, Reform, and Insurrection in Late Tokugawa Japan, 1790–1864.* Berkeley: University of California Press.

Lidin, Olof, trans. 1970. *Ogyu Sorai's Distinguishing the Way.* Tokyo: Sophia University Press.

_____. 1973. *The Life of Ogyu Sorai: A Tokugawa Confucian Philosopher*. Lund: Scandinavian Institute of Asian Studies.

Maruyama, Masao. 1974. *Studies in the Intellectual History of Tokugawa Japan*. Translated by Mikiso Hane. Princeton: Princeton University Press.

McEwan, J. R., trans. 1969. *The Political Writings of Ogyu Sorai*. Cambridge: Cambridge University Press.

McMullen, Ian James. 1968. "Kumazawa Banzan: The Life and Thought of a Seventeenth-Century Japanese Confucian." Ph.D. diss., Cambridge University.

Mercer, Rosemary, trans. 1991. *Deep Words: Miura Baien's System of Natural Philosophy*. Leiden: E. J. Brill.

Najita, Tetsuo. 1987. *Visions of Virtue in Tokugawa Japan: The Kaitokudo Merchant Academy of Osaka*. Chicago: University of Chicago Press.

Najita, Tetsuo, and Irwin Scheiner, eds. 1978. *Japanese Thought in the Tokugawa Period, 1600–1868: Methods and Metaphors*. Chicago: University of Chicago Press.

Nakai, Kate Wildman. 1980. "The Naturalization of Confucianism in Tokugawa Japan: The Problem of Sinocentrism." *Harvard Journal of Asian Studies* 40:157–199.

_____. 1988. *Shogunal Politics: Arai Hakuseki and the Premises of Tokugawa Rule*. Cambridge: Harvard University Press.

Nakamura, Hajime. 1969. *A History of the Development of Japanese Thought from A.D. 592 to 1868*. Tokyo: Japan Cultural Society.

Nosco, Peter, ed. 1984. *Confucianism and Tokugawa Culture*. Princeton: Princeton University Press.

Odin, Steve. 1996. *The Social Self in Zen and American Pragmatism*. Albany: State University of New York Press.

Ooms, Herman. 1985. *Tokugawa Ideology: Early Constructs, 1570–1680*. Princeton: Princeton University Press.

Pollack, David. 1986. *The Fracture of Meaning: Japan's Synthesis of China from the Eighth to the Eighteenth Centuries*. Princeton: Princeton University Press.

Rubinger, Richard. 1982. *Private Academies of Tokugawa Japan*. Princeton: Princeton University Press.

Sansom, George. 1958–1963. *A History of Japan*. 3 vols. Stanford: Stanford University Press.

Sawada, Janine Anderson. 1993. *Confucian Values and Popular Zen: Sekimon Shingaku in Eighteenth-Century Japan*. Honolulu: University of Hawaii Press.

Smith, Warren W. 1973. *Confucianism in Modern Japan: A Study of Conservatism in Japanese Intellectual History*. 2d ed. Tokyo: Hokuseido Press.

Spae, Joseph. 1967. *Ito Jinsai: A Philosopher, Educator, and Sinologist of the Tokugawa Period*. New York: Paragon.

Taylor, Rodney L. 1988. *The Confucian Way of Contemplation: Okada Takehiko and the Tradition of Quiet-Sitting*. Columbia: University of South Carolina Press.

Tominaga, Nakamoto. 1990. *Emerging from Meditation*. Translated, with an introduction by Michael Pye. London: Duckworth.

Totman, Conrad. 1993. *Early Modern Japan*. Berkeley: University of California Press.

Tucker, Mary Evelyn. 1989. *Moral and Spiritual Cultivation in Japanese Neo-Confucianism: The Life and Thought of Kaibara Ekken (1630–1714)*. Albany: State University of New York Press.

Walthall, Anne. 1986. *Social Protest and Popular Culture in Eighteenth-Century Japan*. Tuscon: University of Arizona Press.

Yamashita, Ryuji. 1979. "Nakae Toju's Religious Thought and Its Relation to 'Jitsugaku.'" In *Principle and Practicality: Essays in Neo-Confucianism and Practical Learning*, edited by Wm. Theodore de Bary and Irene Bloom. New York: Columbia University Press.

Yamashita, Samuel H. 1994. *Master Sorai's Responsals: Annotated Translation of Sorai Sensi Tomonsho*. Honolulu: University of Hawaii Press.

Yoshikawa, Kojiro. 1983. *Jinsai, Sorai, Horinaga: Three Classical Philologists of Mid-Tokugawa Japan*. Tokyo: Toho Gakkai.

Index